Open-String Guitar Chords

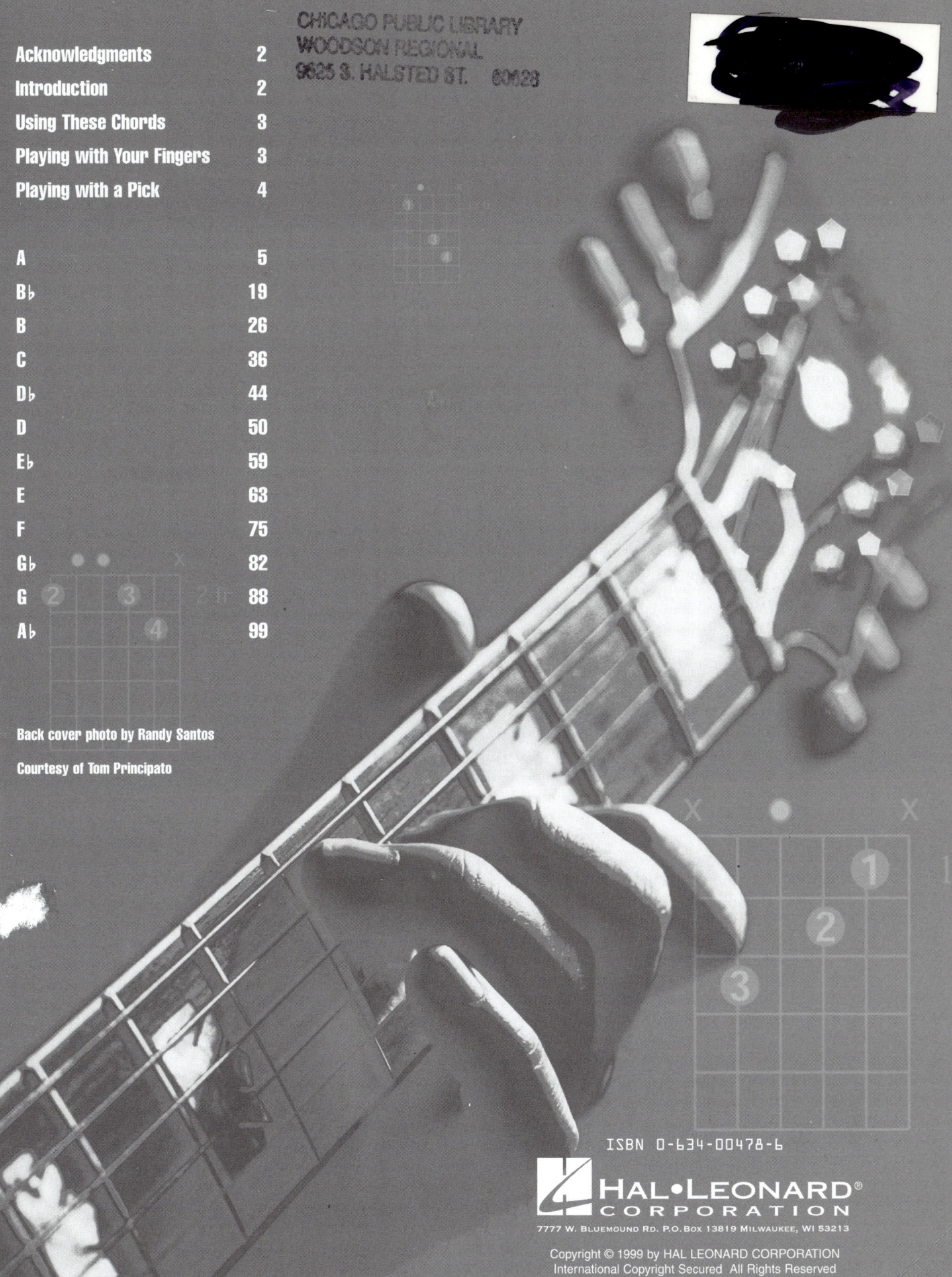

Acknowledgments	2
Introduction	2
Using These Chords	3
Playing with Your Fingers	3
Playing with a Pick	4
A	5
B♭	19
B	26
C	36
D♭	44
D	50
E♭	59
E	63
F	75
G♭	82
G	88
A♭	99

Back cover photo by Randy Santos

Courtesy of Tom Principato

ISBN 0-634-00478-6

HAL•LEONARD® CORPORATION

7777 W. BLUEMOUND RD. P.O. BOX 13819 MILWAUKEE, WI 53213

Copyright © 1999 by HAL LEONARD CORPORATION
International Copyright Secured   All Rights Reserved

No part of this publication may be reproduced in any form or by any means
without the prior written permission of the Publisher.

Visit Hal Leonard Online at
www.halleonard.com

Acknowledgments

I would like to send a special "thank you" to Rob Powell at Design Revolution—without his expertise, this book would not have been possible.

Introduction

I first became aware of open-string chords through the music of Chet Atkins and Merle Travis when I began playing guitar in the mid 1960s. Later in the 1970s, I heard Lenny Breau using much "jazzier" and extended open-string guitar chord voicings in his music. This intrigued me enough in 1978 to begin this book. I was well into it when I performed a show at the Cellar Door nightclub in Washington, D.C. with Danny Gatton, Buddy Emmons, and Lenny Breau in April 1979. In fact, that night in April, Lenny Breau and I had a discussion about open-string guitar chords—I even gave him a sampler sheet of some of the more intriguing open-string chords I had compiled up to that point. Even though Lenny and I did not have any further discussion about open-string chords, I noticed that he did a series of columns in *Guitar Player* magazine on this subject from November 1981 to January 1982.

An increasingly busier schedule throughout the 1980s, and the realization that this book would be a considerably larger undertaking than first imagined, slowed down progress for quite a while. But I always kept a near-finished rough draft for use and reference, and every time I discovered another good open-string voicing, I'd add it. Finally in 1997, nearly twenty years later, I mustered the determination and perseverance to expand and finish this book—and here it is. Refer to it whenever you need something special or different for a particular musical situation. I hope it opens some new doors for you as a guitarist.

—*Tom Principato*

Using These Chords

The chord diagrams in this book follow a standard format. The strings run vertically, and the frets run horizontally across the page. Fingerings are indicated by finger numbers on the fretboard—which show you both where to fret the strings and which fingers to use. Xs and Os at the top of the frame indicate which strings to mute and which to sound as open strings, respectively.

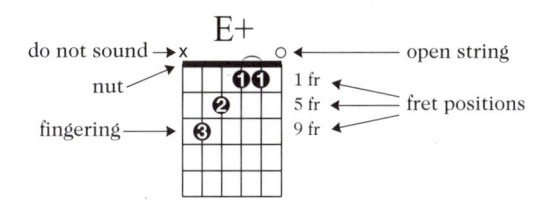

Fret positions, when necessary, are indicated by a number appearing to the right of the frame. Some voicings can be played in more than one position, in which case multiple fret positions are indicated (e.g., "1fr, 4fr, 7fr, 10fr").

Playing with Your Fingers

Open-string chords really lend themselves to being played in a "fingerstyle" manner, where the notes are plucked simultaneously with the fingers, as opposed to being strummed in succession with a pick. Here are a few options for you to consider when playing fingerstyle:

- Sometimes, such as with this E6/9 chord, an arpeggiated sound can be achieved by playing the notes in succession from lowest to highest pitch:

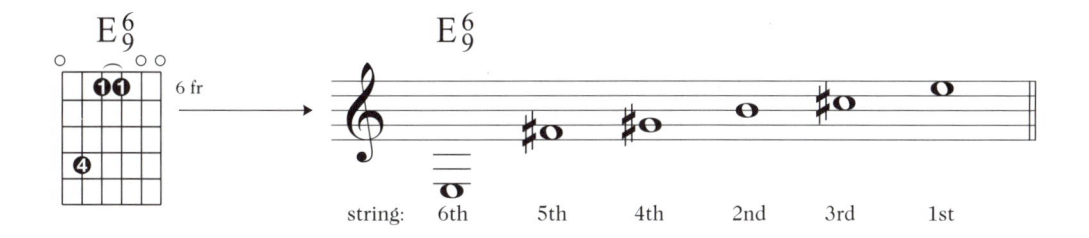

Allow the notes to ring together to create a more "harp-like" and "chimey" sound.

- Open-string chords also sound great played Travis/Atkins-style, especially if you use voicings in a chord progression that all have an open string in common, such as this I-VI-ii-V turnaround in G:

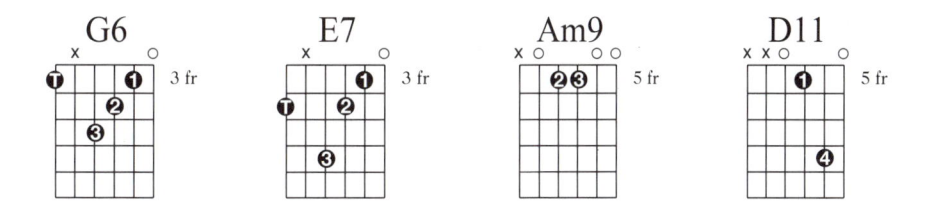

Playing with a Pick

Because of the unusual voicings that can occur with open-string chords, many times you'll find that which direction you strum the chord—i.e., from low to high, or from high to low—can make a big difference in how the chord sounds:

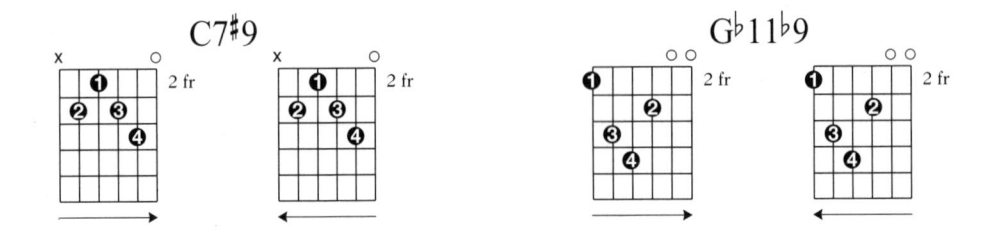

C7♯9   G♭11♭9

For "fingerstyle" playing, try running the back of your thumbnail across the strings from high to low à la flamenco music.

> NOTE: Many of the chords in this book do not have a root, in which case they may not work for solo playing—however, these same chords typically lend themselves well to ensemble playing, where the bass or other instrument may fill in the root. You'll also find these chords create great colors when combined with traditional chords. Experiment—there's a whole new world of sounds out there!

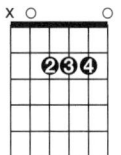

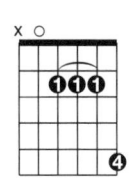

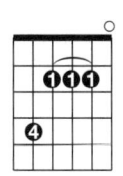

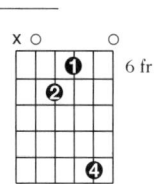

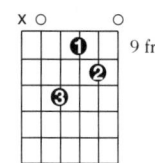

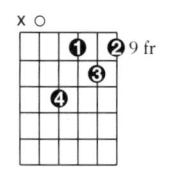

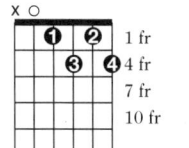

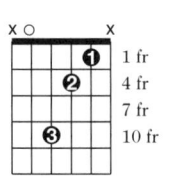

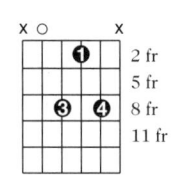

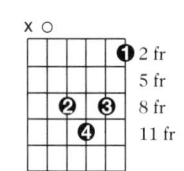

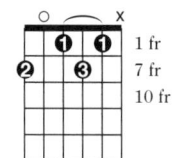

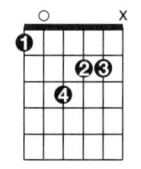

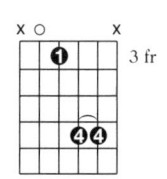

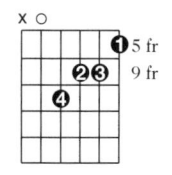

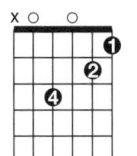

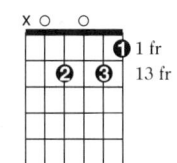

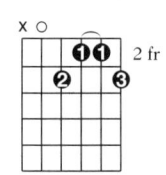

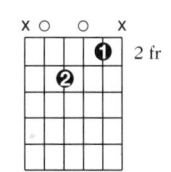

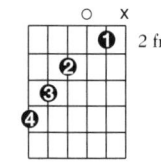

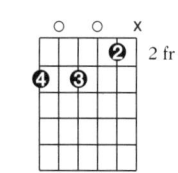

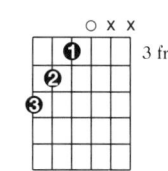

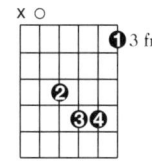

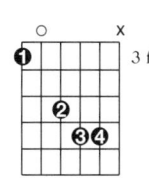

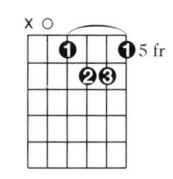

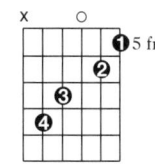

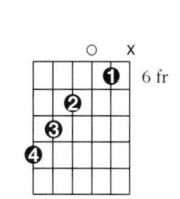

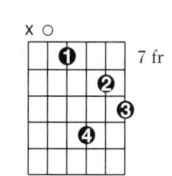

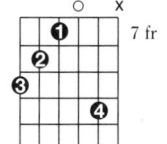

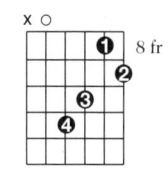

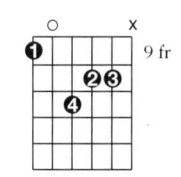

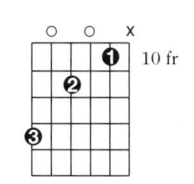

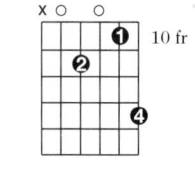

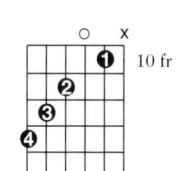

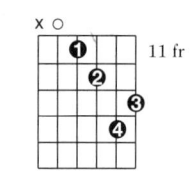

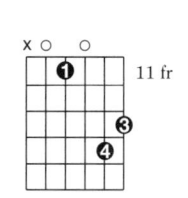

A

A

A°

A+

A+7

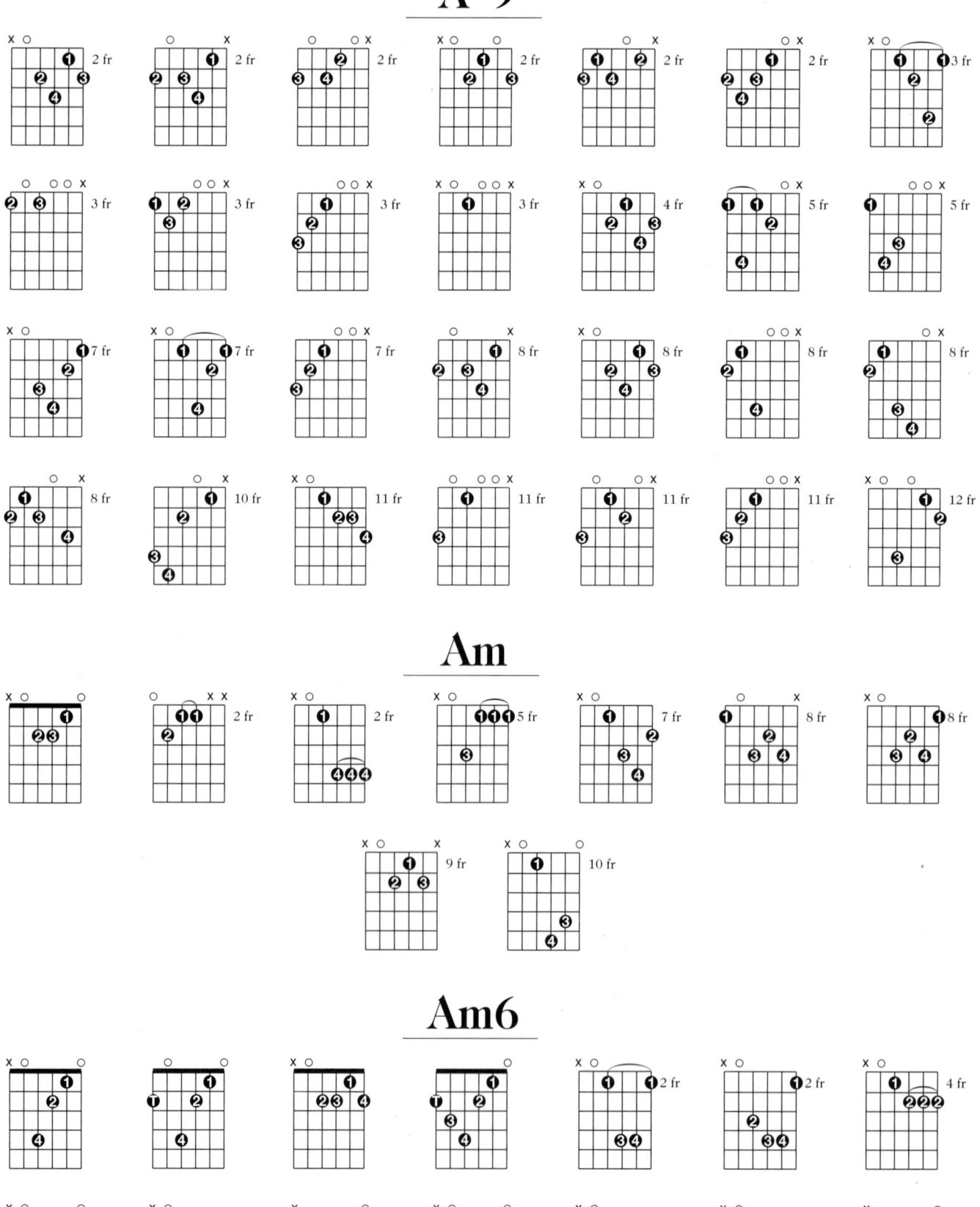

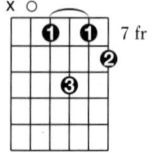

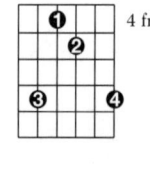

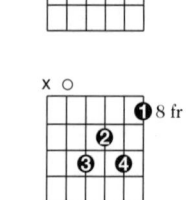

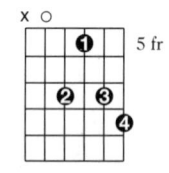

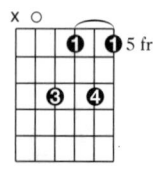

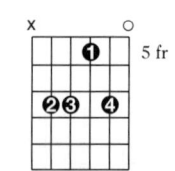

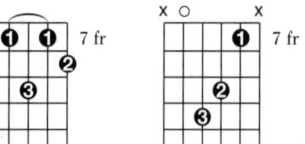

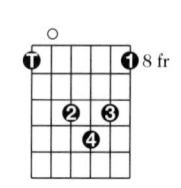

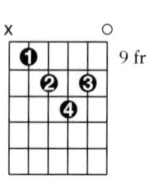

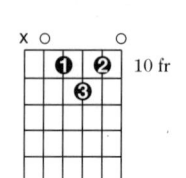

A

A+9

Am

Am6

Am6 (cont'd)

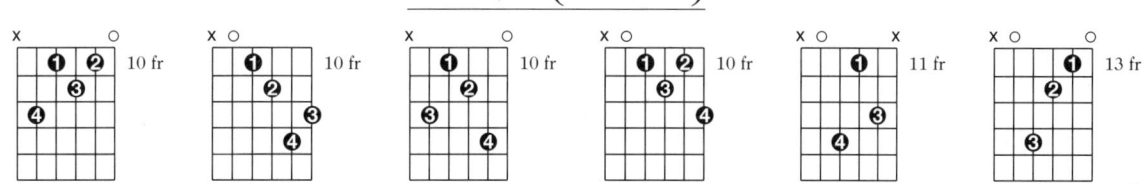

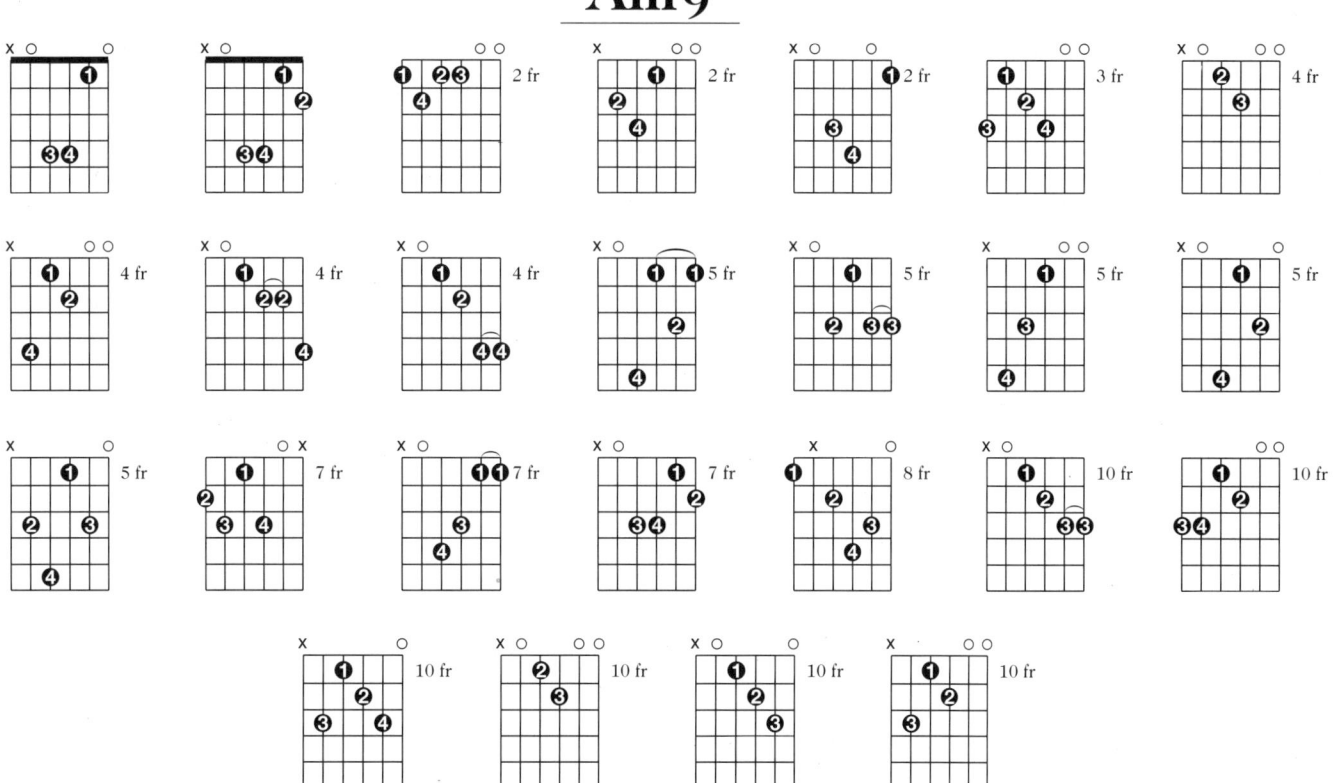

Am⁶⁄₉

Am13

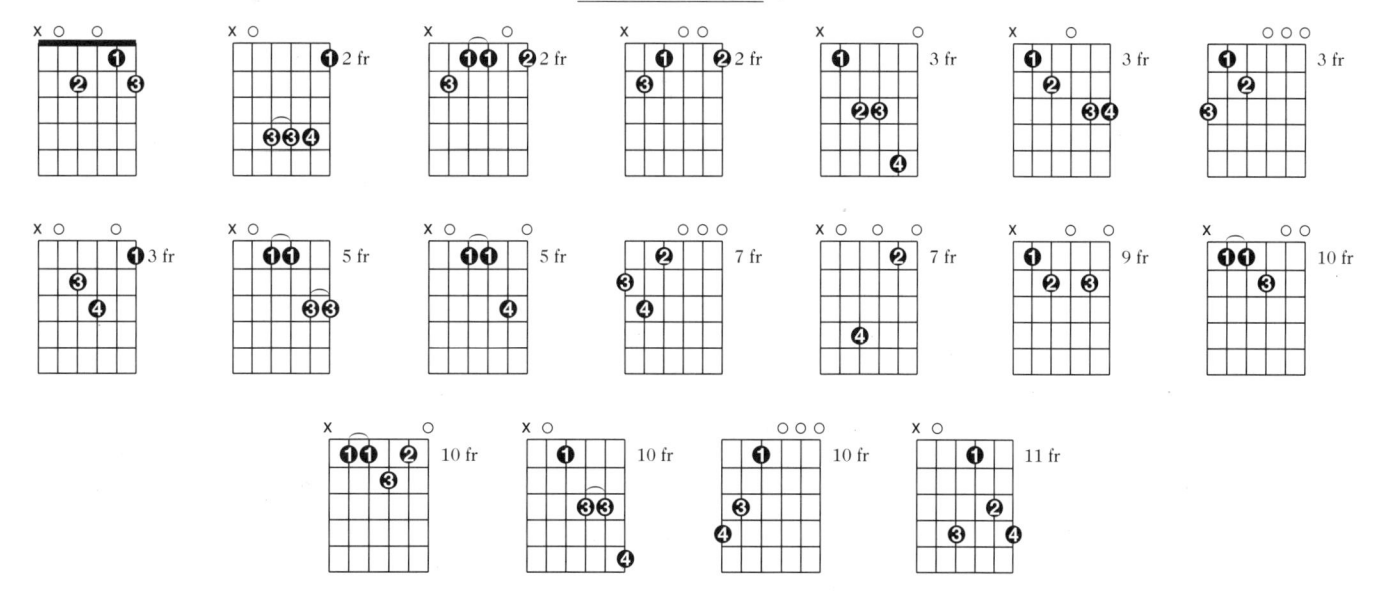

A

Am7

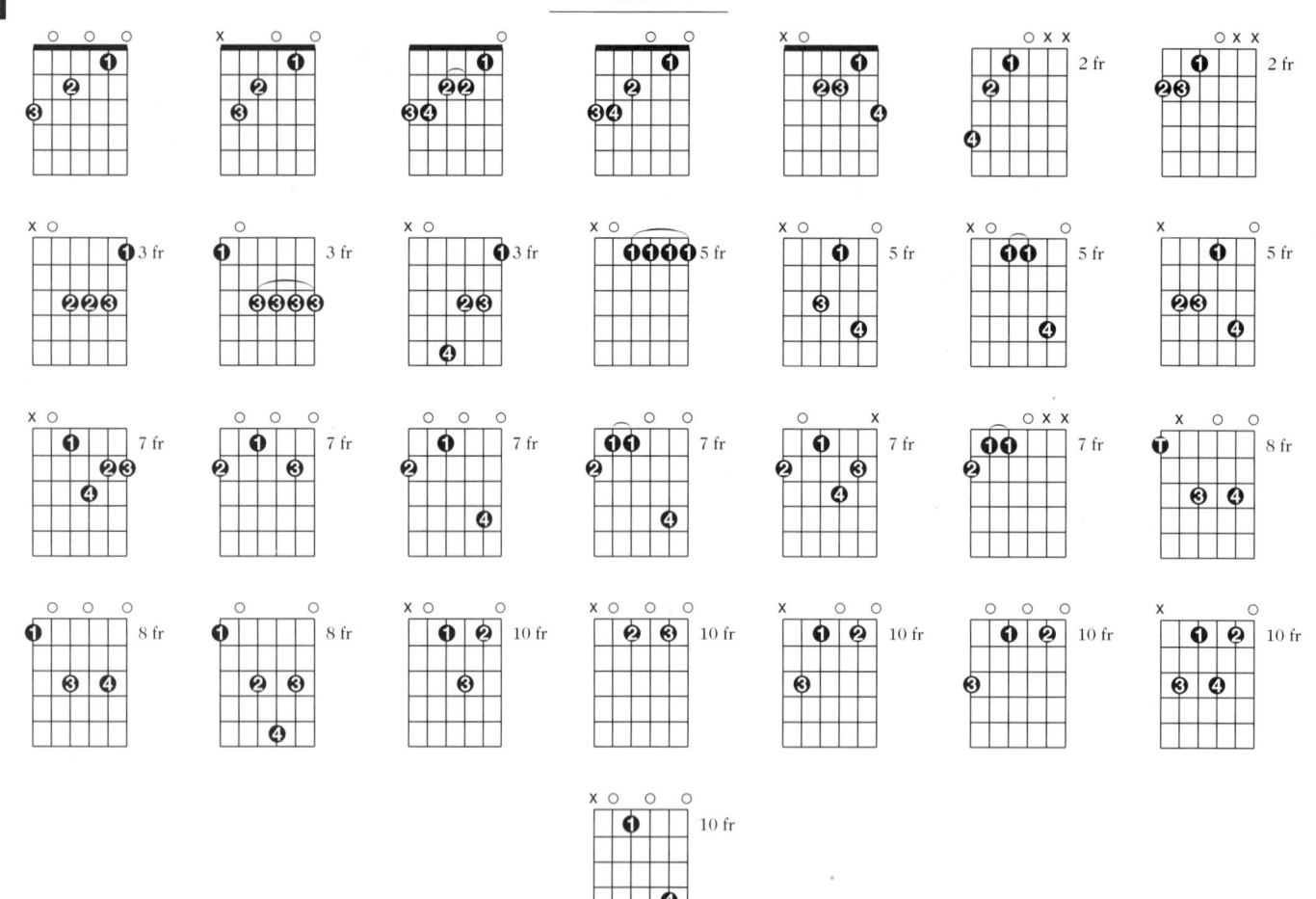

Am(add9)

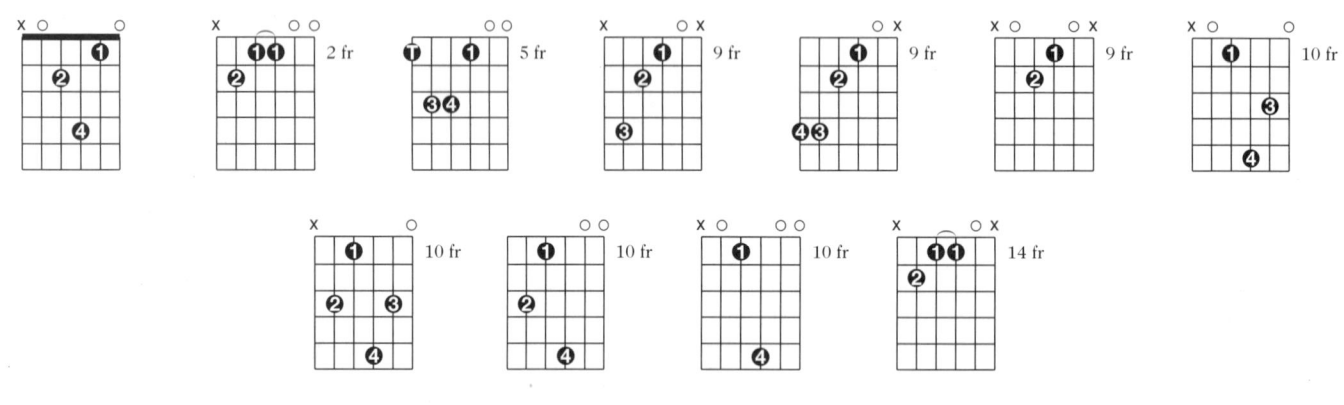

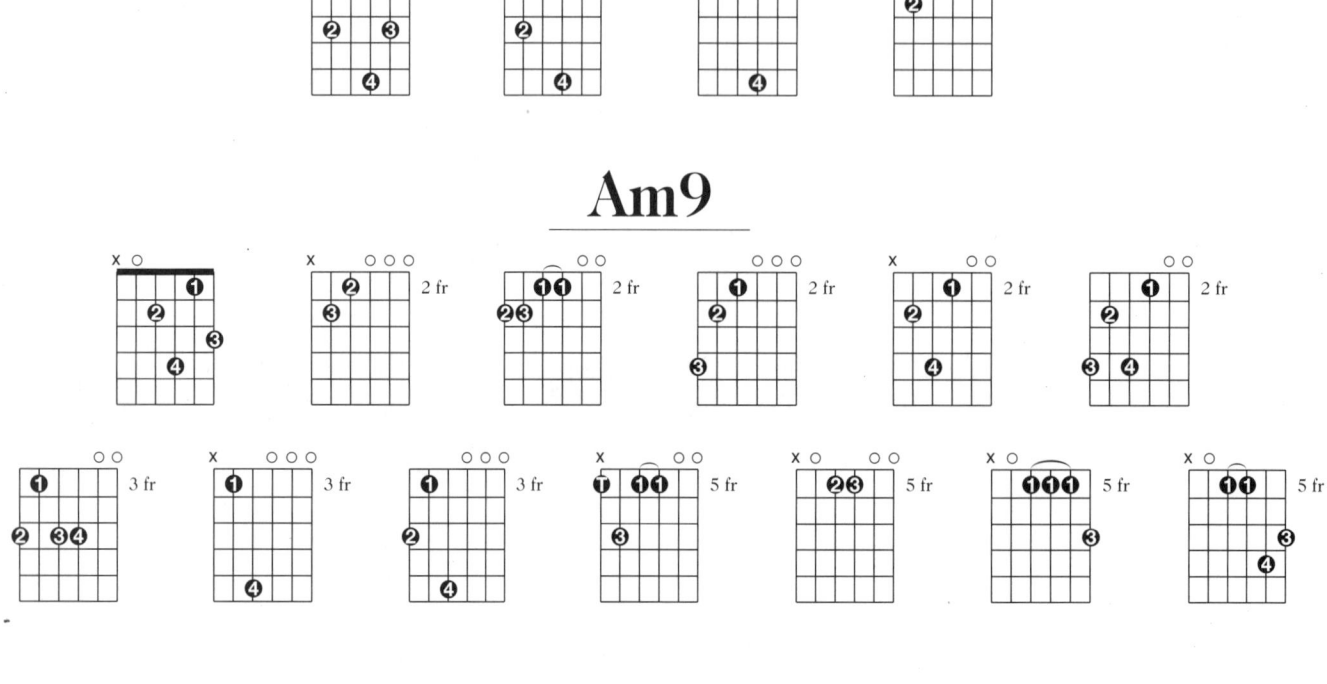

Am9

Am9 (cont'd)

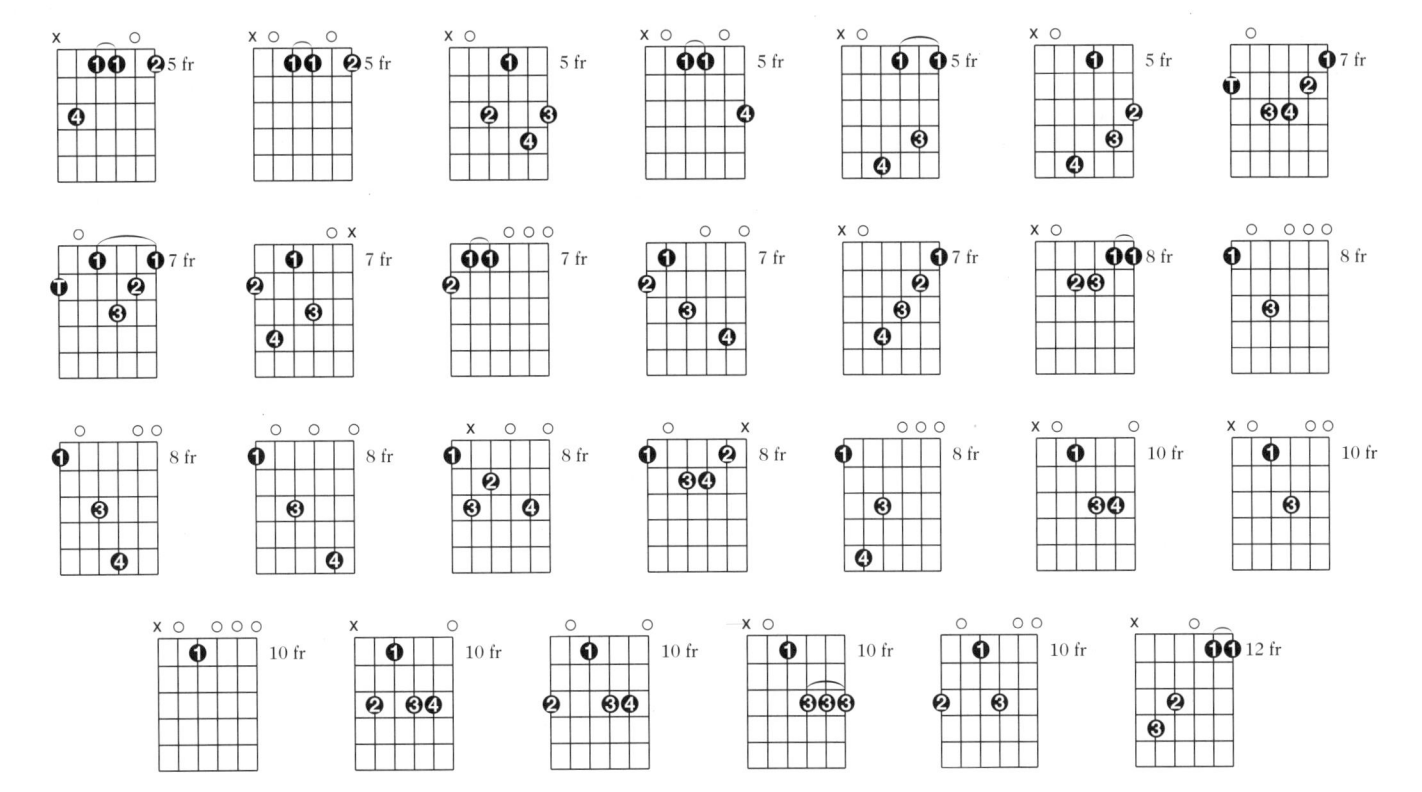

Am11

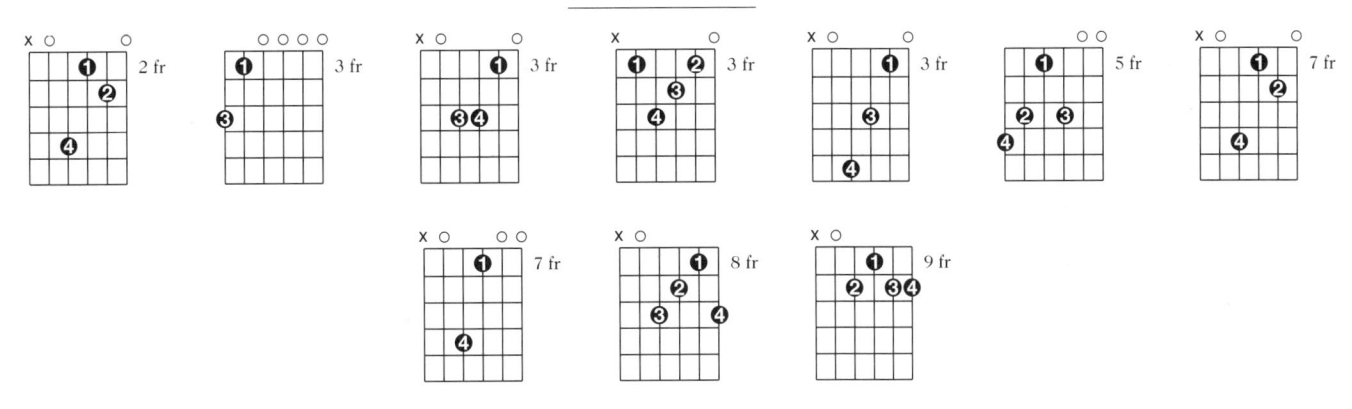

Am7♭5

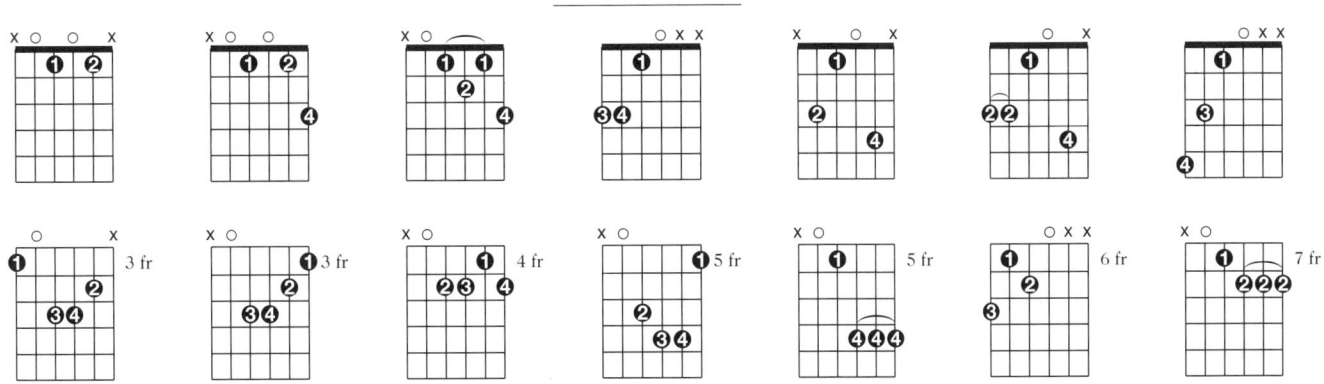

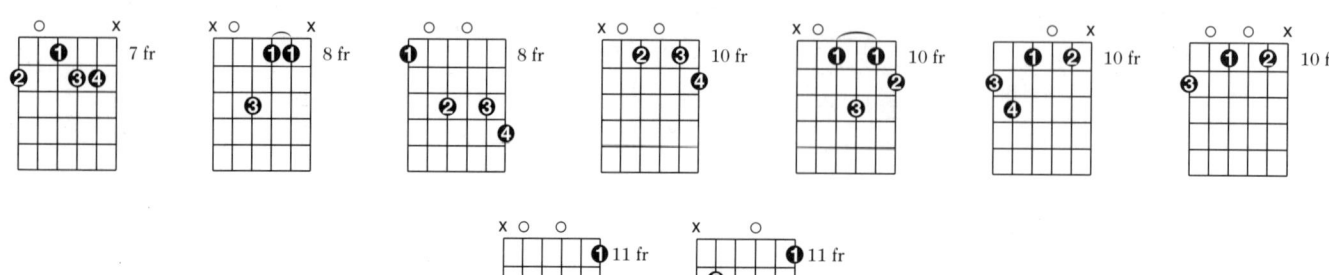

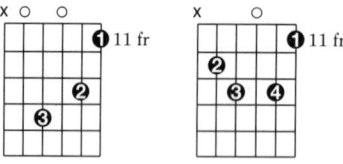

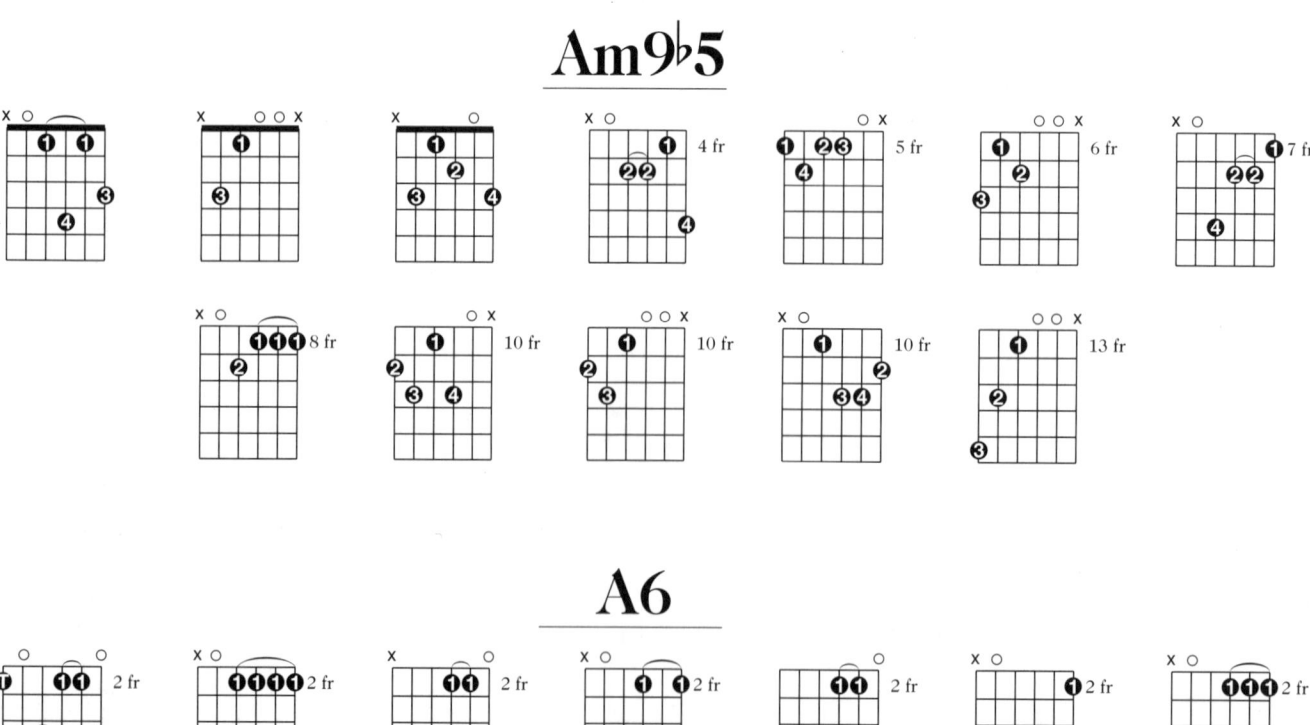

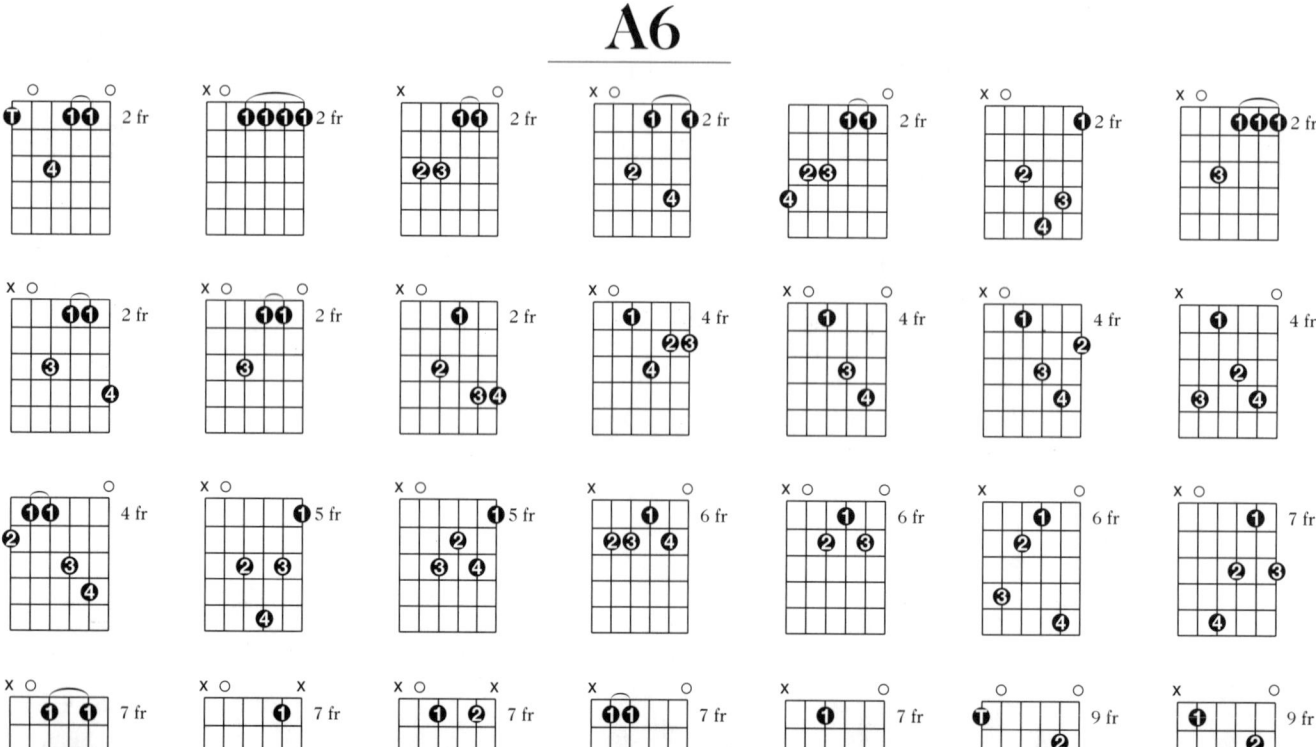

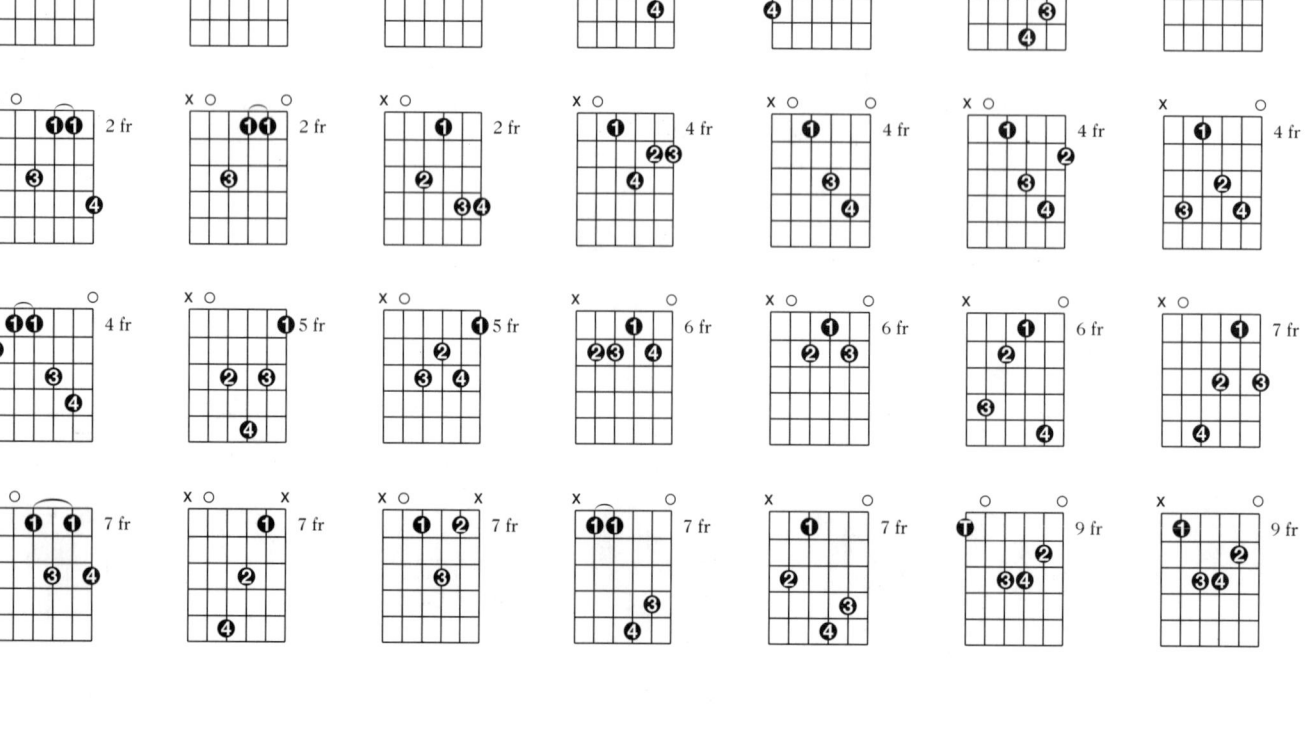

A

Am7♭5 (cont'd)

Am9♭5

A6

A6 (cont'd)

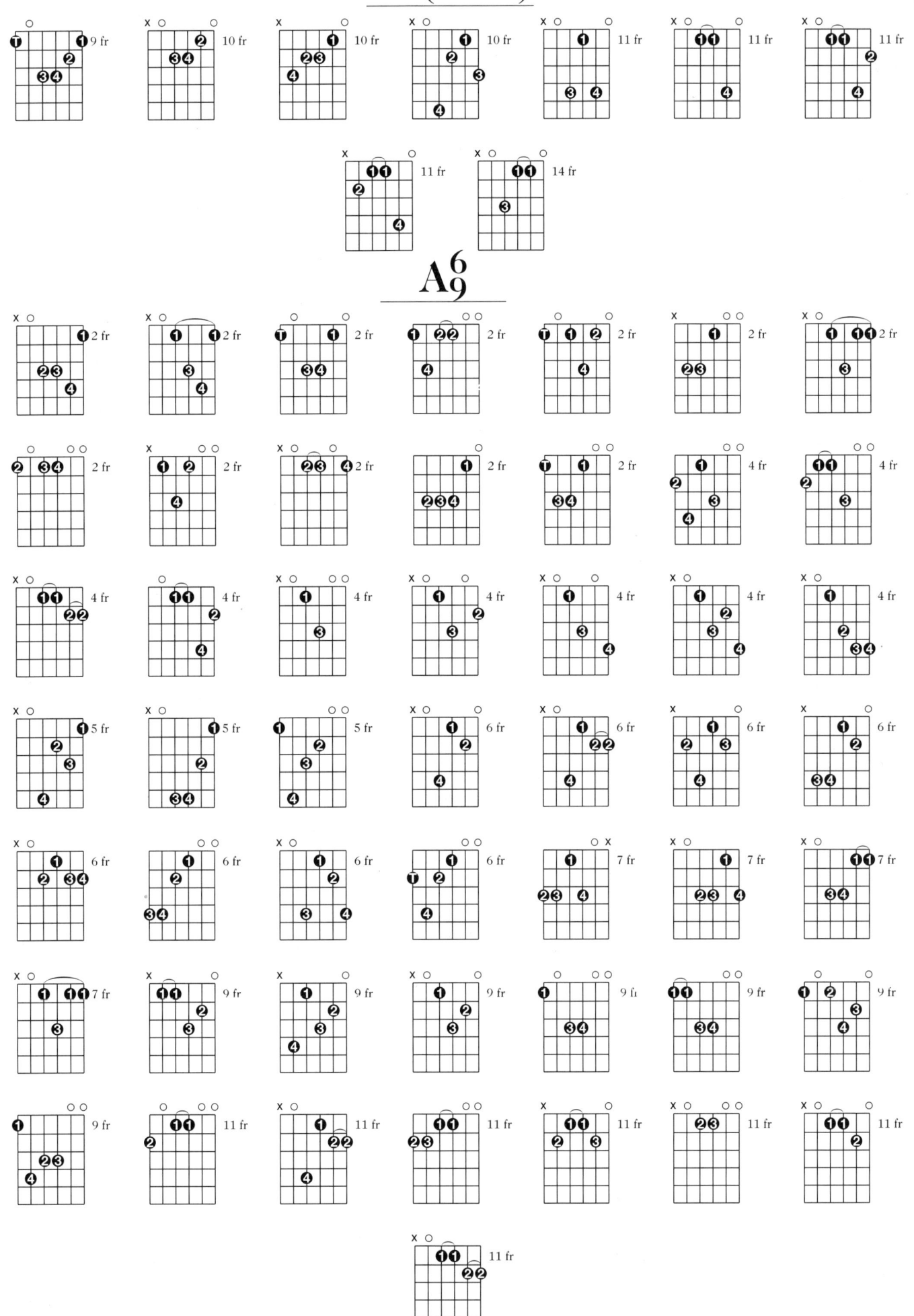

A⁶/₉

A

A13

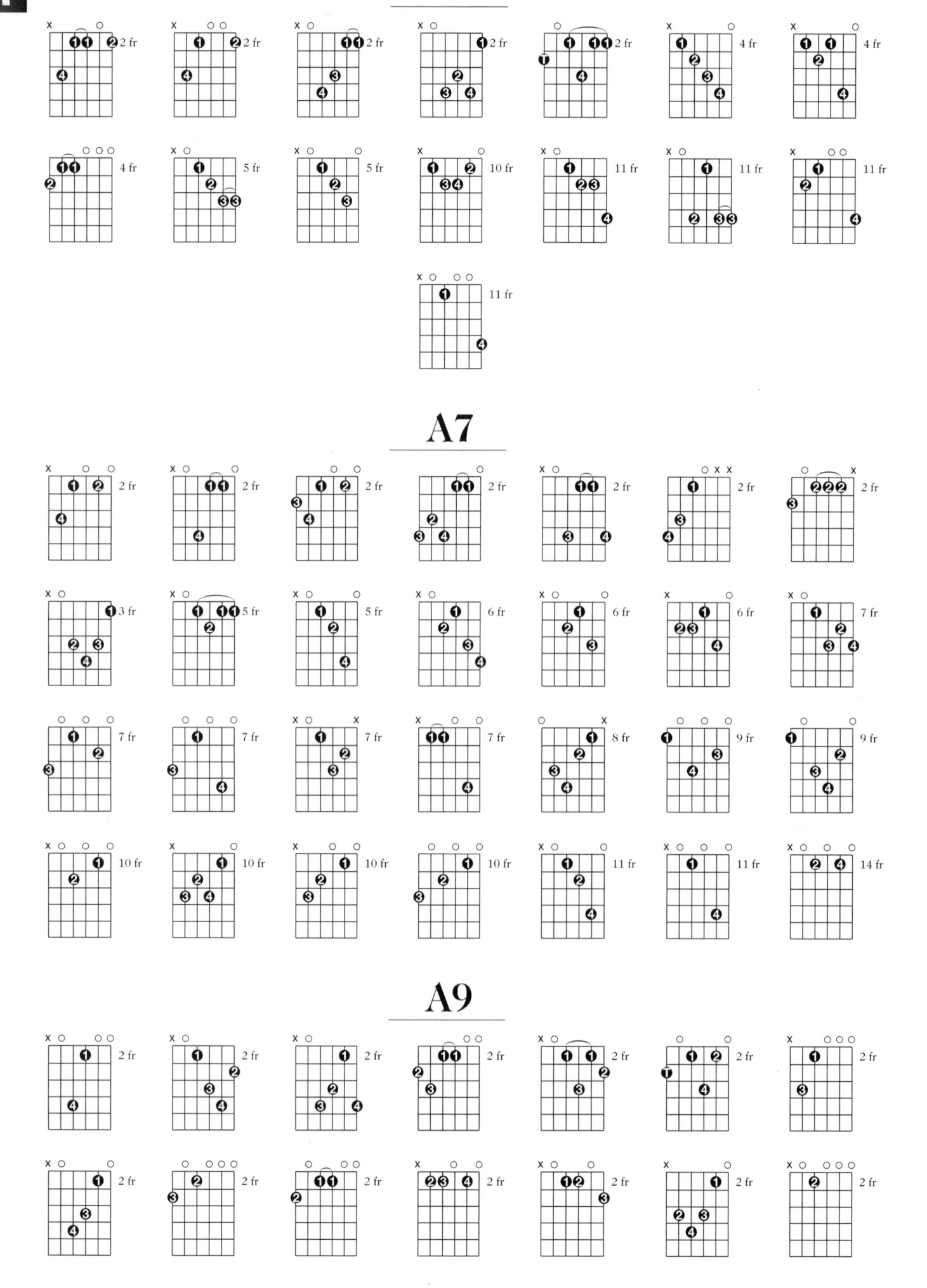

A7

A9

A9 (cont'd)

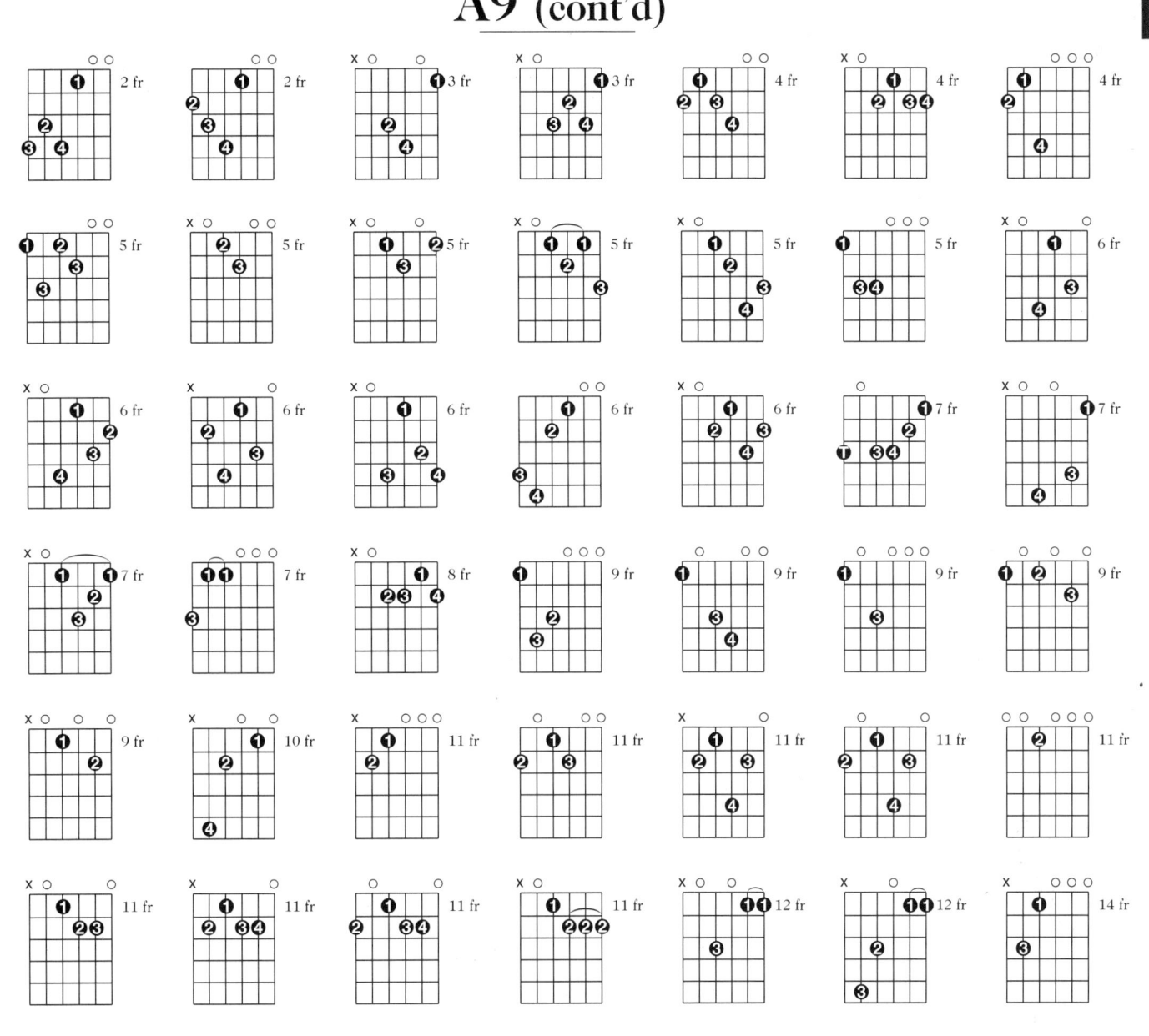

Aadd9

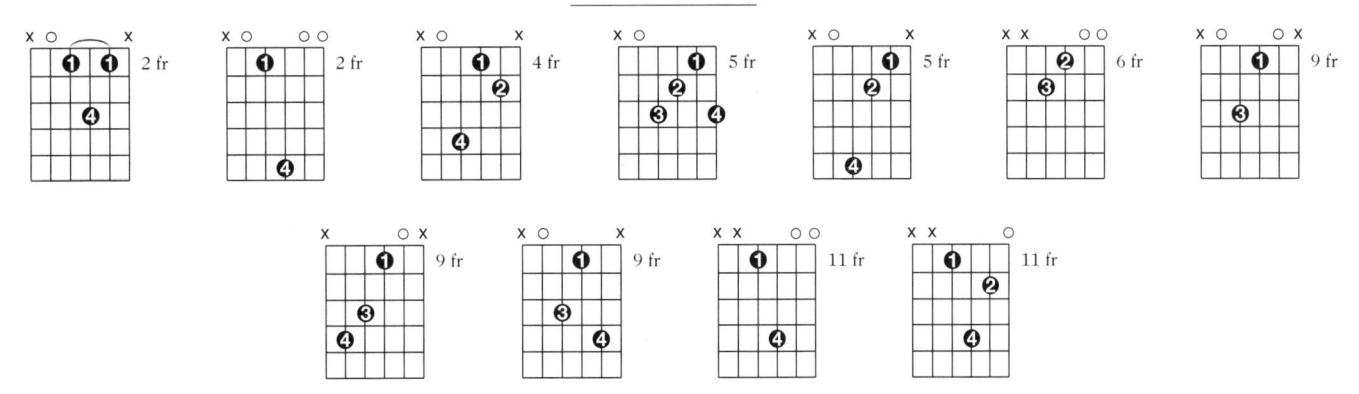

A

Amaj7

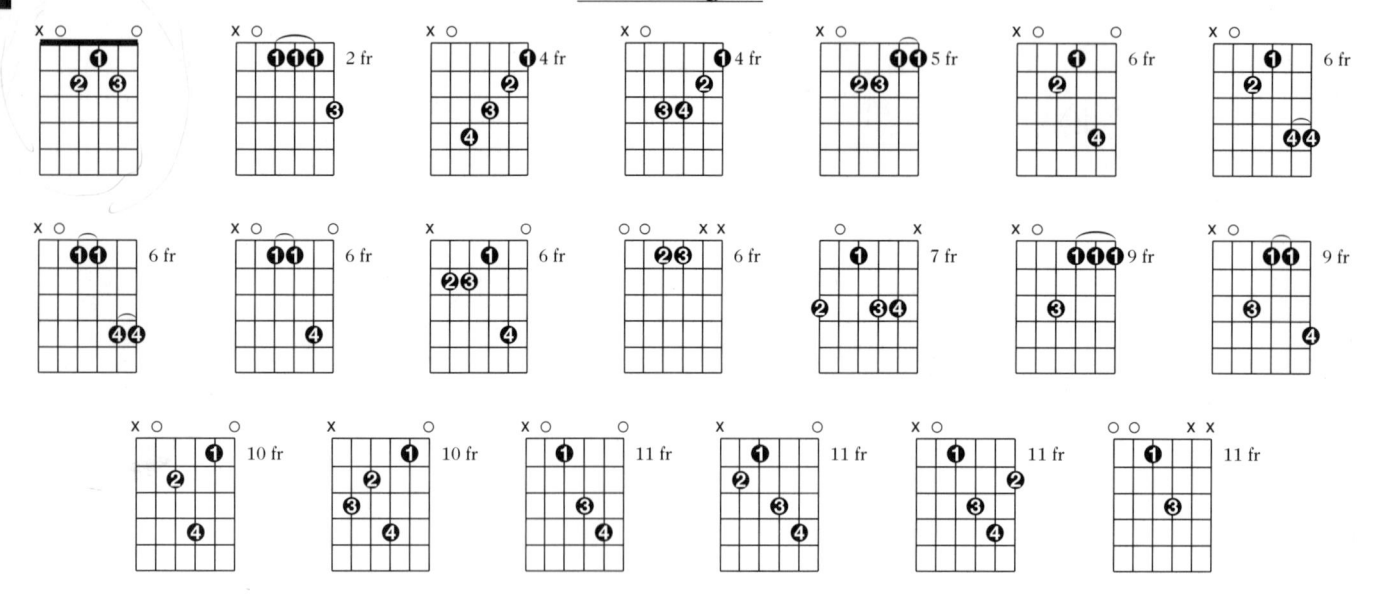

Amaj9

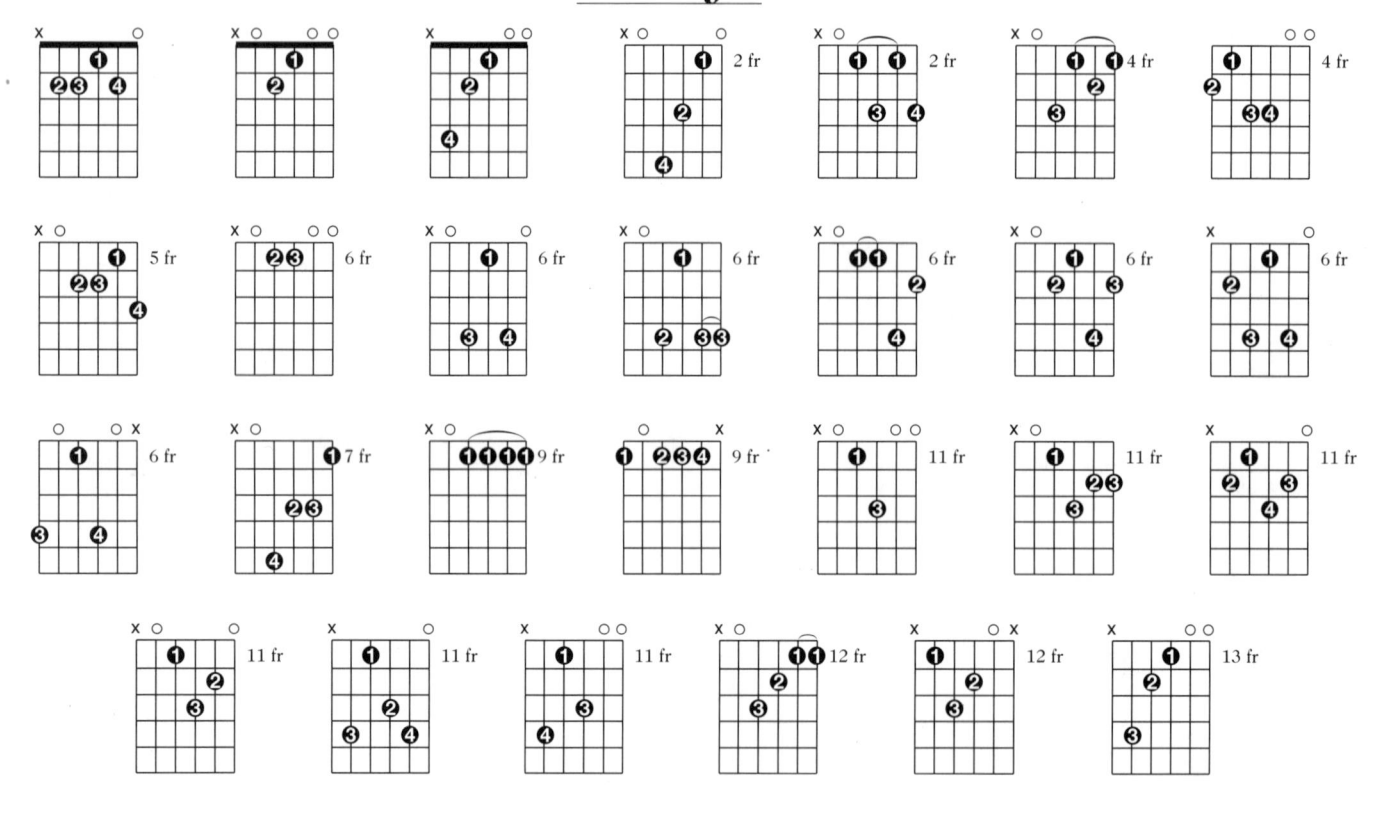

Amaj13

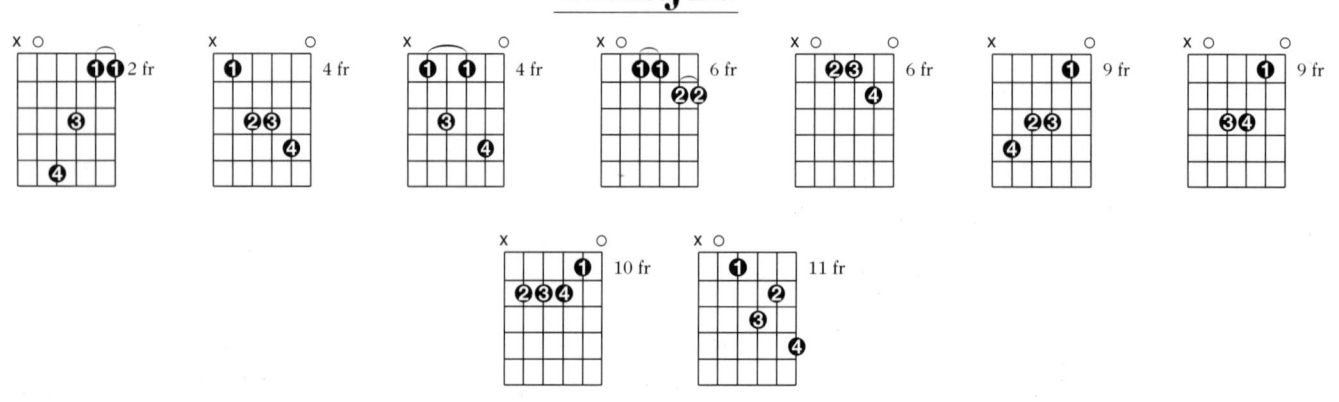

A7sus4

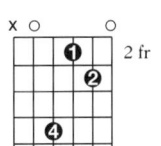

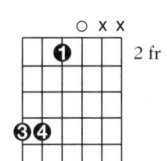

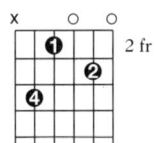

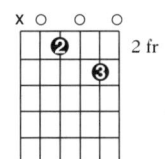

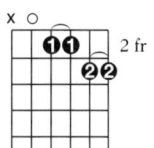

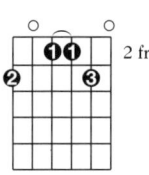

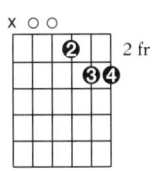

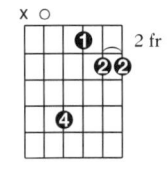

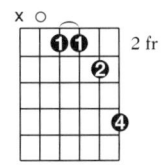

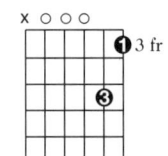

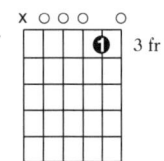

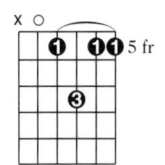

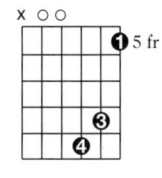

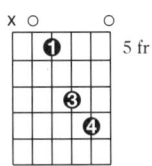

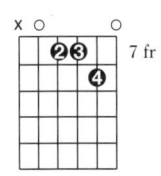

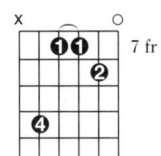

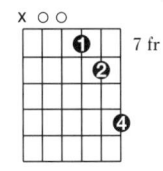

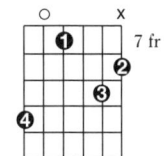

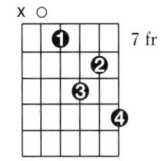

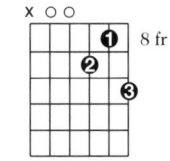

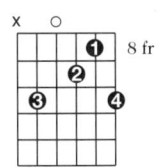

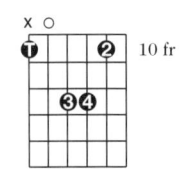

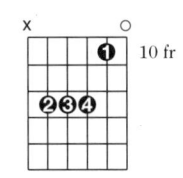

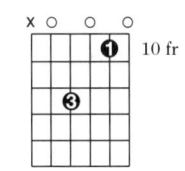

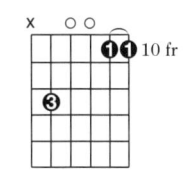

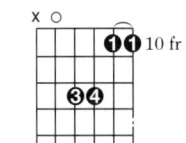

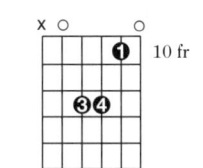

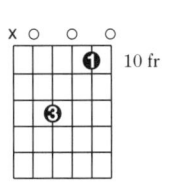

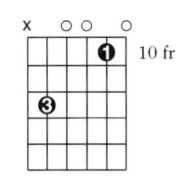

A11

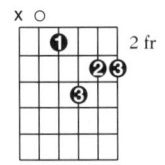

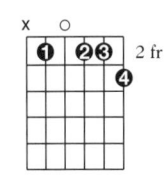

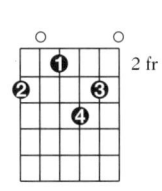

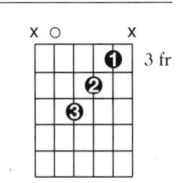

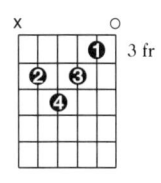

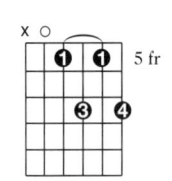

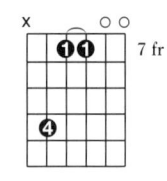

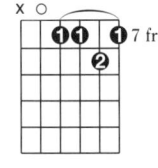

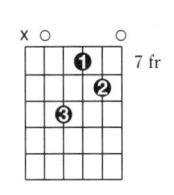

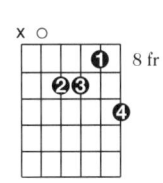

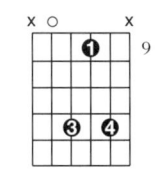

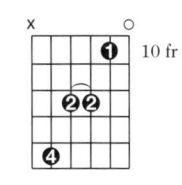

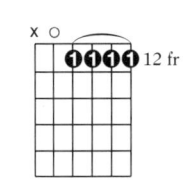

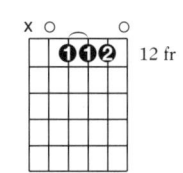

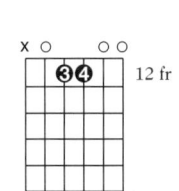

A7♭5

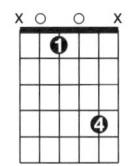

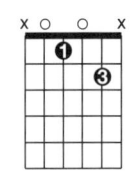

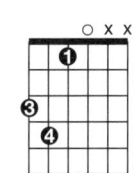

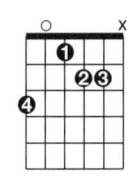

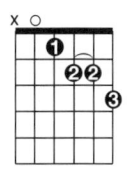

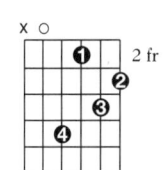

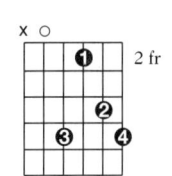

A

A7♭5 (cont'd)

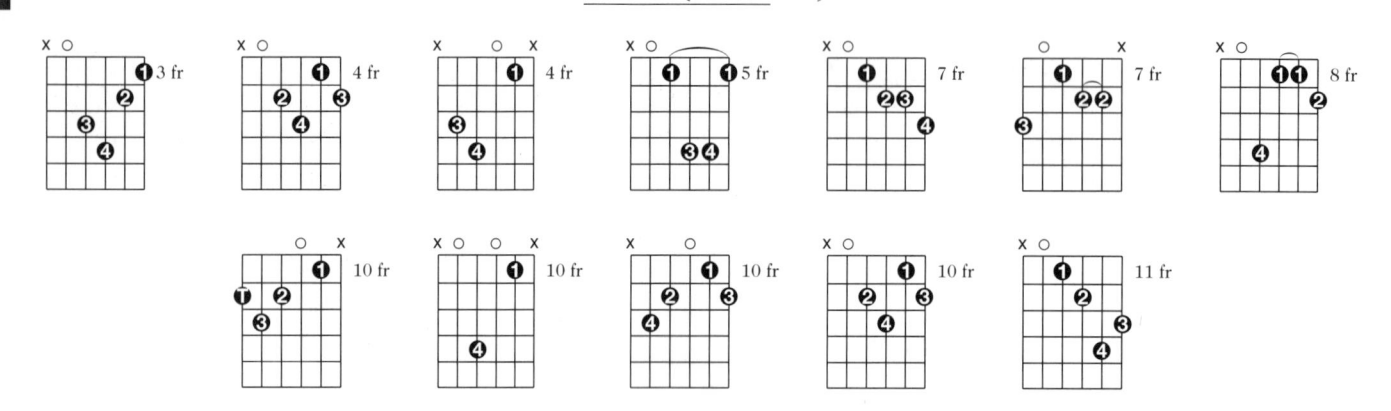

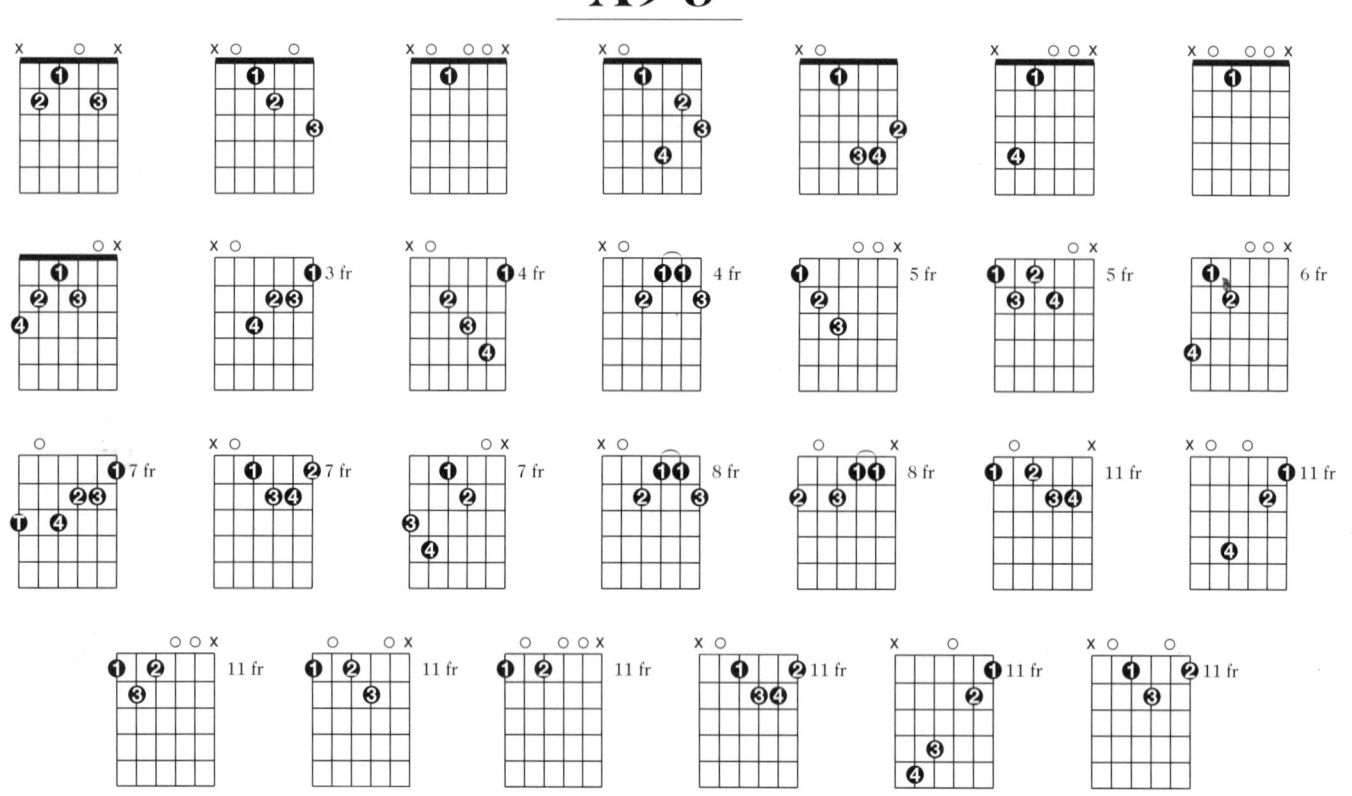

A9♭5

A9♯11

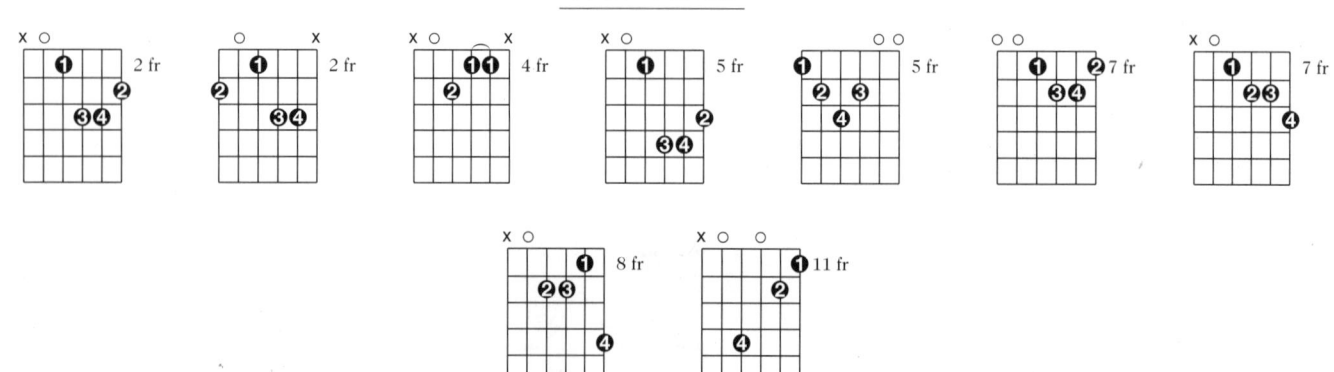

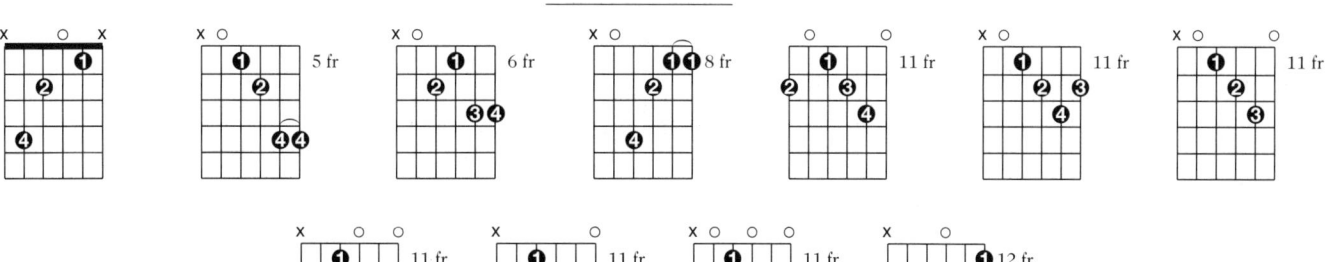

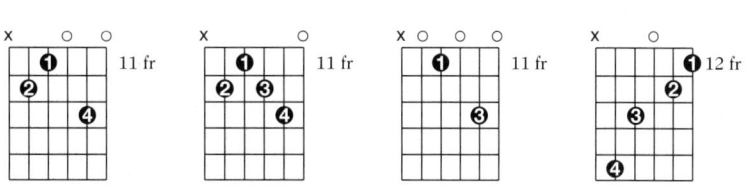

A7#9

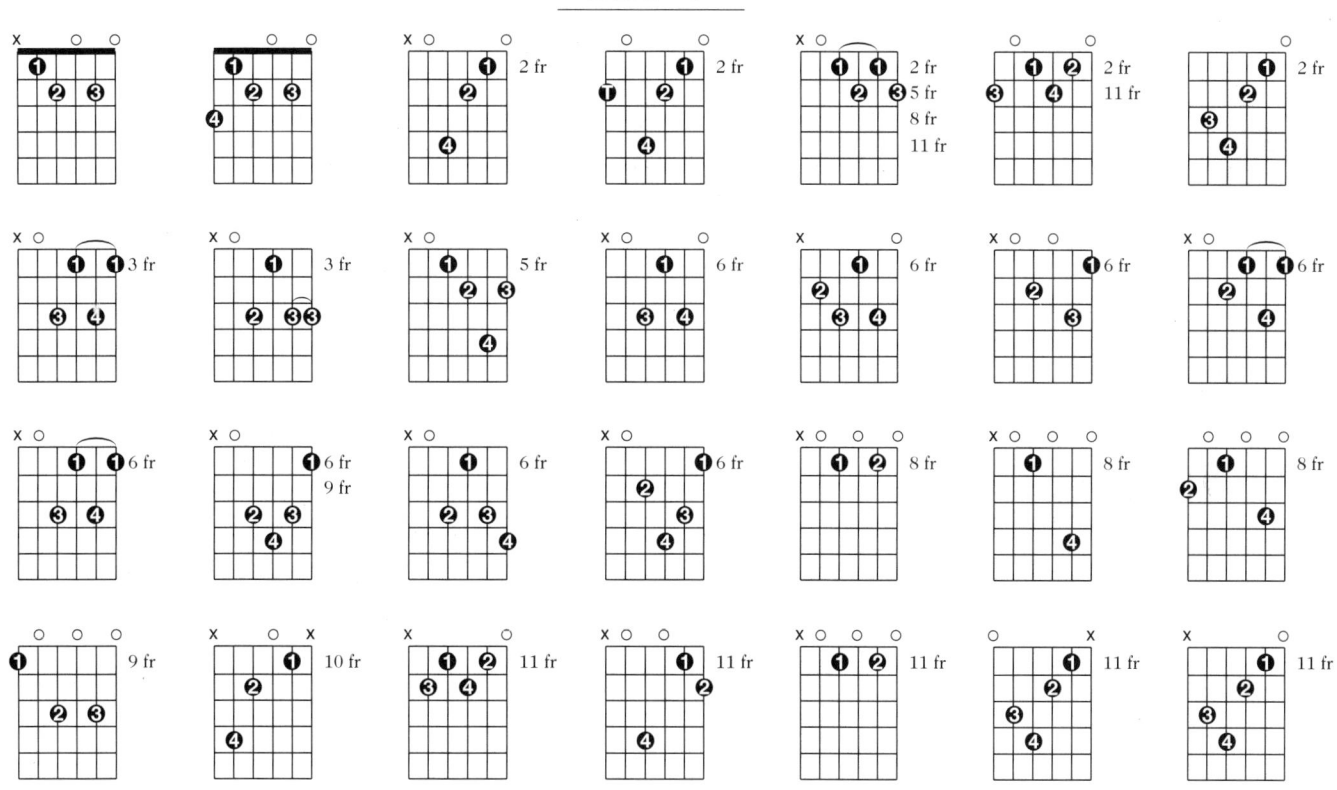

A7♭9

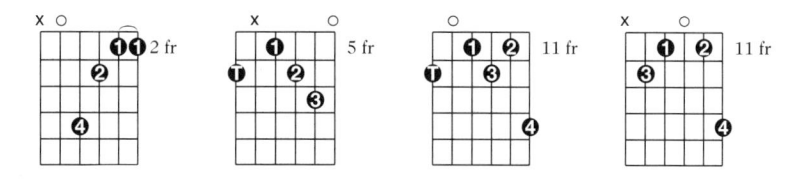

A13♭9

Am(maj7)

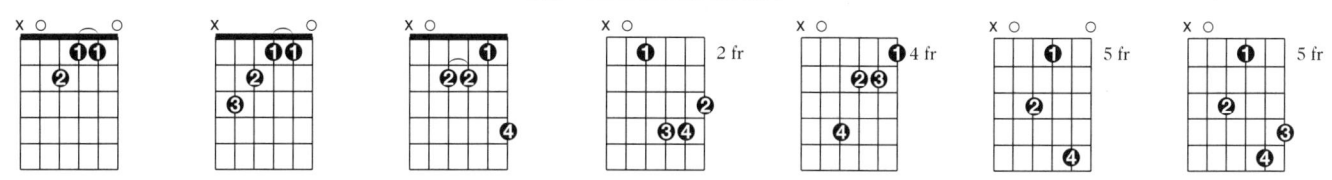

Am(maj7) (cont'd)

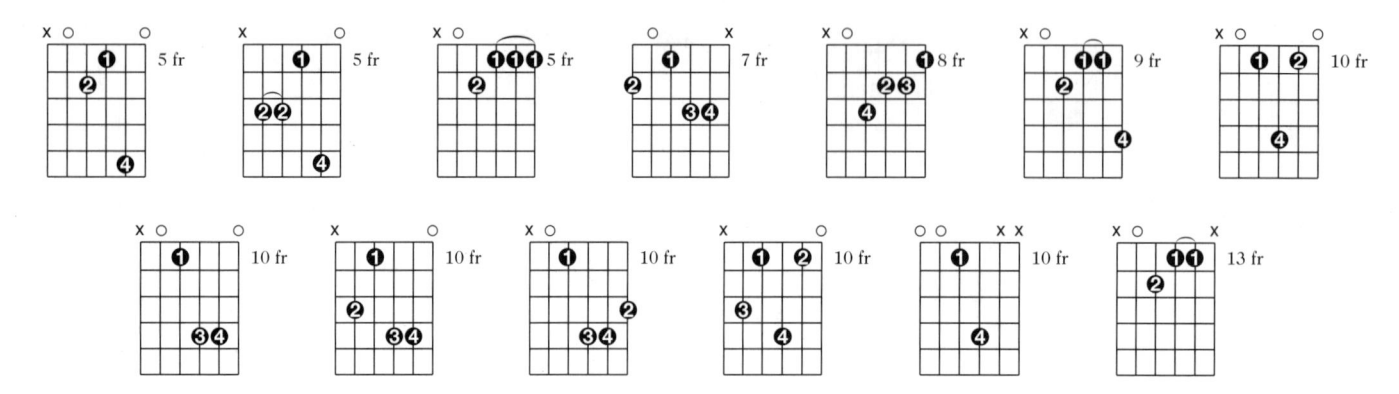

Am(maj9)

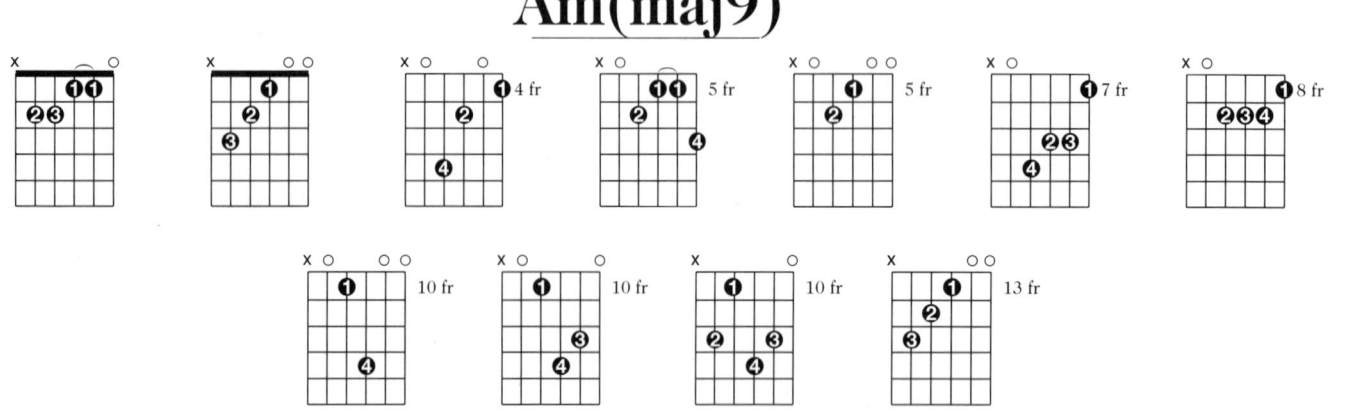

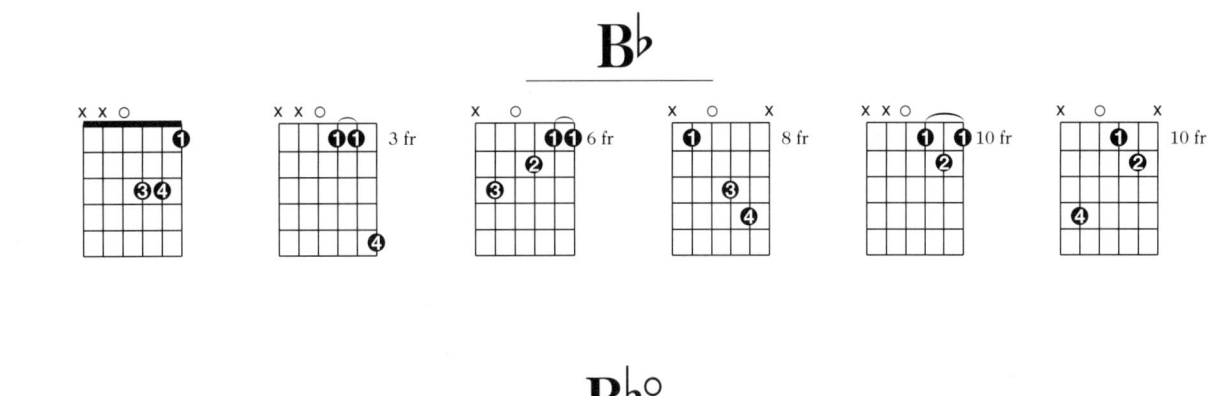

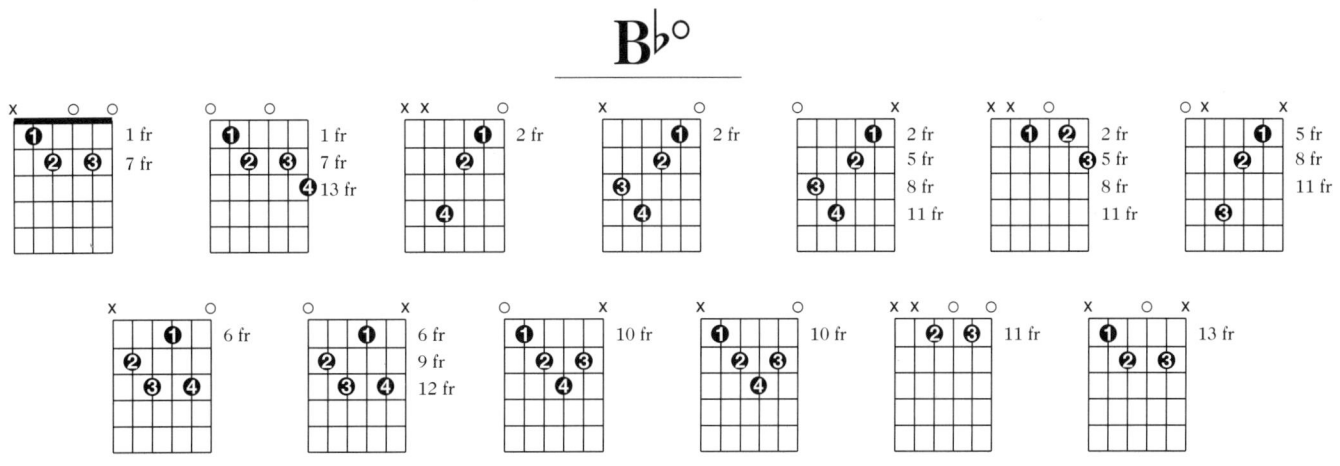

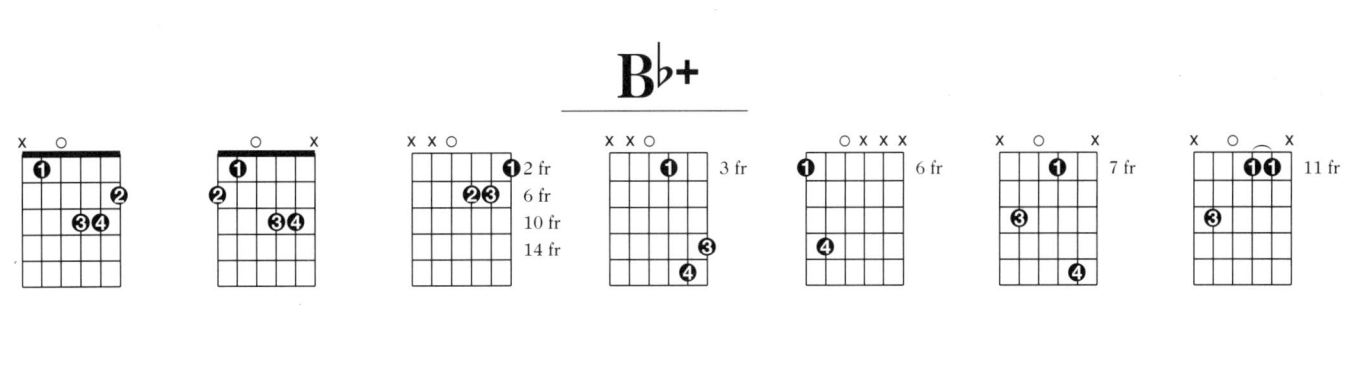

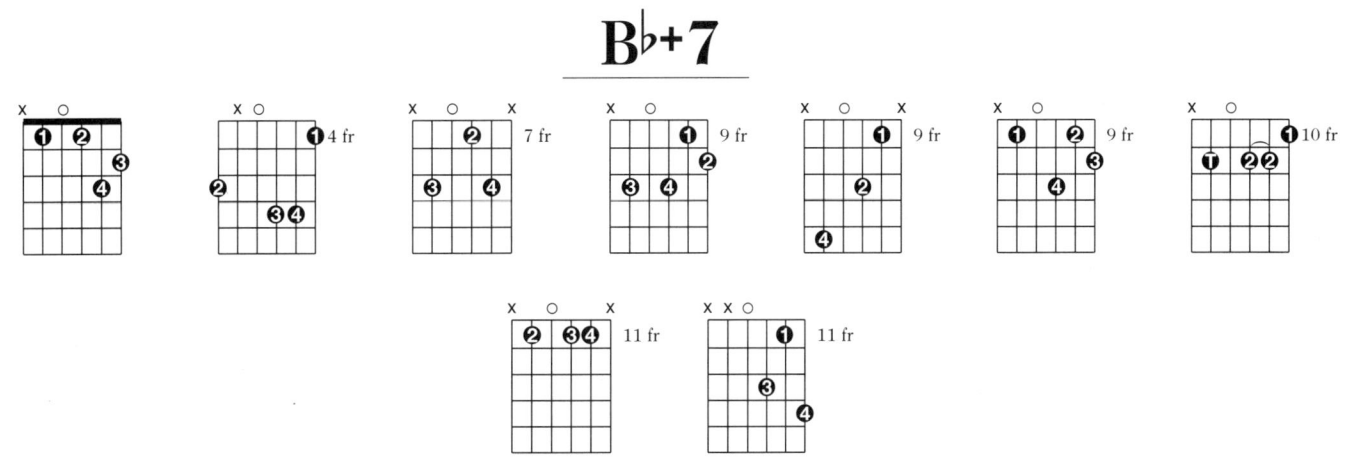

B♭

B♭

B♭°

B♭+

B♭+7

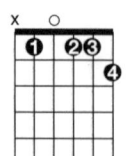

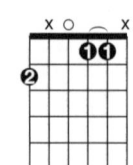

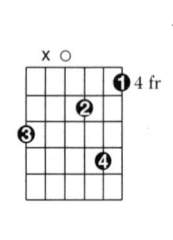

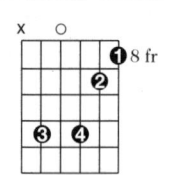

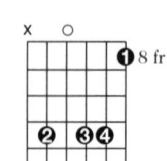

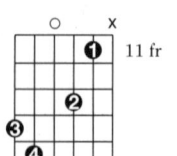

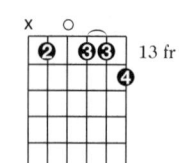

B♭+9

B♭m6

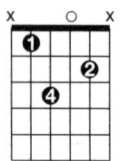

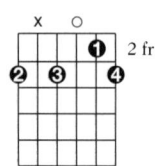

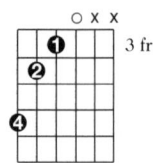

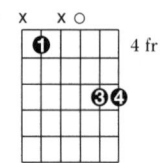

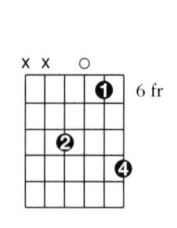

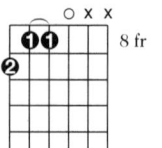

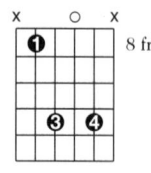

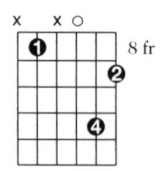

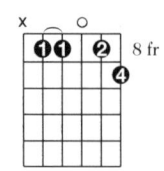

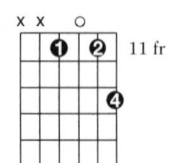

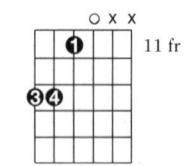

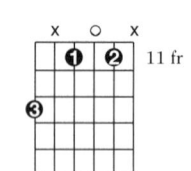

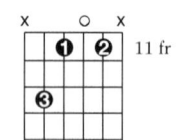

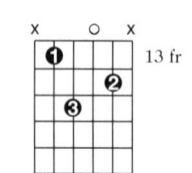

B♭m6/9

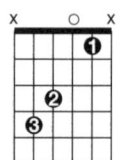

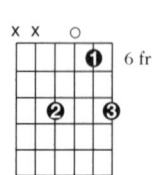

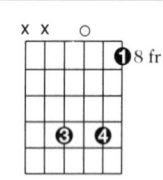

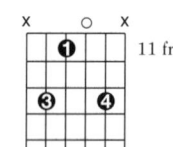

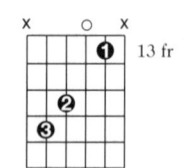

B♭m13

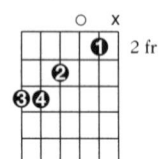

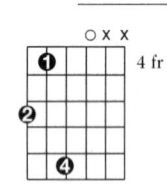

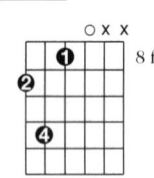

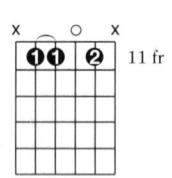

B♭m7♭5

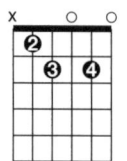

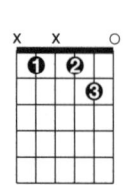

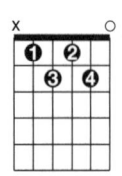

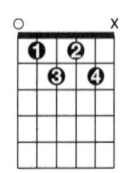

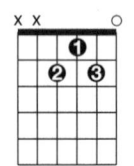

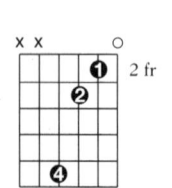

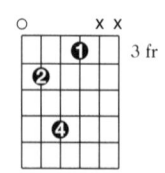

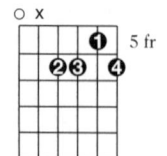

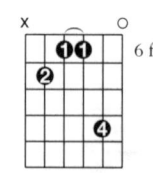

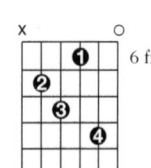

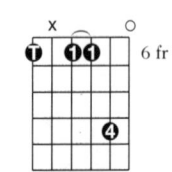

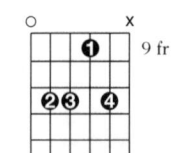

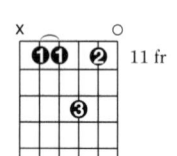

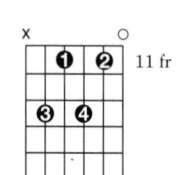

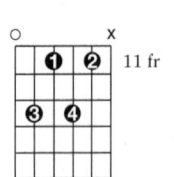

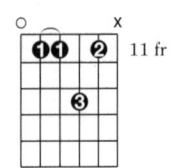

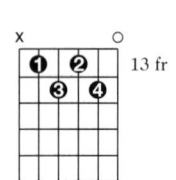

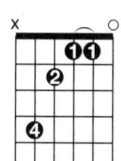

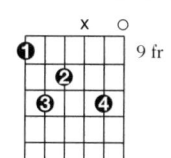

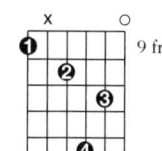

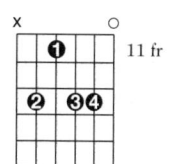

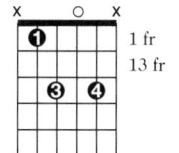

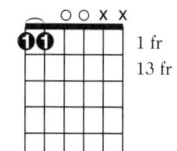

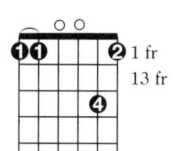

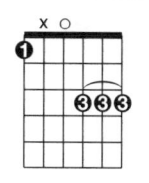

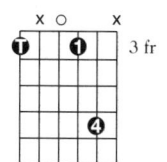

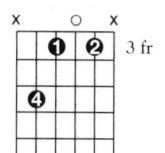

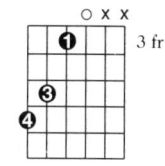

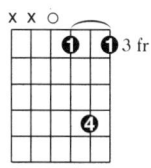

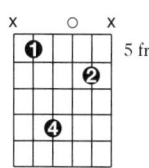

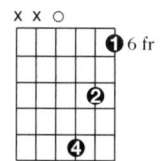

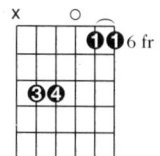

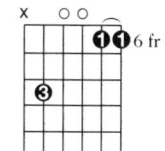

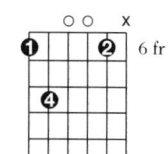

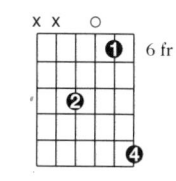

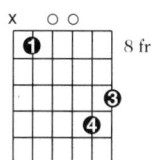

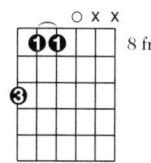

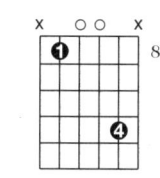

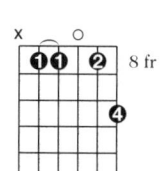

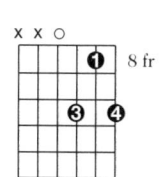

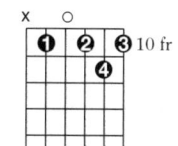

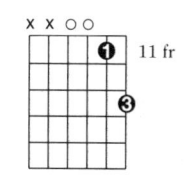

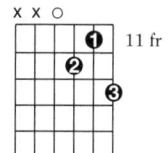

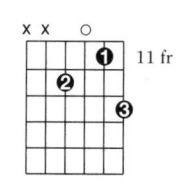

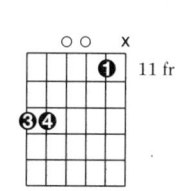

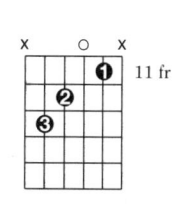

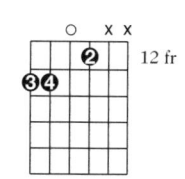

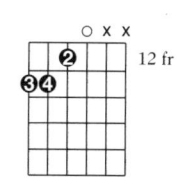

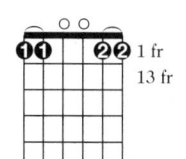

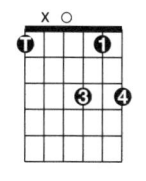

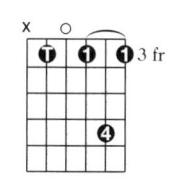

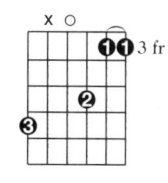

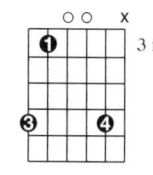

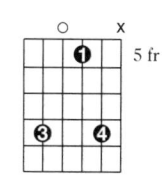

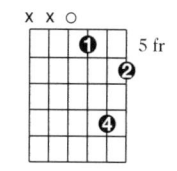

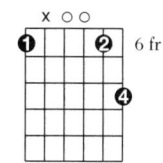

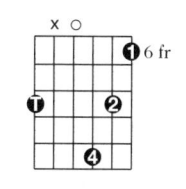

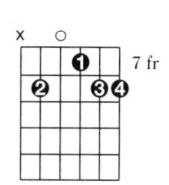

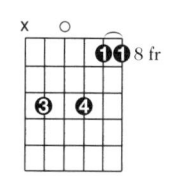

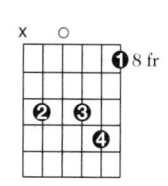

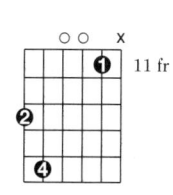

B♭m9♭5

B♭6

B♭6/9

B♭

B♭13

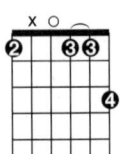

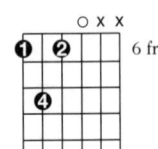

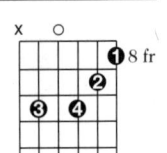

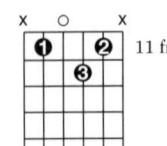

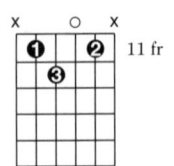

B♭7

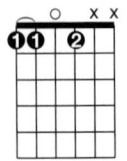

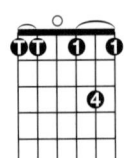

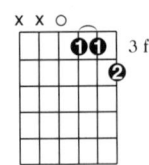

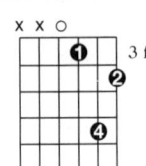

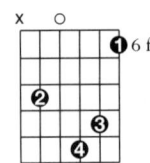

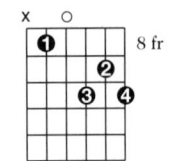

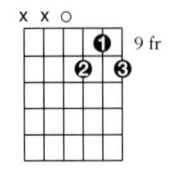

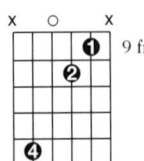

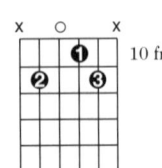

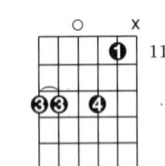

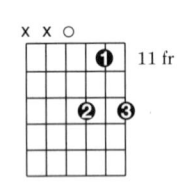

B♭9

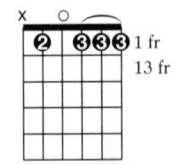

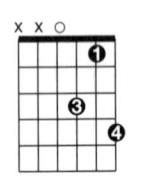

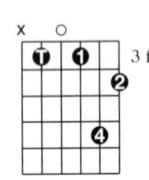

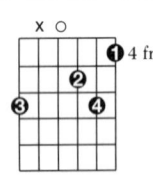

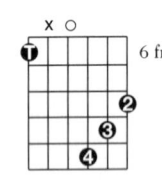

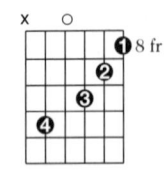

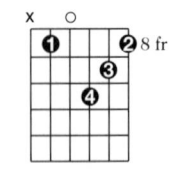

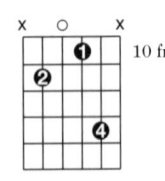

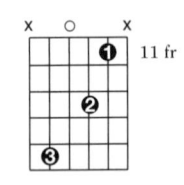

B♭add9

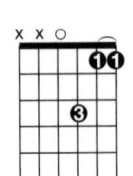

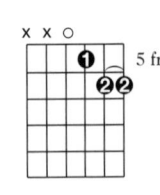

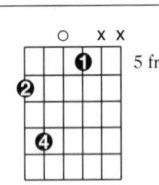

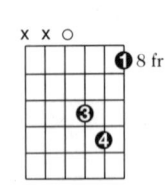

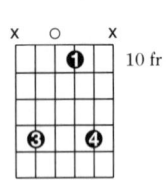

B♭maj7

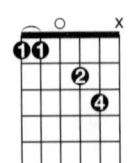

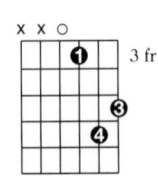

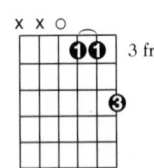

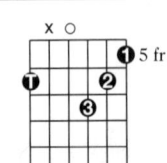

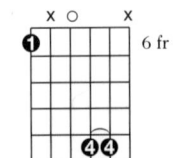

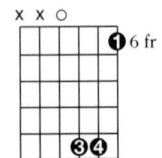

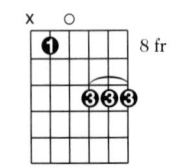

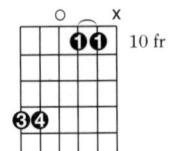

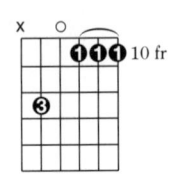

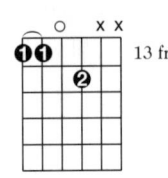

B♭maj9

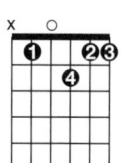

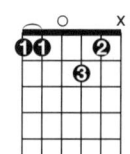

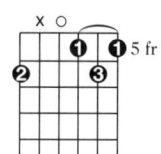

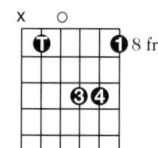

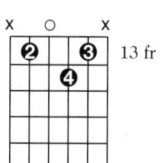

B♭maj13

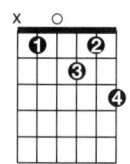

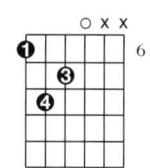

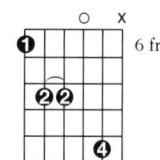

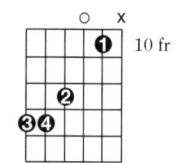

B♭11

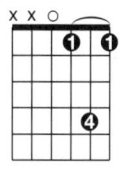

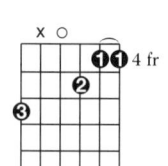

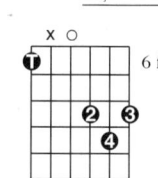

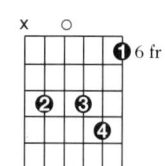

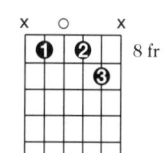

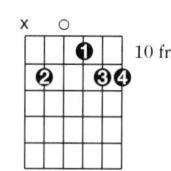

B♭7♭5

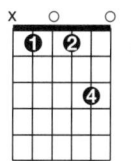

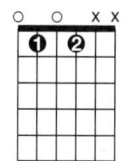

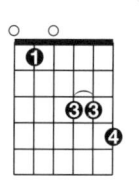

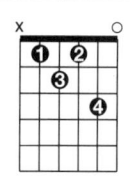

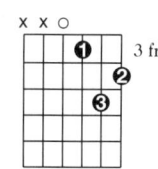

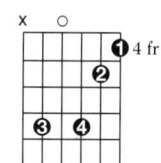

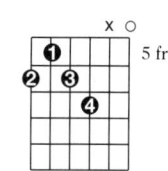

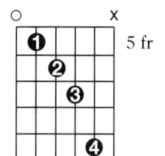

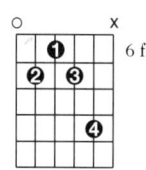

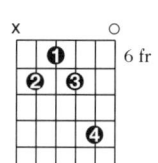

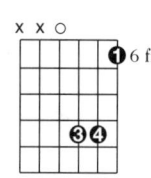

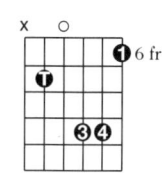

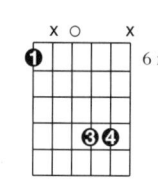

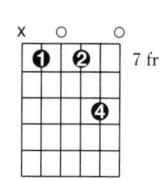

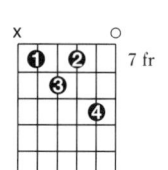

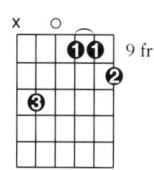

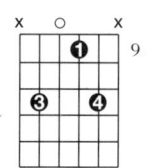

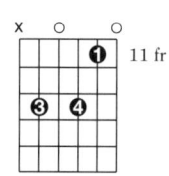

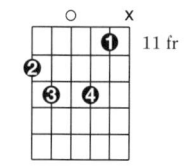

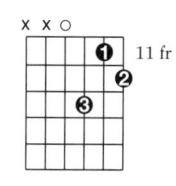

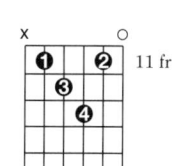

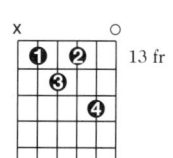

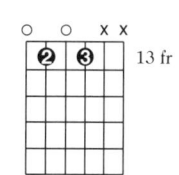

B♭9♭5

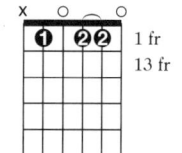

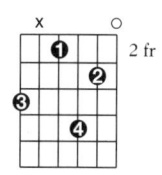

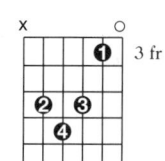

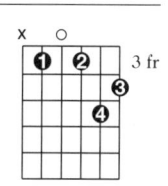

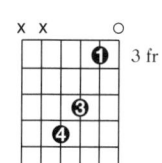

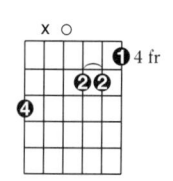

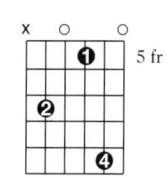

B♭9♭5 (cont'd)

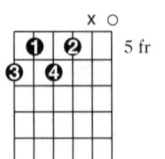

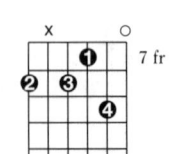

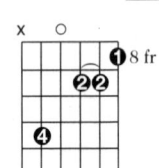

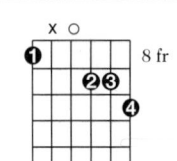

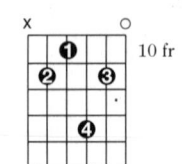

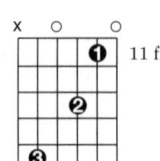

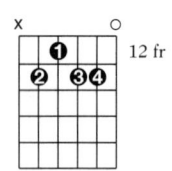

B♭9♯11

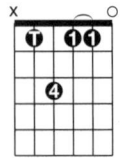

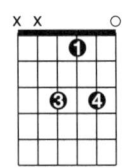

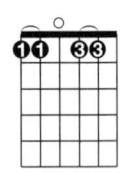

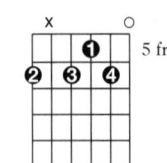

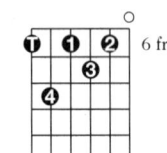

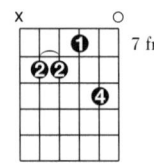

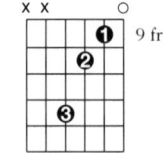

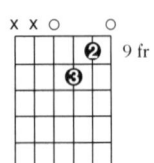

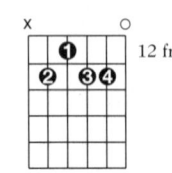

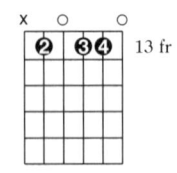

B♭13♭5

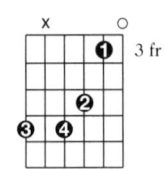

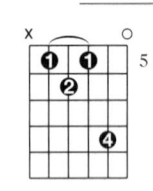

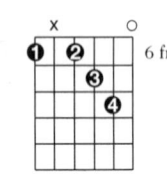

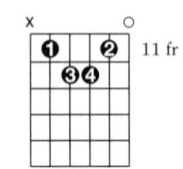

B♭7♯9

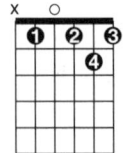

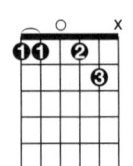

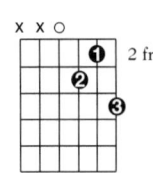

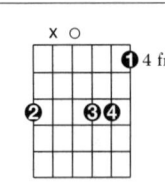

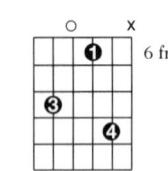

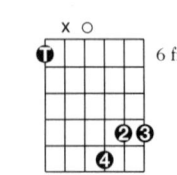

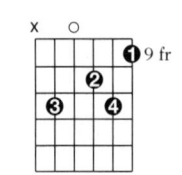

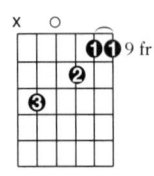

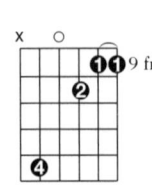

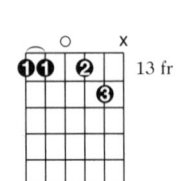

B♭7♭9

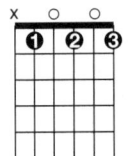

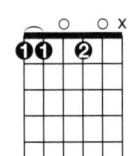

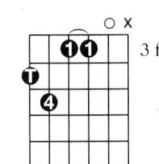

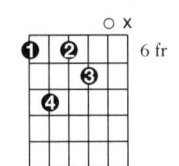

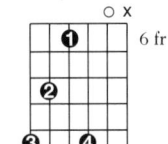

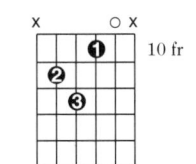

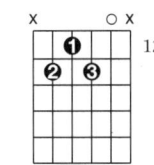

B♭13♭9

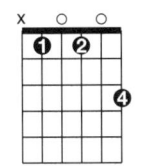

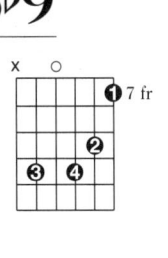

B♭13♭5(♭9)

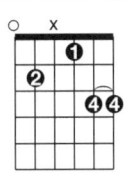

B♭

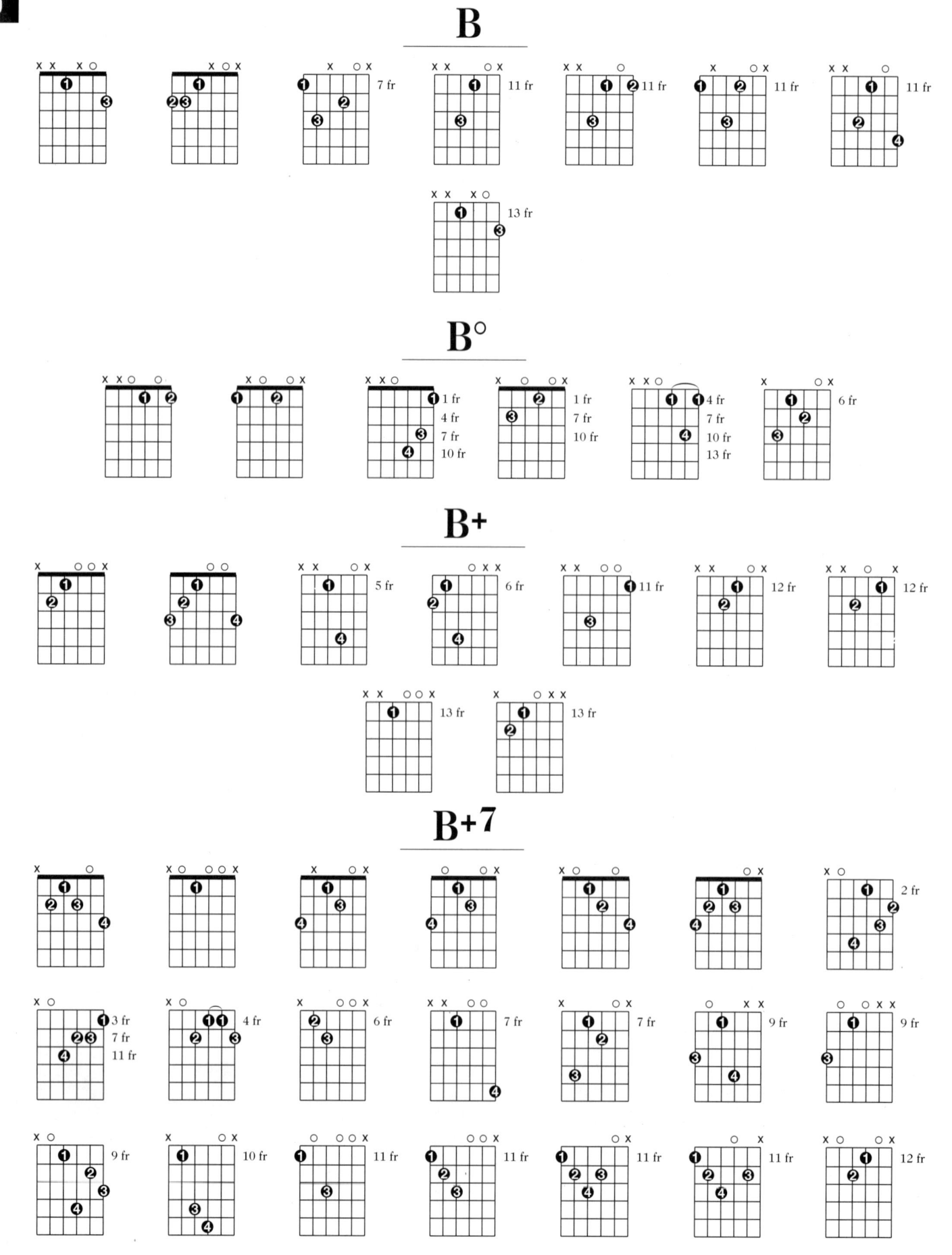

B

B

B°

B+

B+7

B+7 (cont'd)

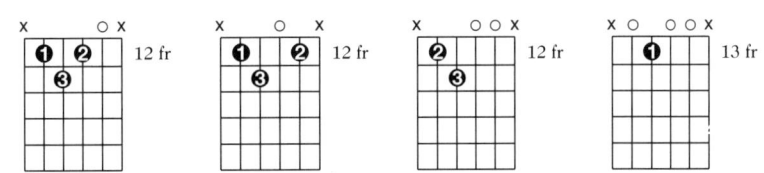

B+9

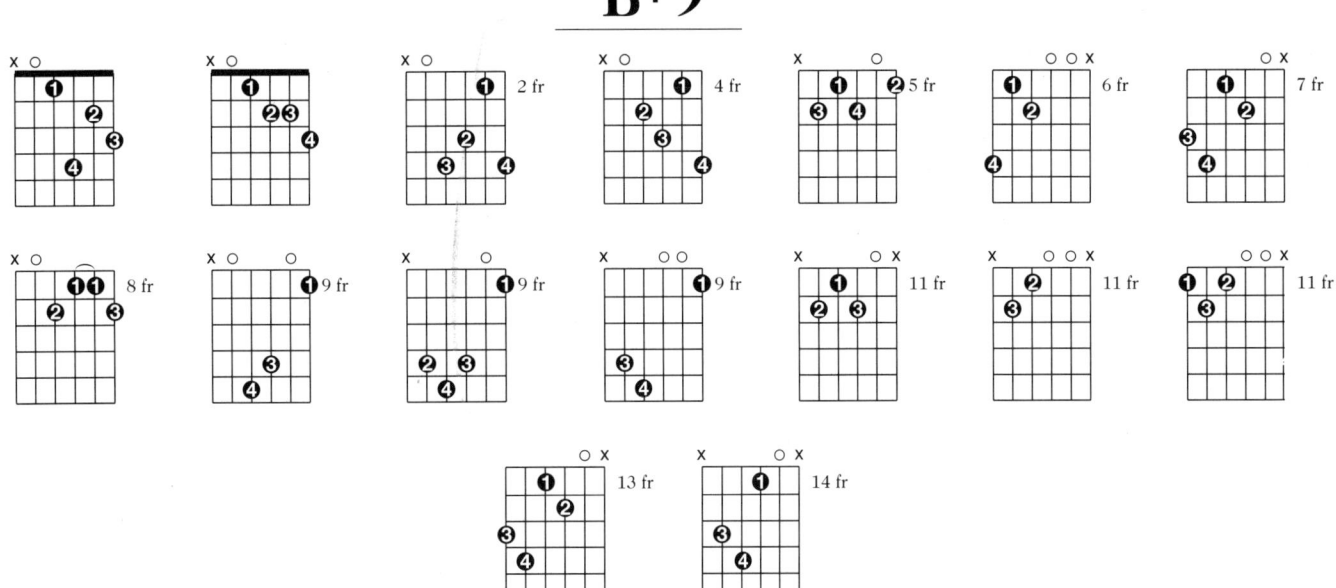

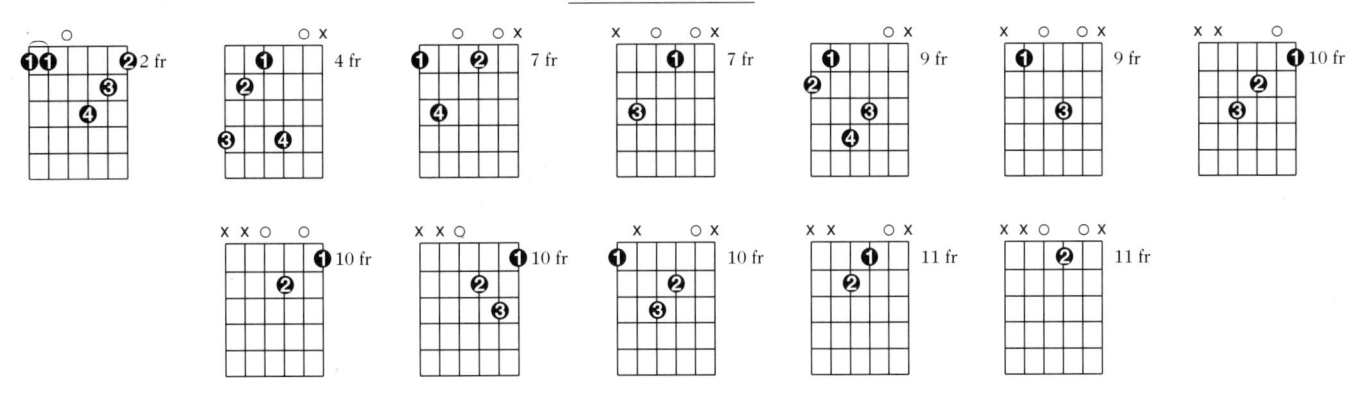

Bm

Bm6

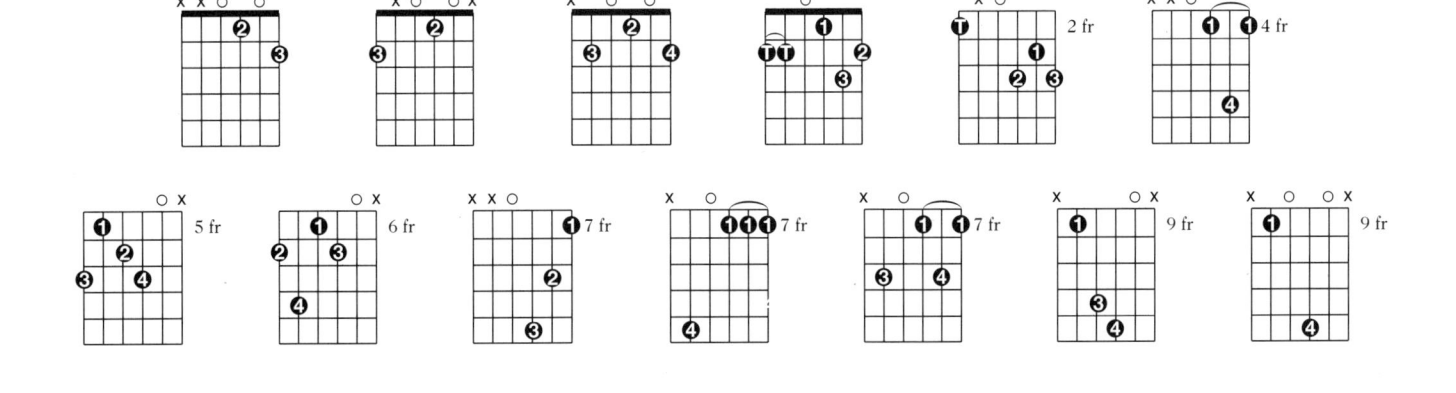

Bm6 (cont'd)

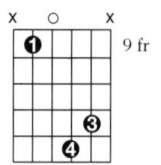

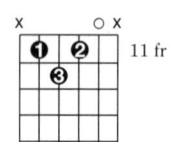

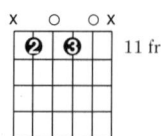

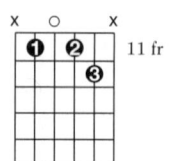

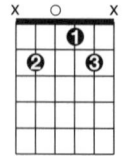

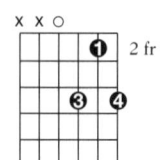

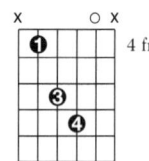

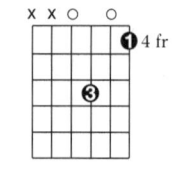

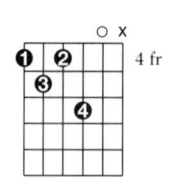

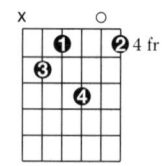

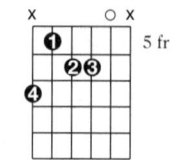

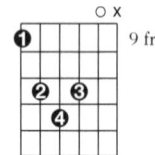

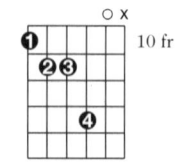

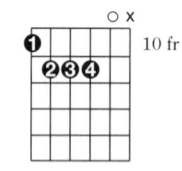

Bm$^6_9$

Bm13

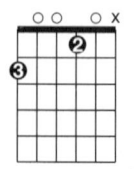

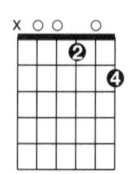

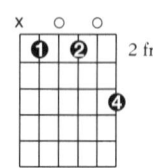

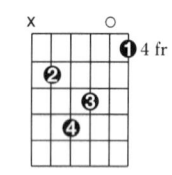

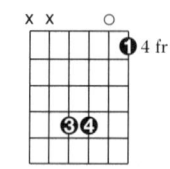

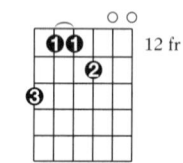

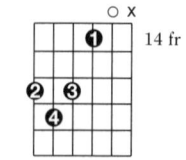

Bm7

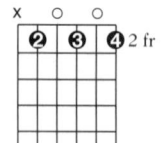

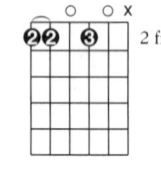

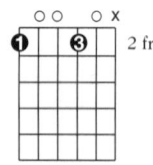

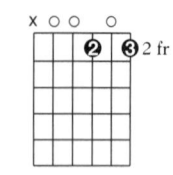

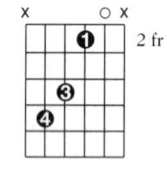

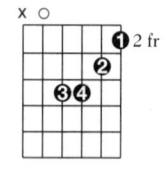

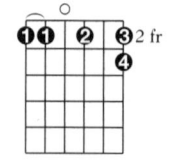

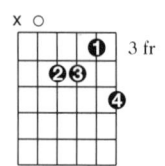

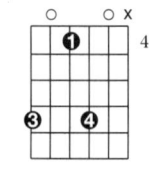

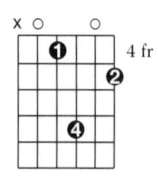

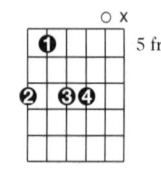

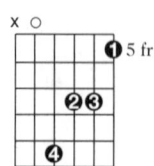

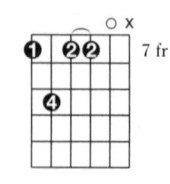

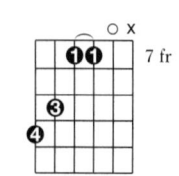

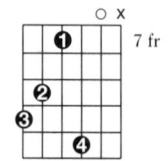

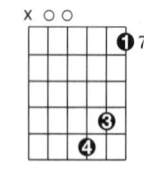

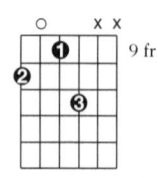

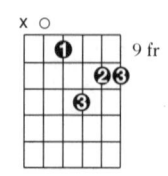

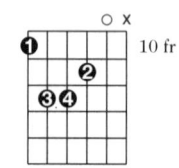

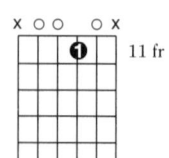

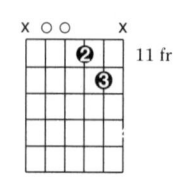

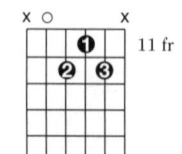

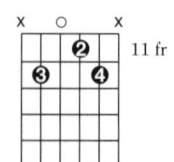

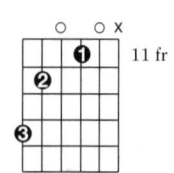

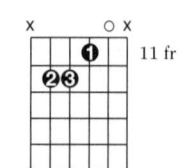

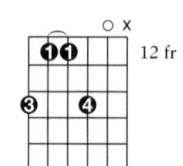

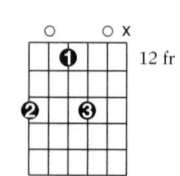

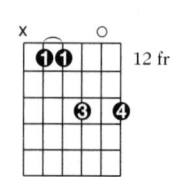

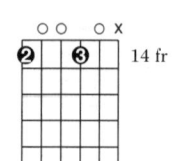

Bm(add9)

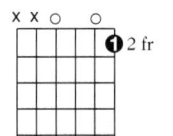

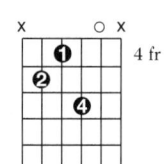

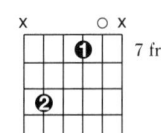

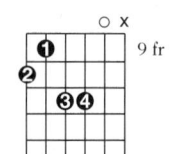

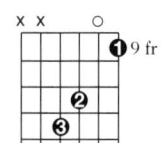

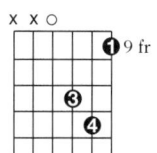

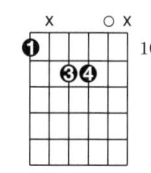

Bm9

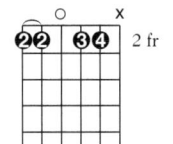

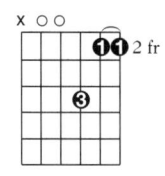

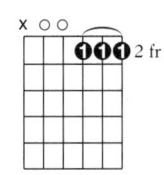

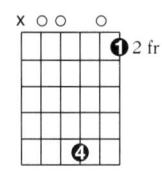

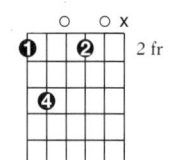

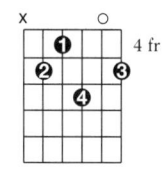

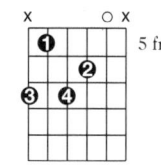

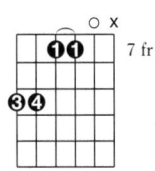

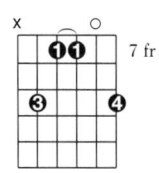

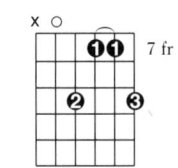

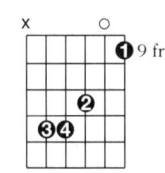

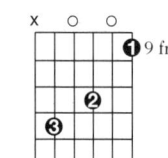

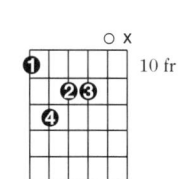

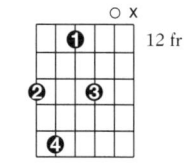

Bm11

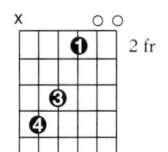

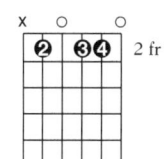

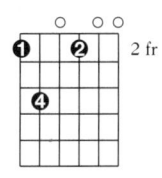

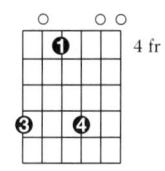

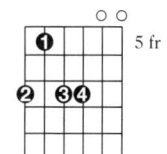

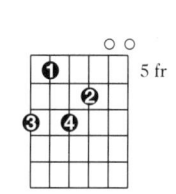

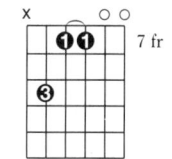

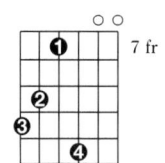

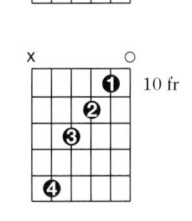

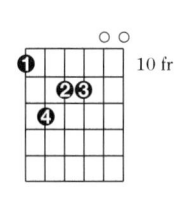

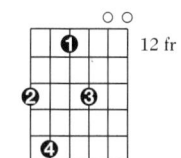

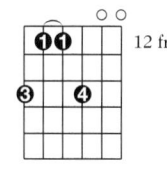

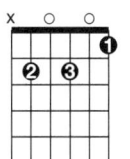

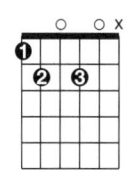

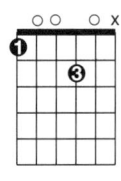

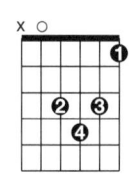

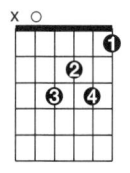

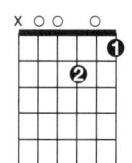

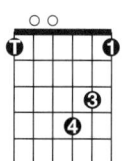

Bm7♭5

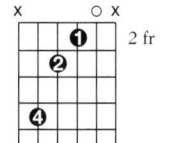

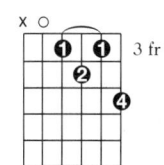

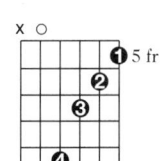

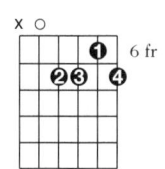

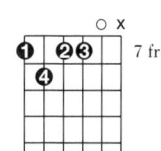

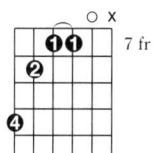

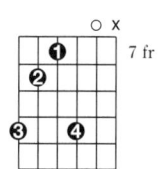

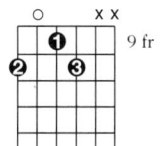

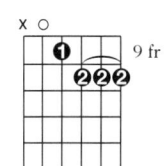

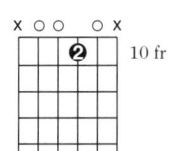

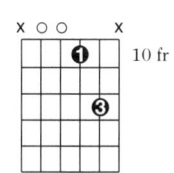

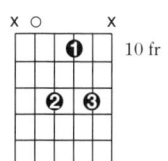

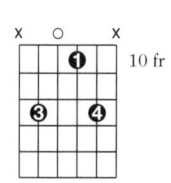

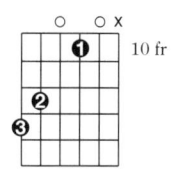

Bm7♭5 (cont'd)

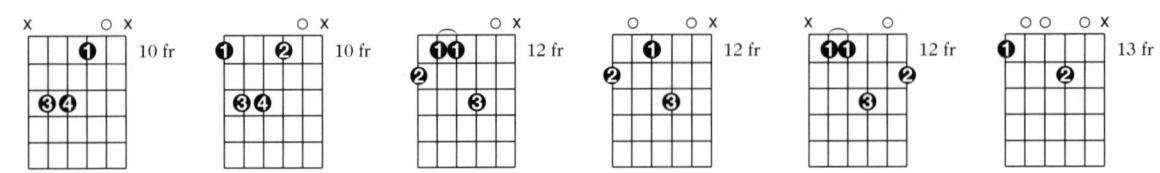

Bm9♭5

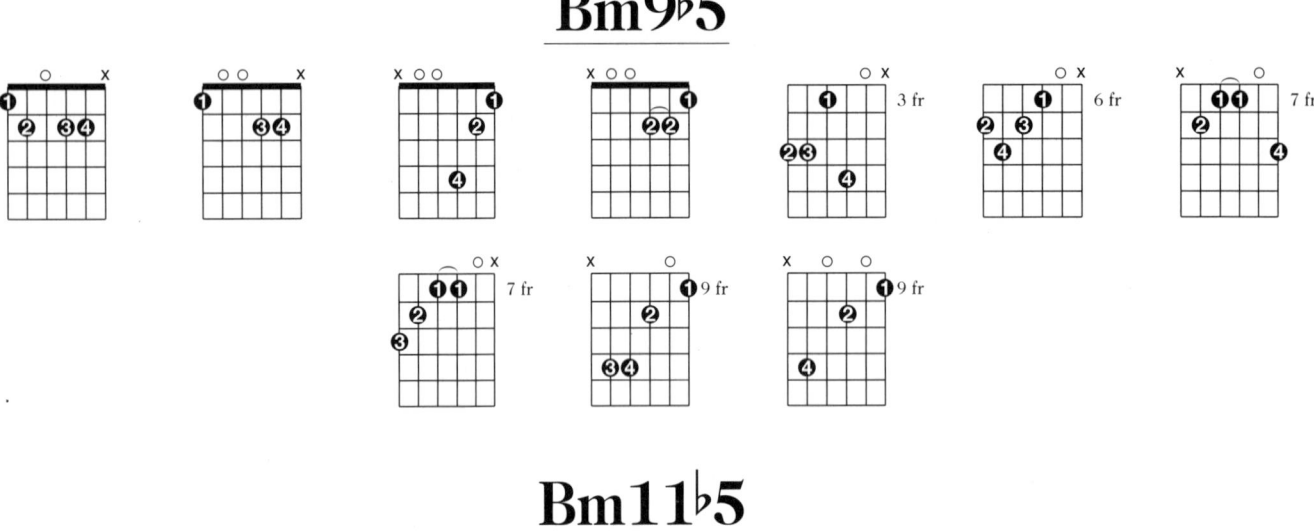

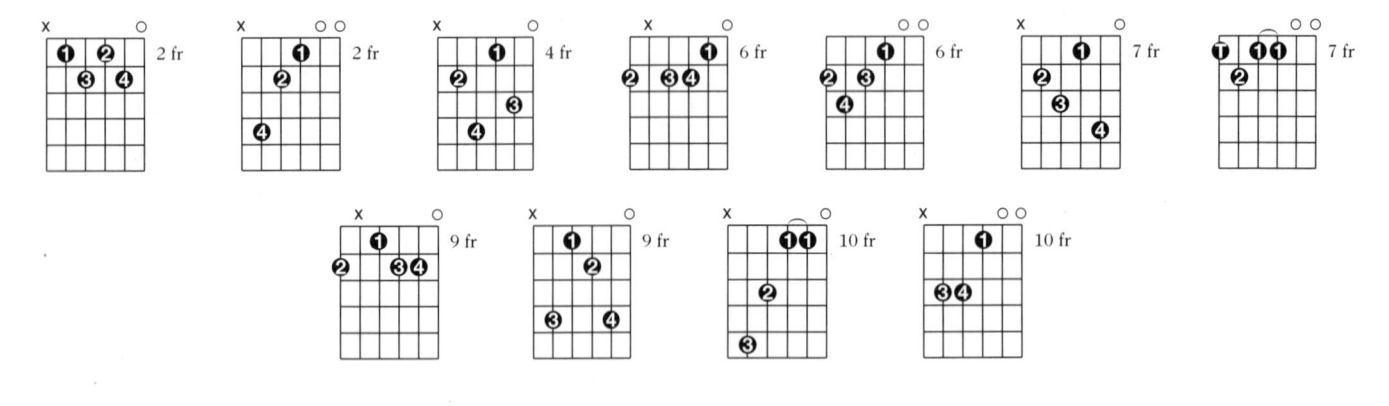

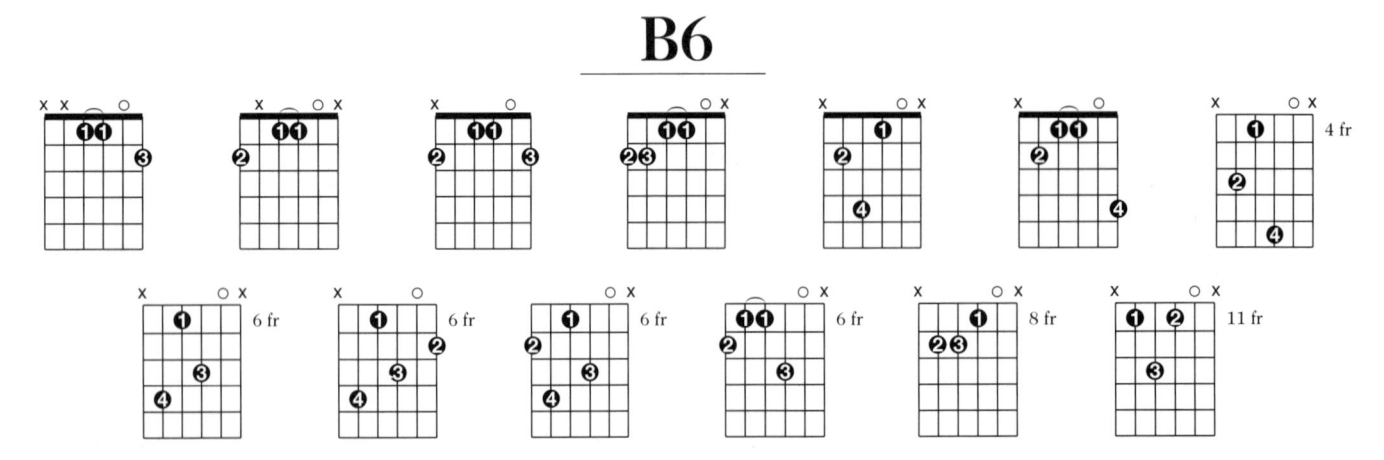

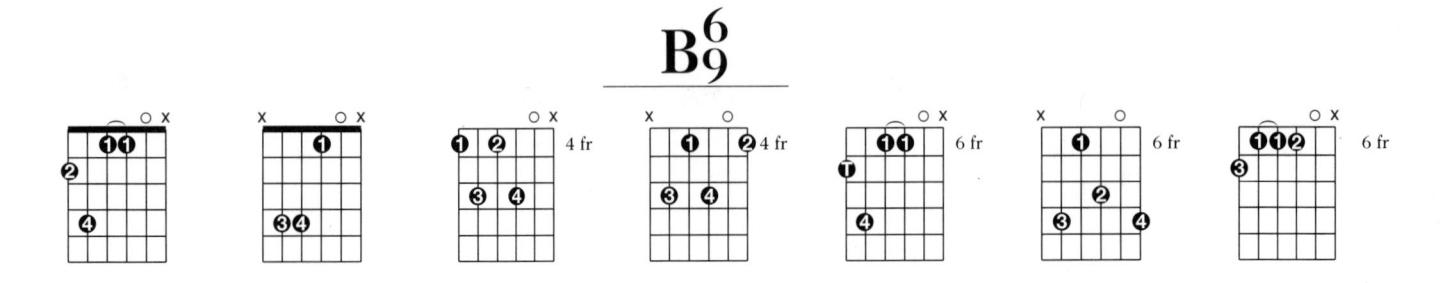

Bm11♭5

B6

B6/9

30

B⁶/₉ (cont'd)

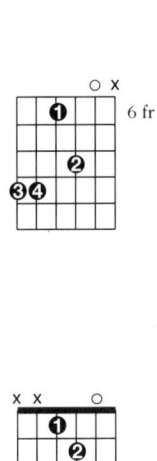

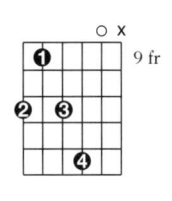

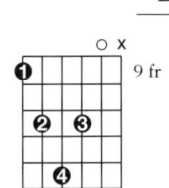

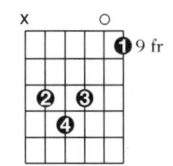

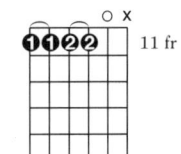

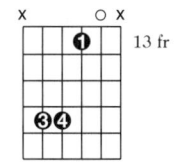

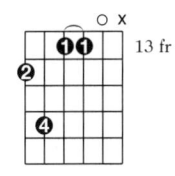

B13

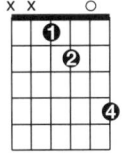

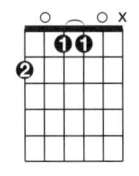

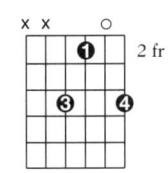

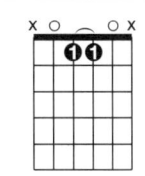

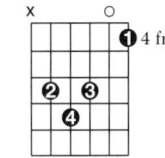

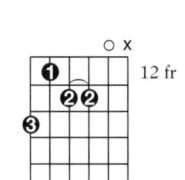

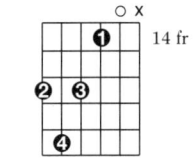

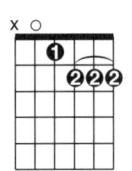

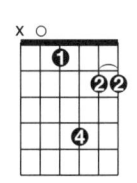

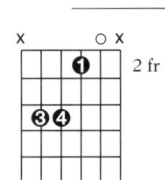

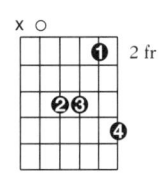

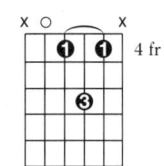

B7

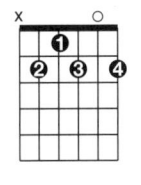

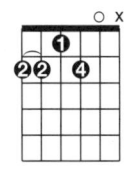

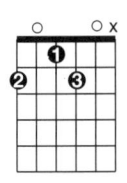

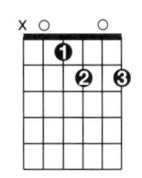

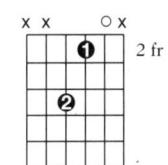

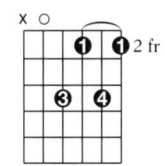

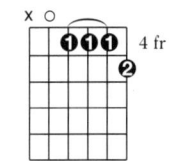

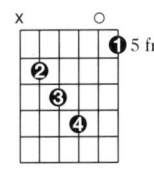

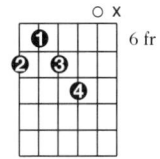

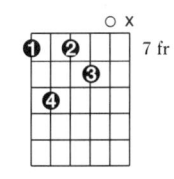

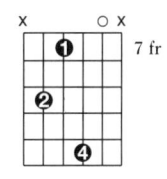

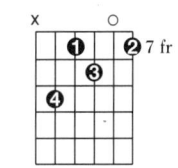

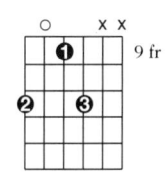

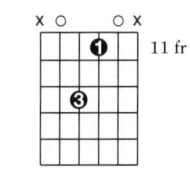

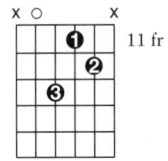

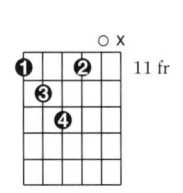

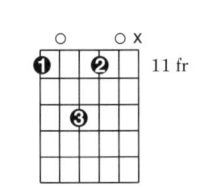

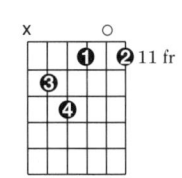

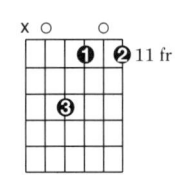

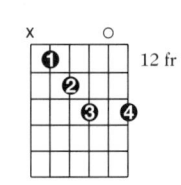

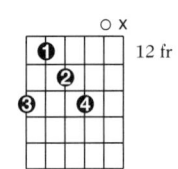

B9

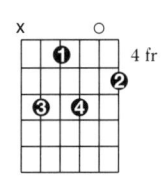

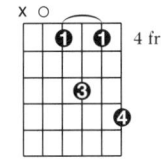

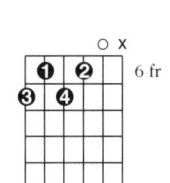

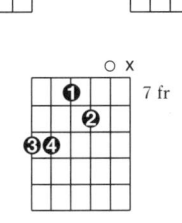

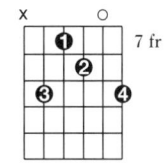

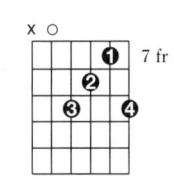

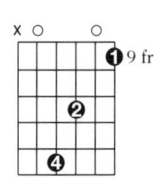

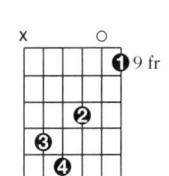

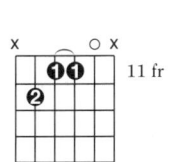

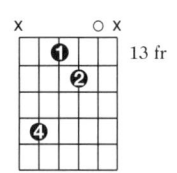

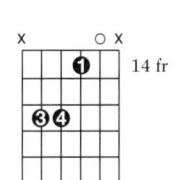

Badd9

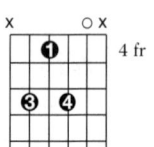

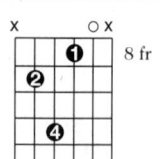

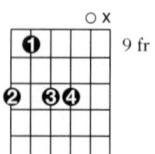

Bmaj7

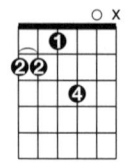

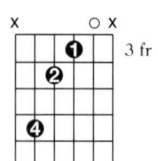

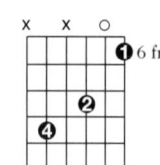

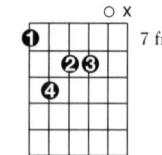

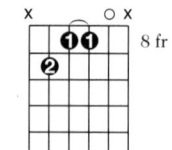

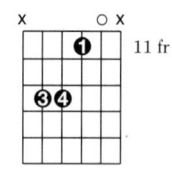

Bmaj9

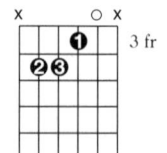

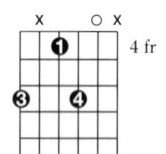

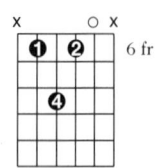

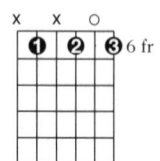

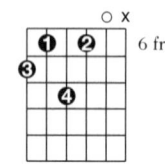

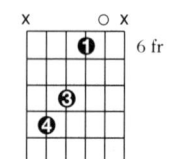

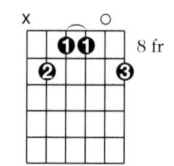

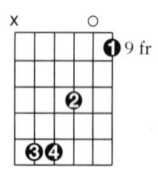

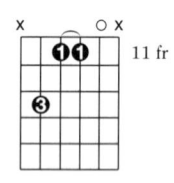

Bmaj13

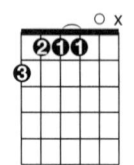

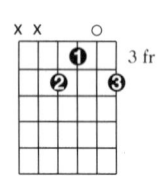

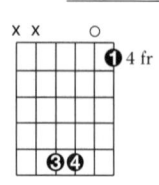

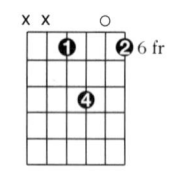

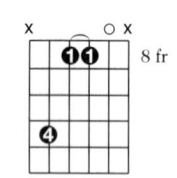

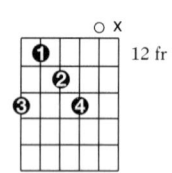

B7sus4

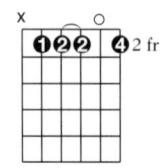

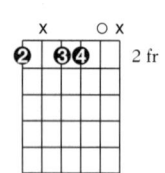

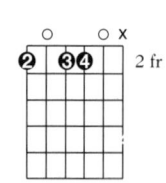

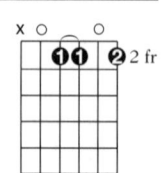

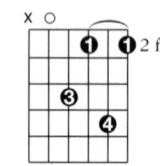

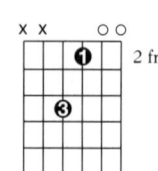

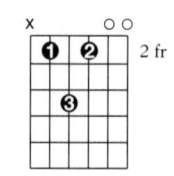

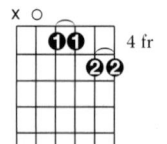

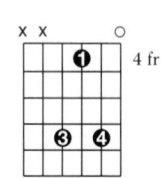

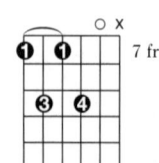

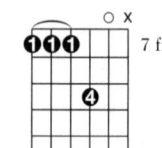

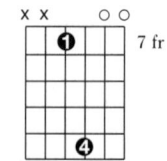

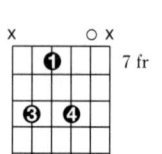

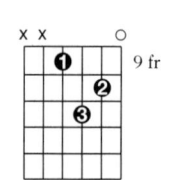

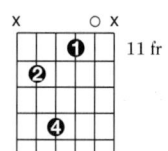

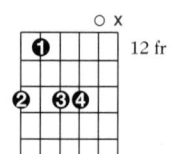

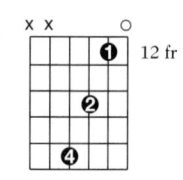

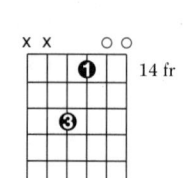

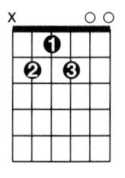

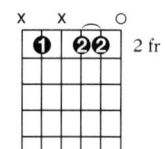

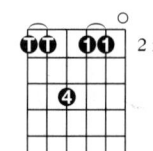

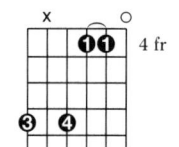

B11

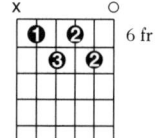

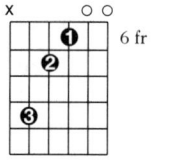

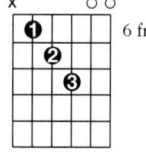

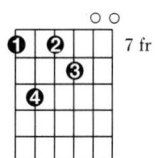

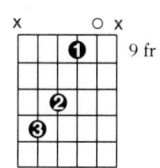

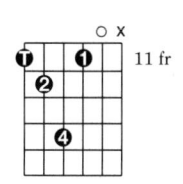

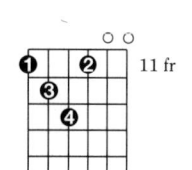

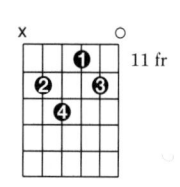

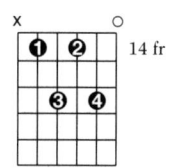

B7♭5

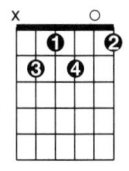

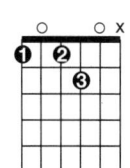

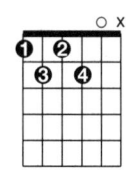

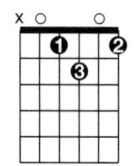

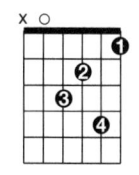

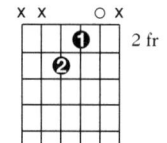

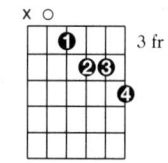

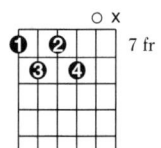

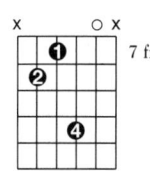

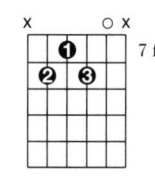

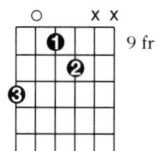

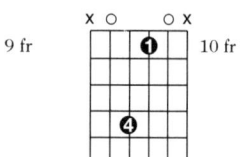

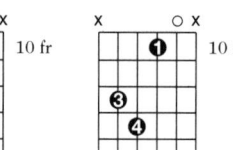

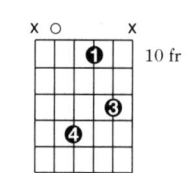

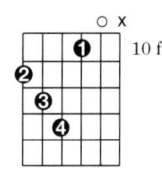

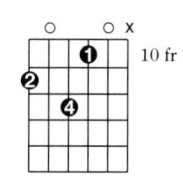

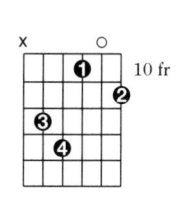

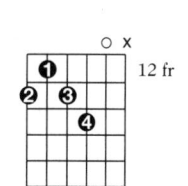

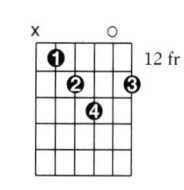

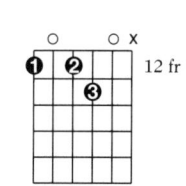

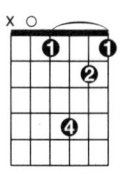

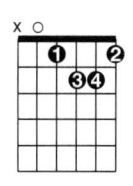

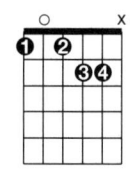

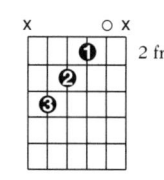

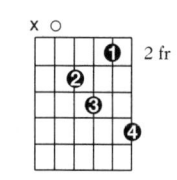

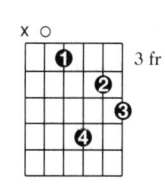

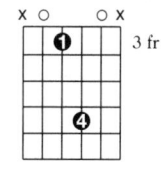

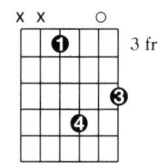

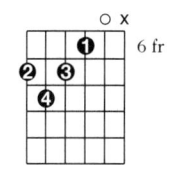

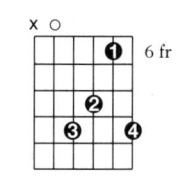

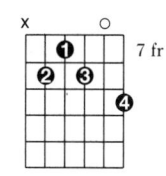

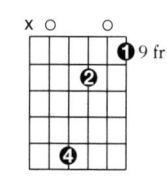

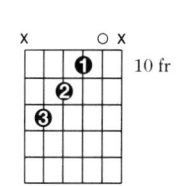

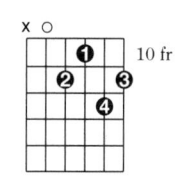

B9♭5

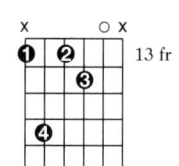

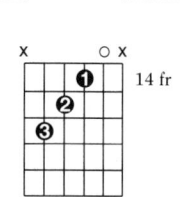

B7♯11

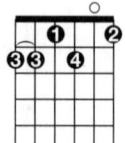

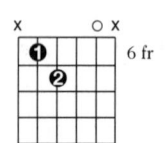

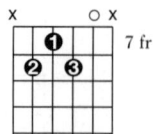

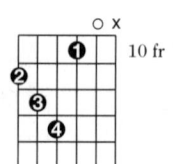

B7♯9

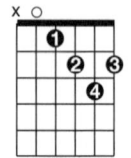

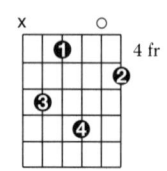

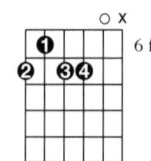

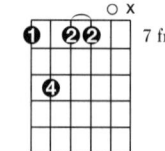

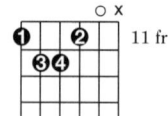

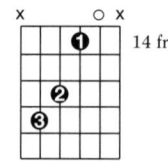

B7♭9

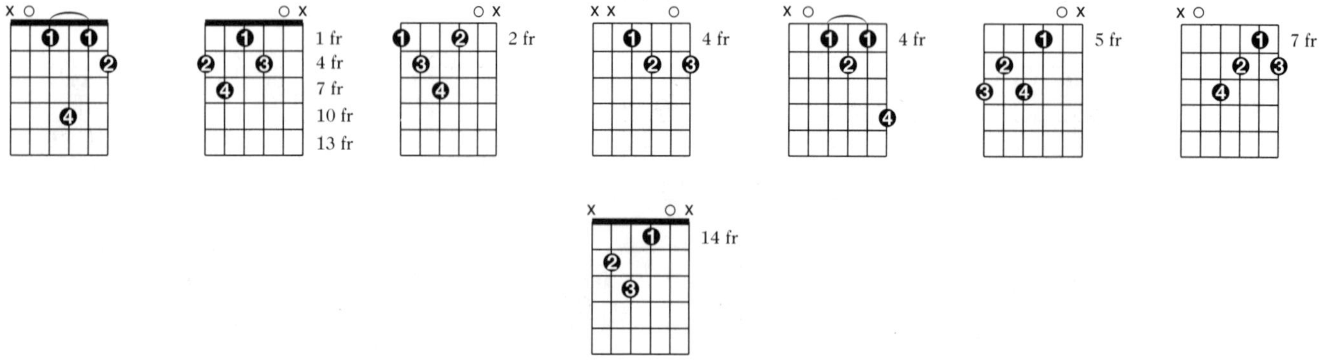

B11♭9

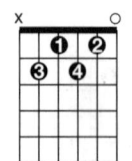

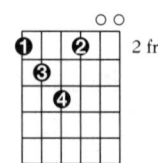

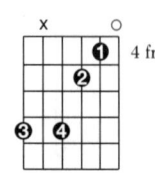

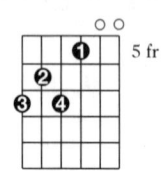

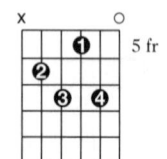

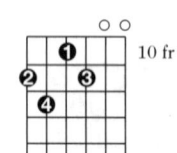

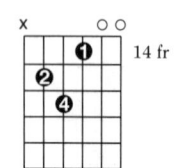

B7sus4(add♭9)

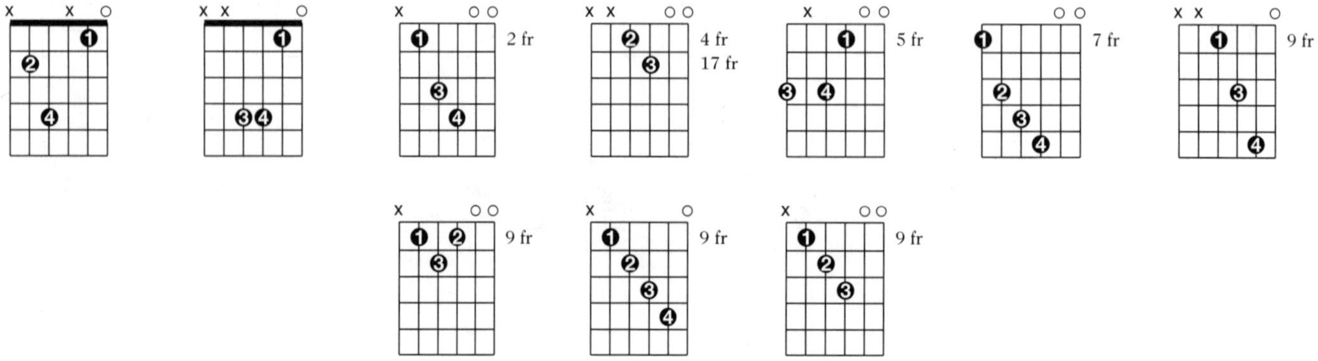

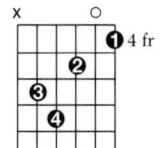

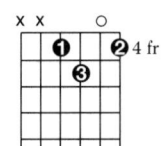

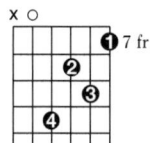

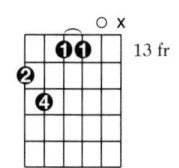

B13♭9

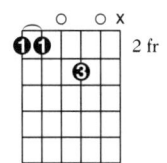

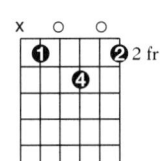

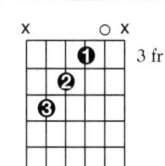

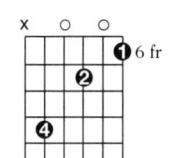

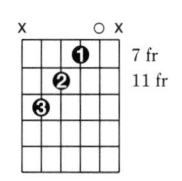

Bm(maj7)

Bm(maj9)

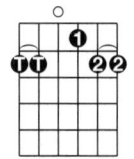

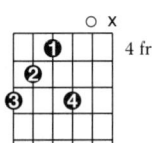

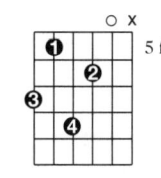

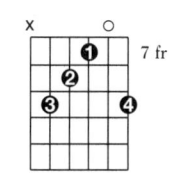

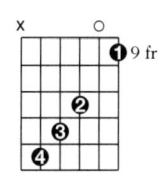

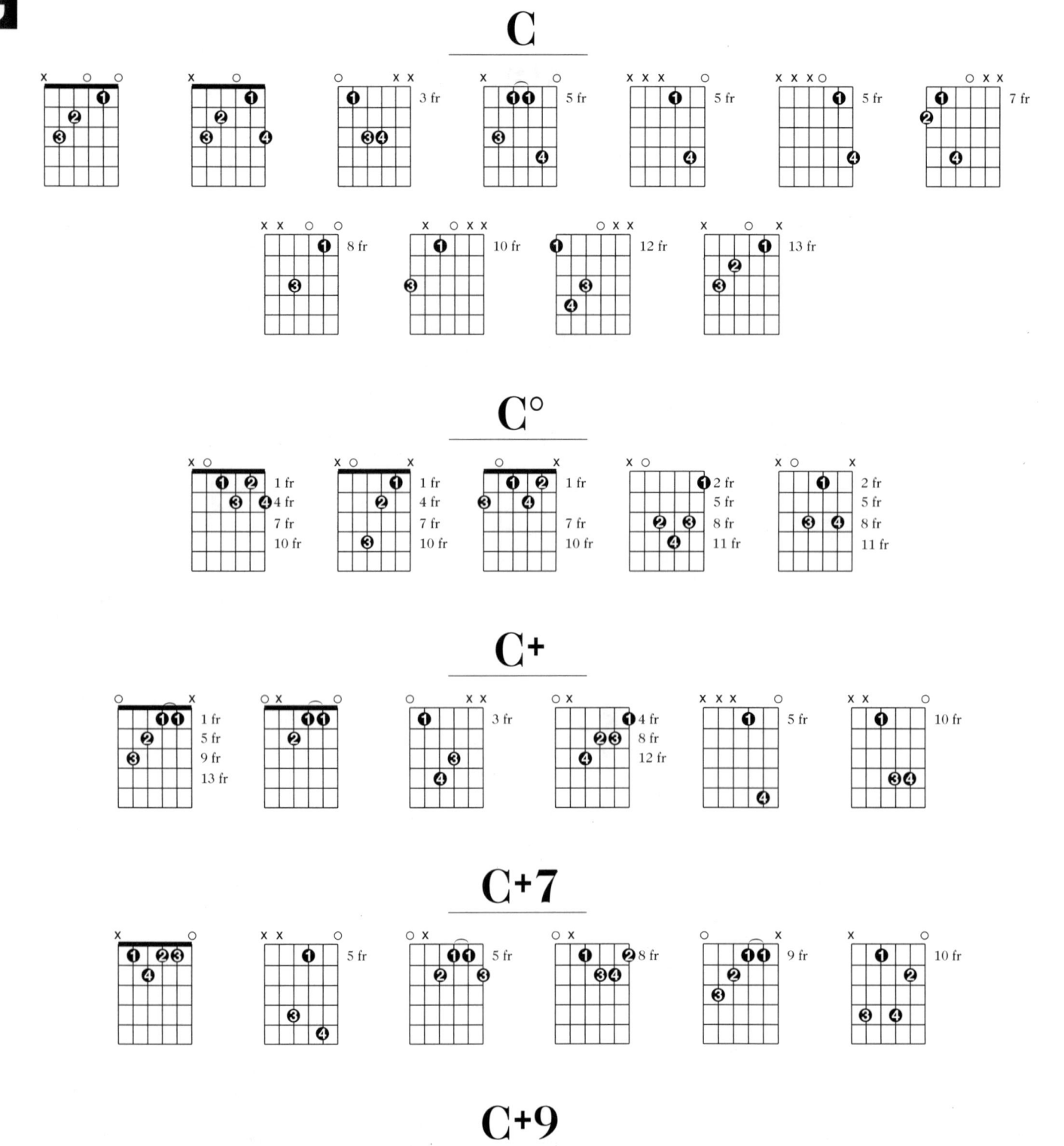

C

C

C°

C+

C+7

C+9

Cm

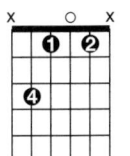

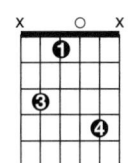

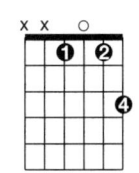

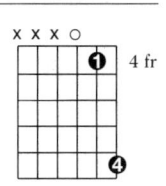

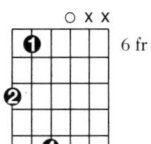

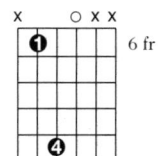

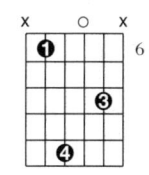

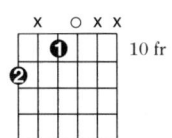

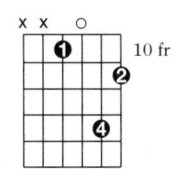

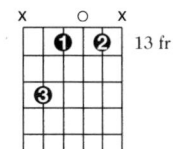

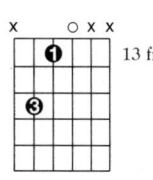

Cm6

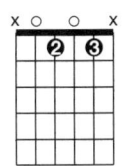

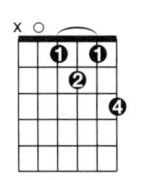

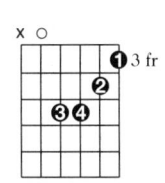

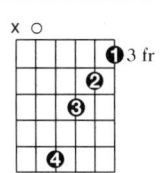

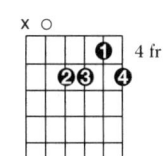

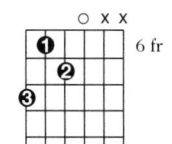

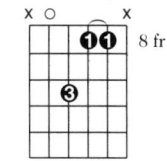

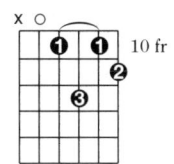

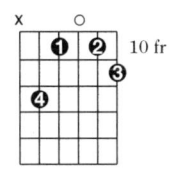

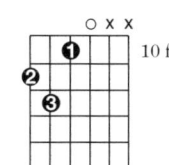

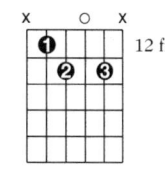

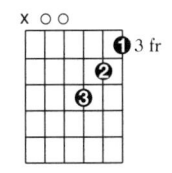

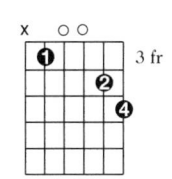

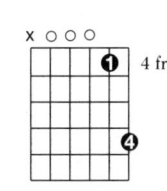

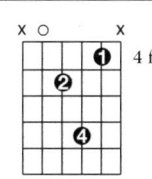

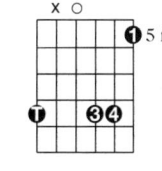

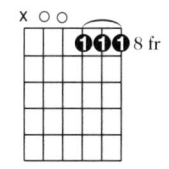

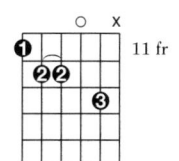

Cm$^6_9$

Cm13

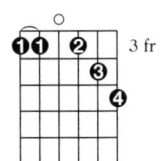

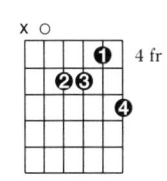

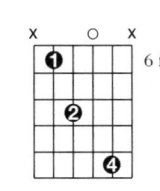

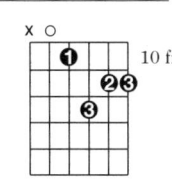

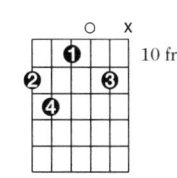

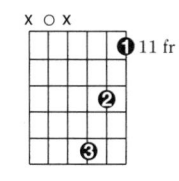

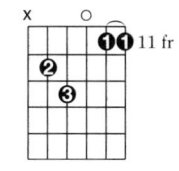

Cm7

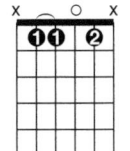

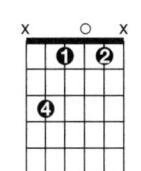

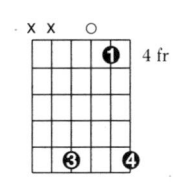

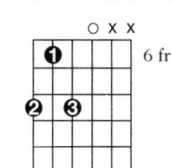

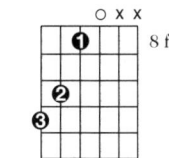

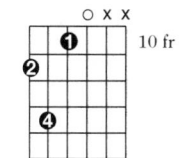

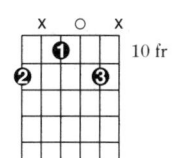

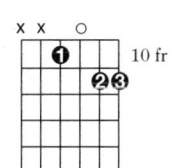

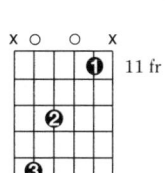

Cm(add9)

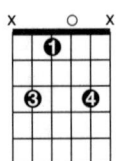

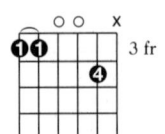

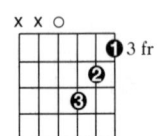

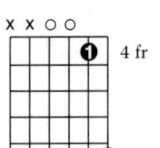

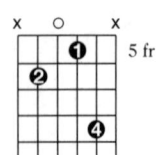

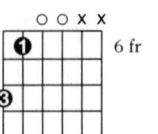

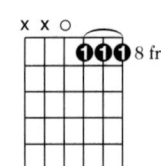

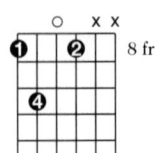

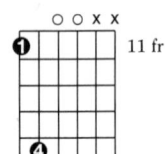

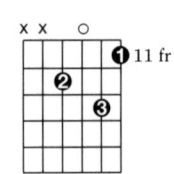

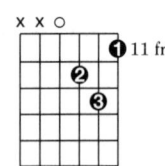

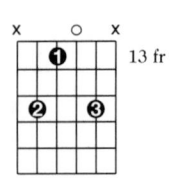

Cm9

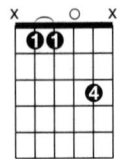

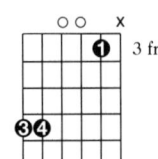

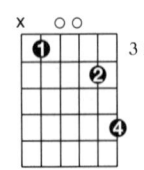

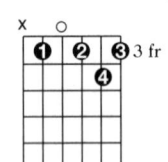

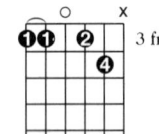

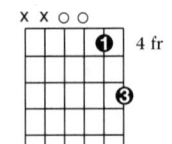

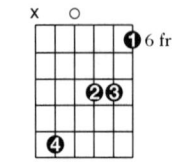

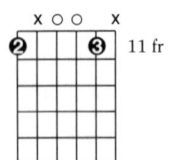

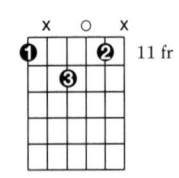

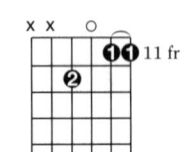

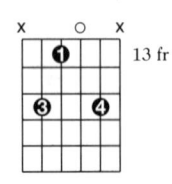

Cm11

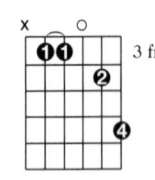

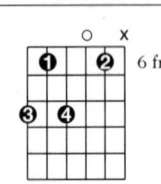

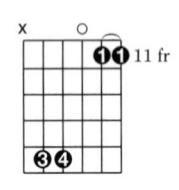

Cm9♭5

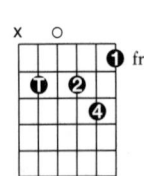

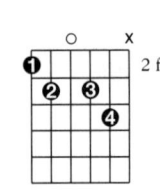

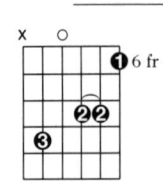

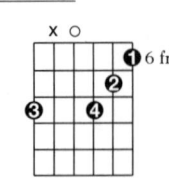

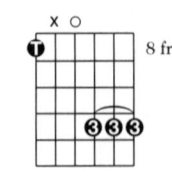

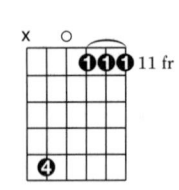

C6

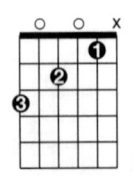

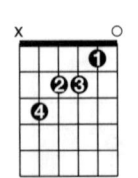

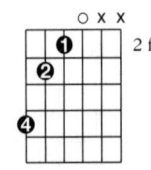

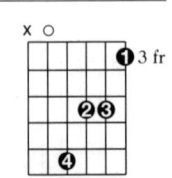

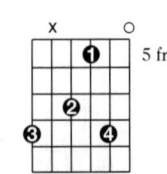

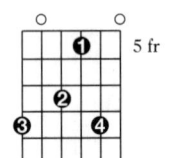

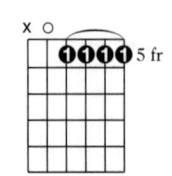

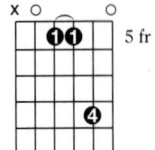

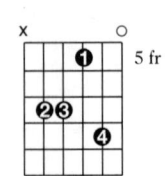

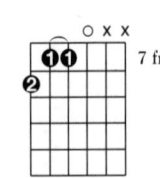

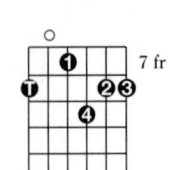

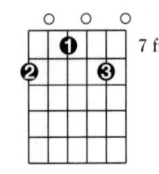

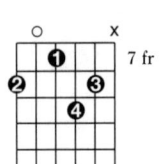

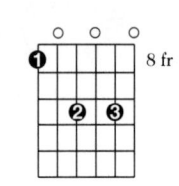

C6 (cont'd)

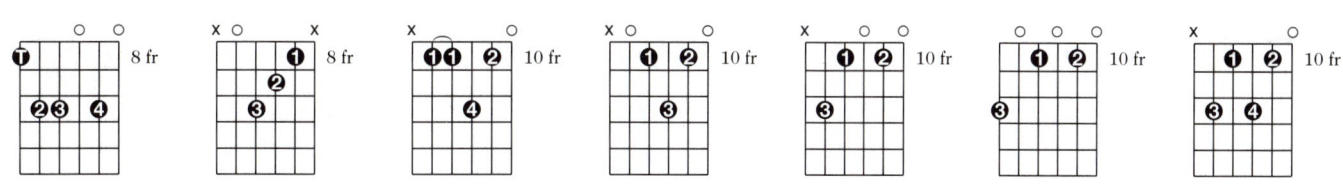

C⁶/₉

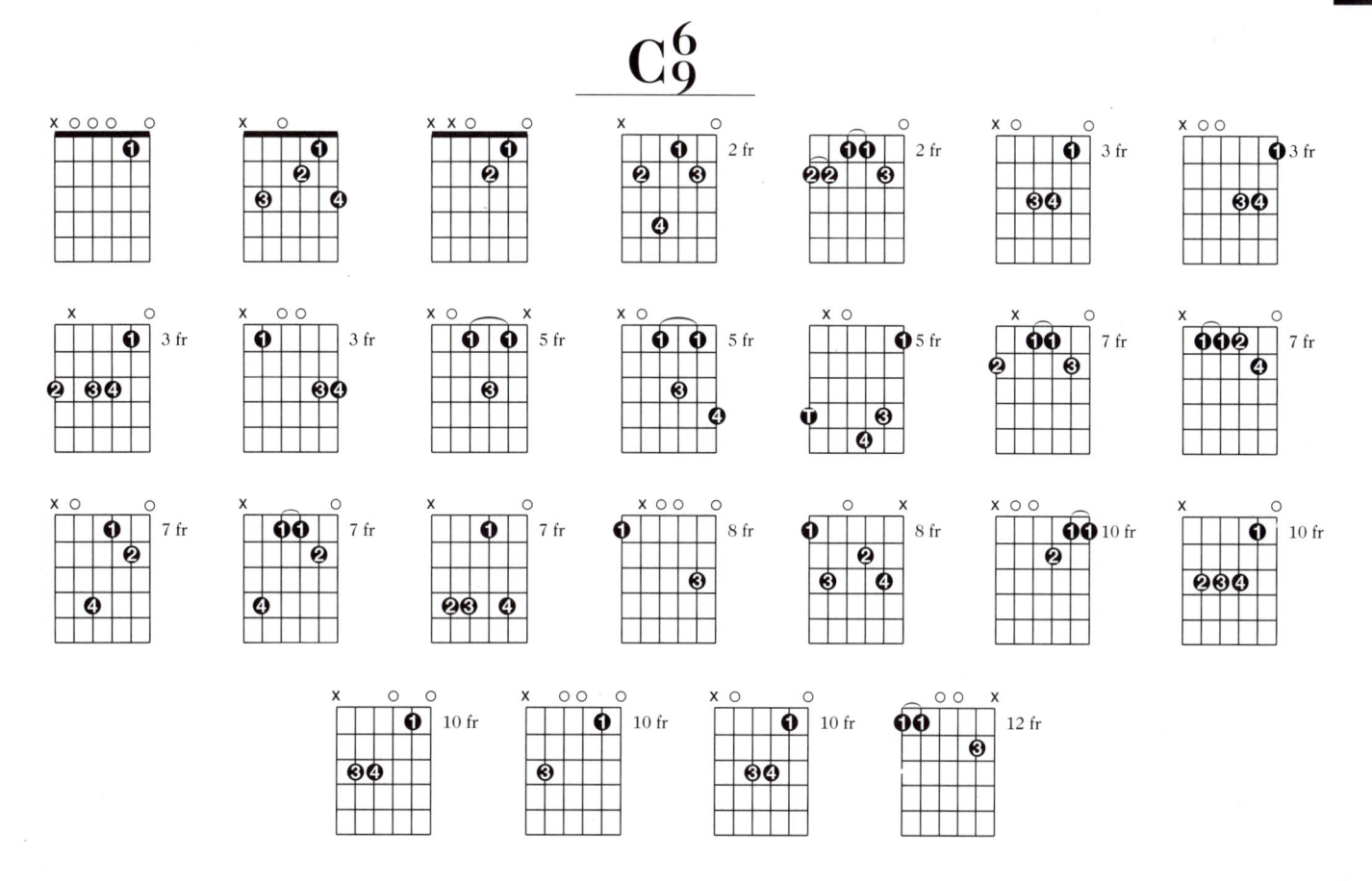

C13

C7

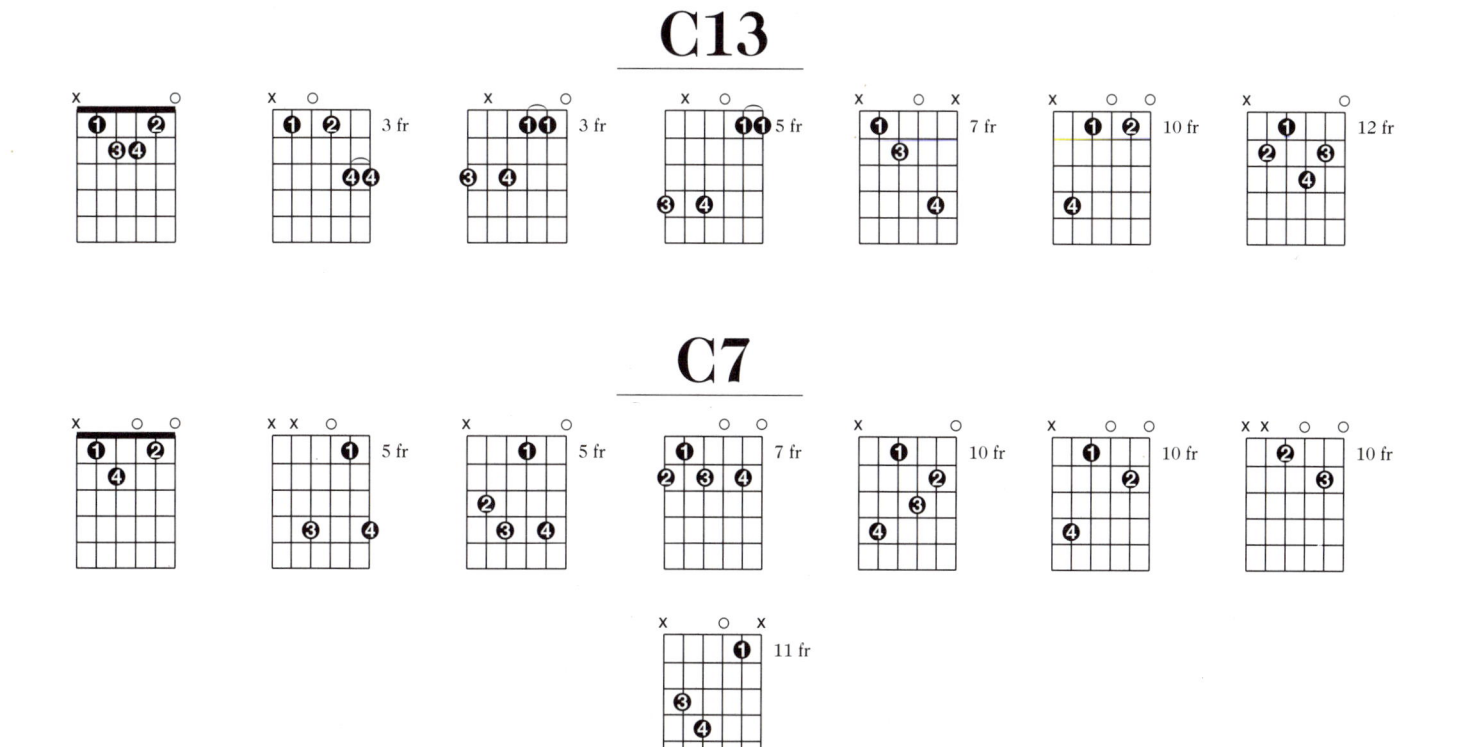

C9

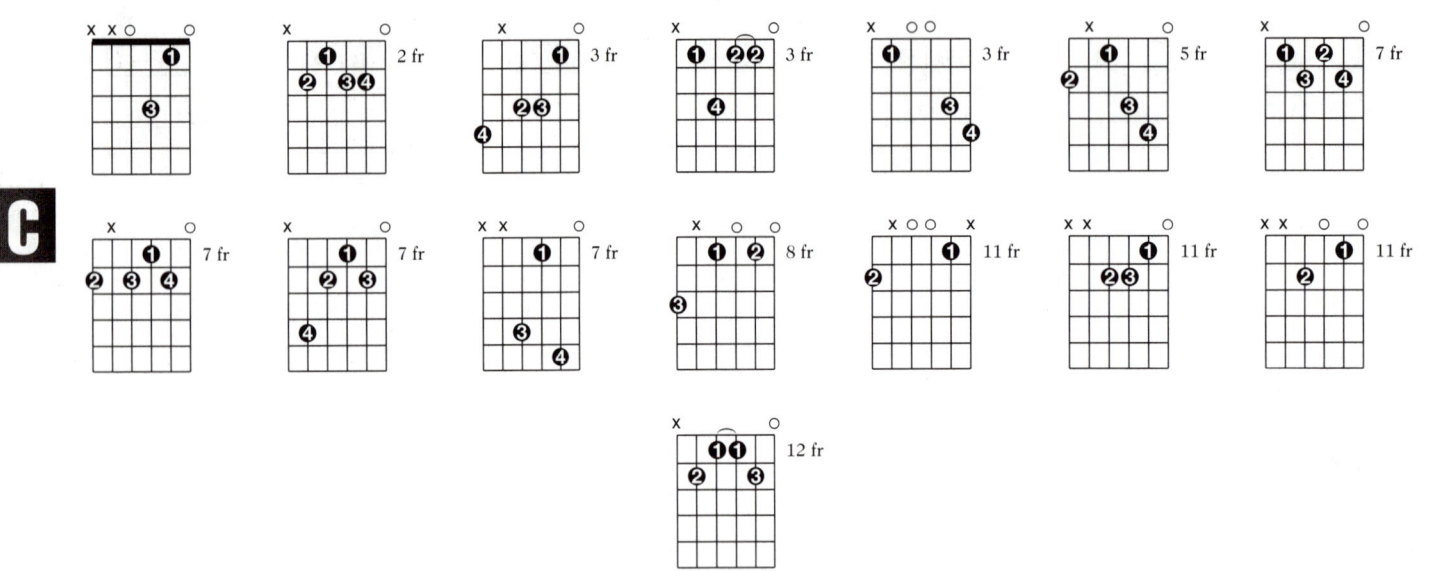

Cadd9

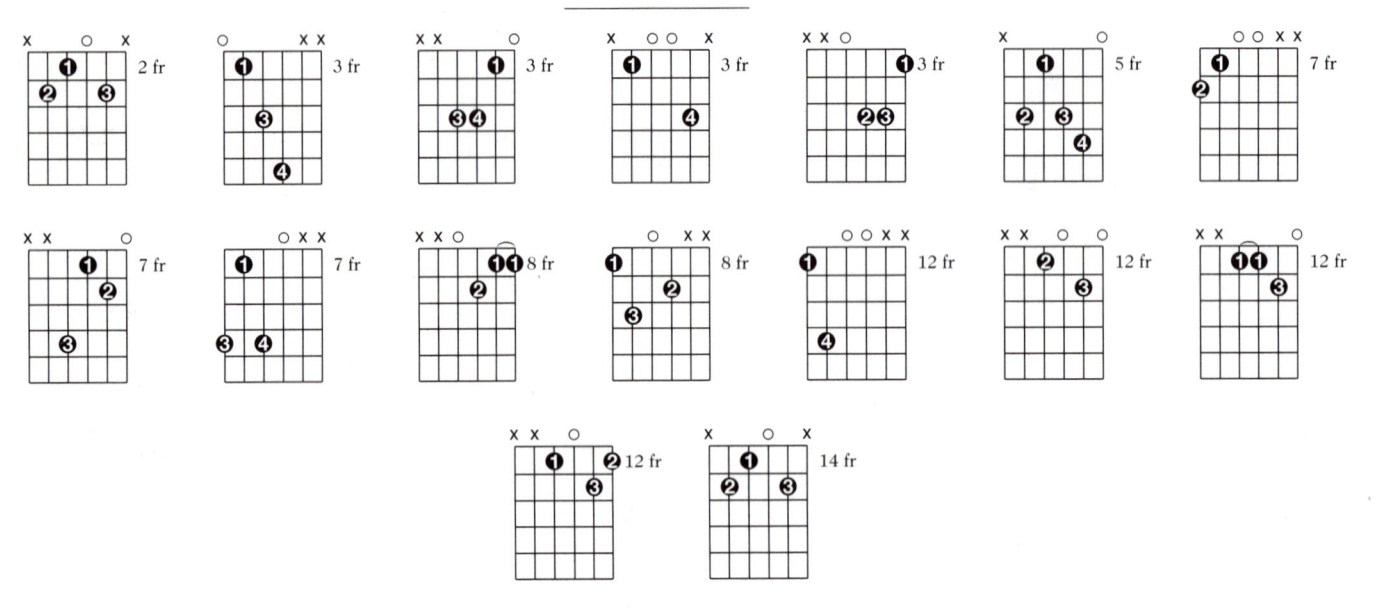

Cmaj7

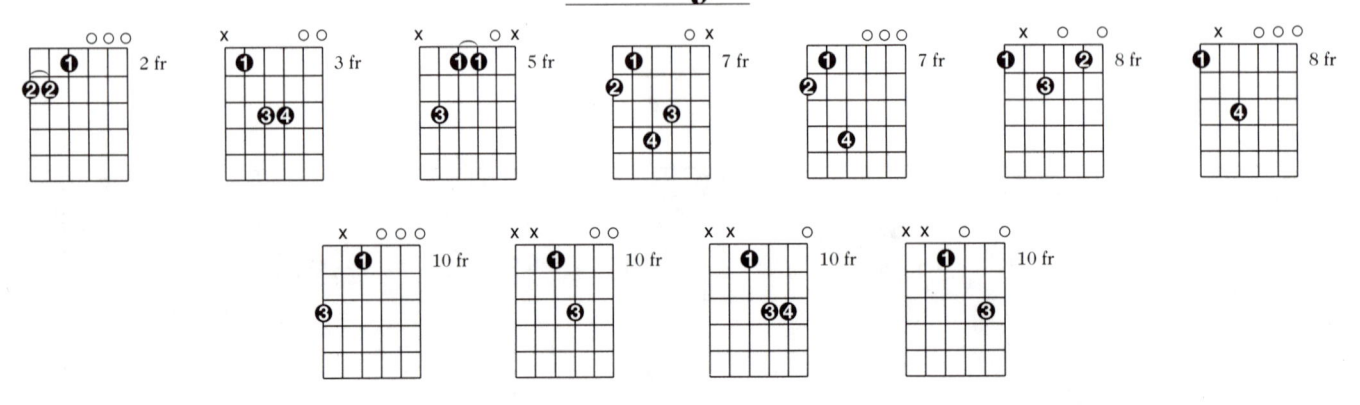

Cmaj9

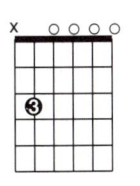

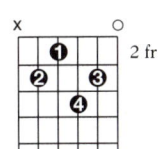

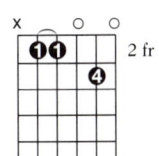

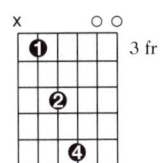

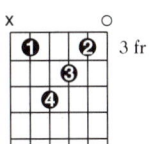

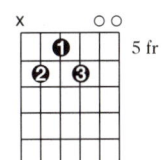

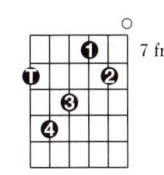

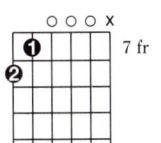

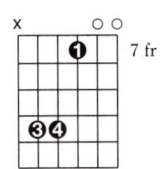

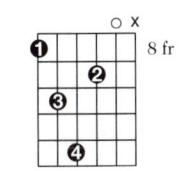

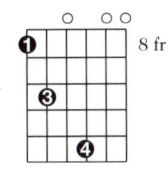

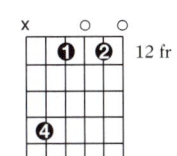

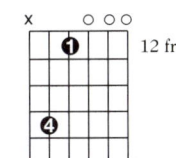

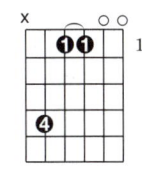

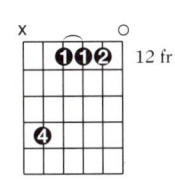

Cmaj13

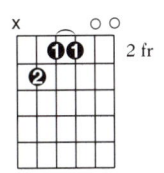

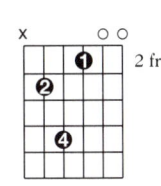

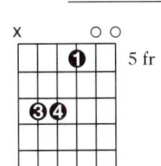

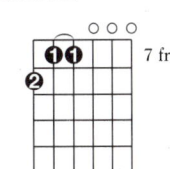

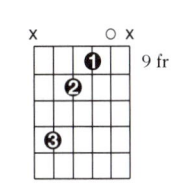

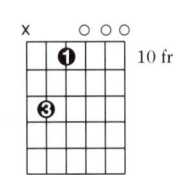

C7sus4

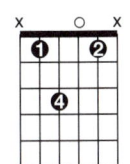

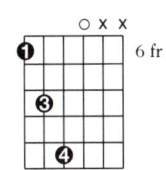

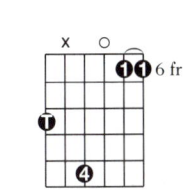

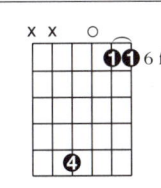

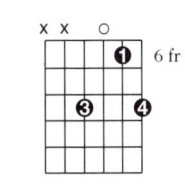

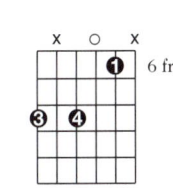

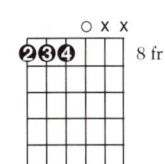

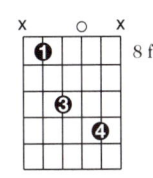

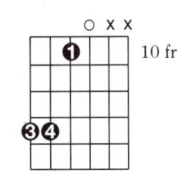

C$^{sus4}_{add9}$

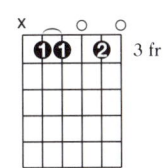

C11

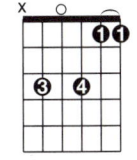

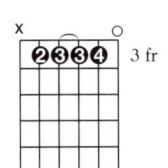

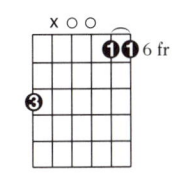

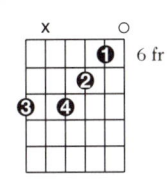

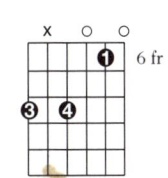

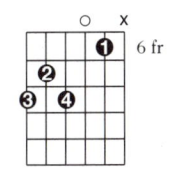

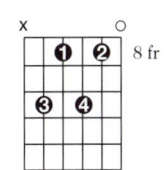

C11 (cont'd)

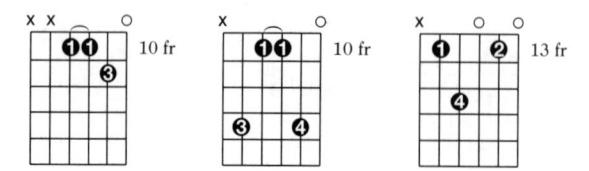

C7♭5

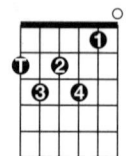

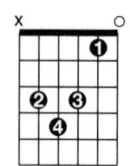

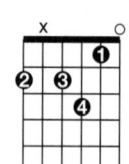

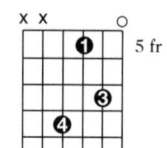

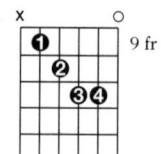

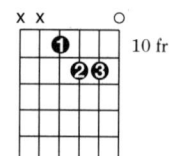

C9♭5

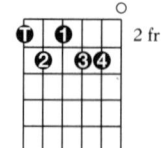

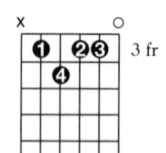

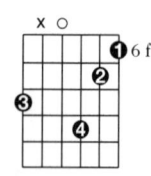

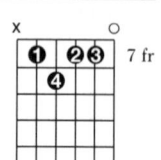

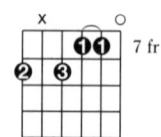

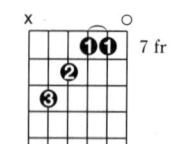

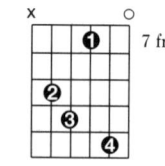

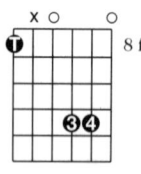

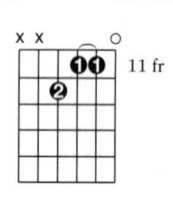

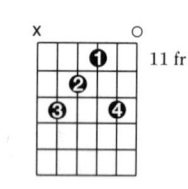

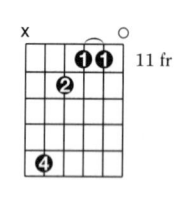

C9♯11

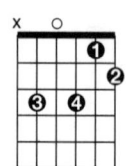

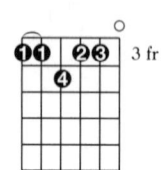

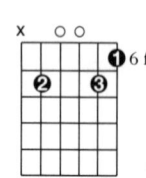

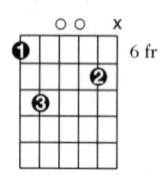

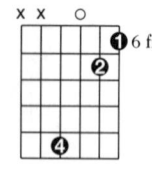

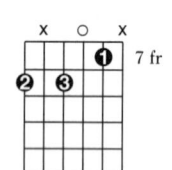

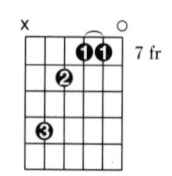

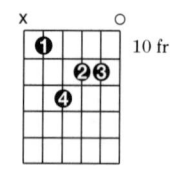

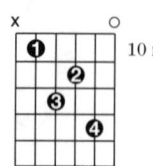

C7♯9

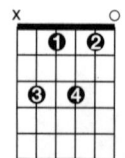

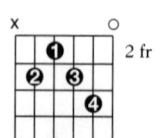

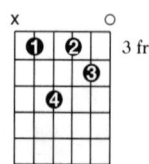

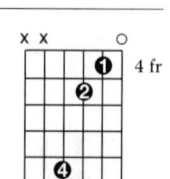

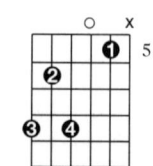

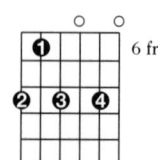

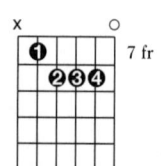

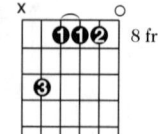

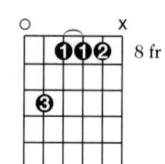

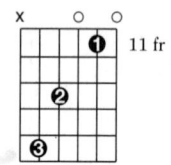

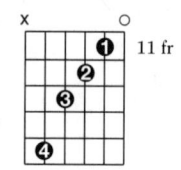

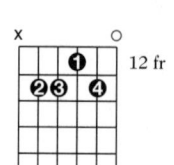

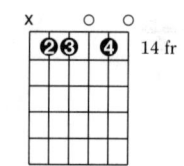

C7♭9

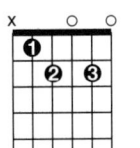

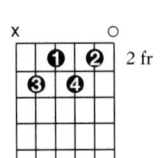

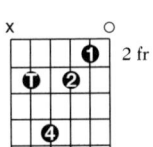

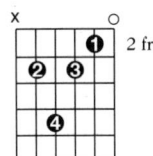

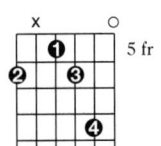

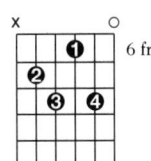

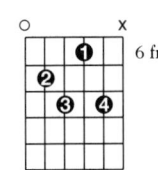

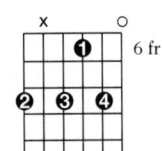

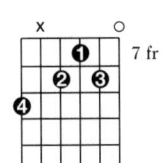

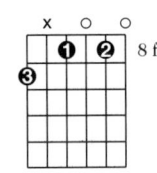

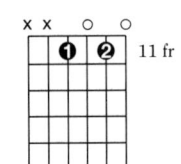

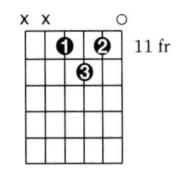

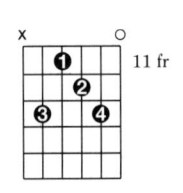

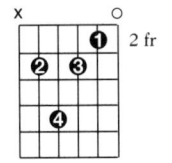

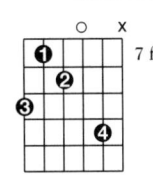

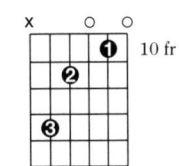

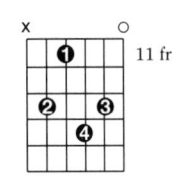

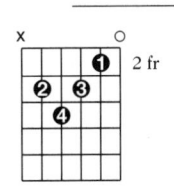

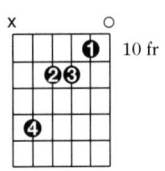

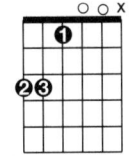

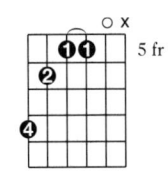

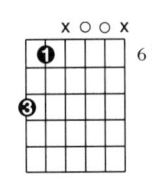

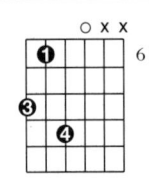

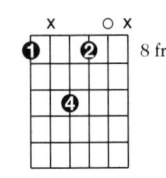

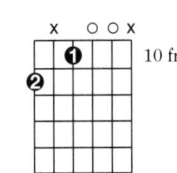

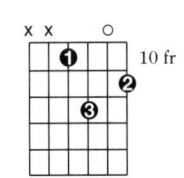

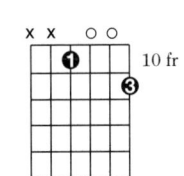

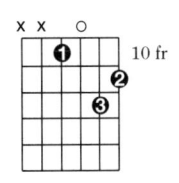

C13♭9

C13♭5(♭9)

Cm(maj7)

Cm(maj9)

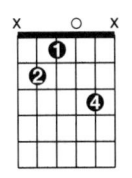

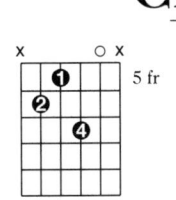

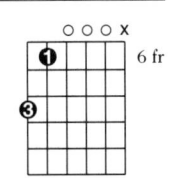

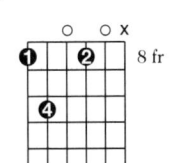

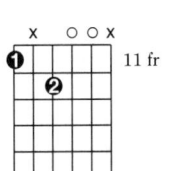

D♭

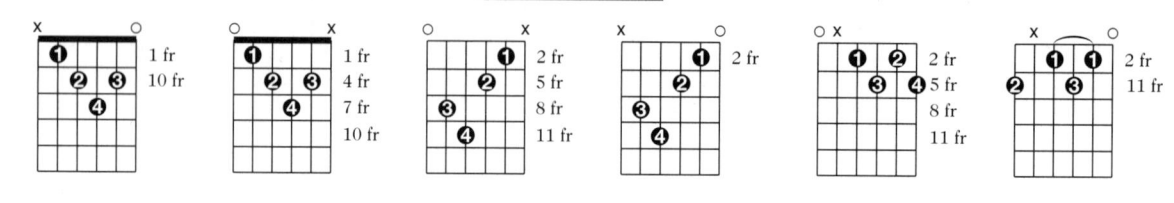

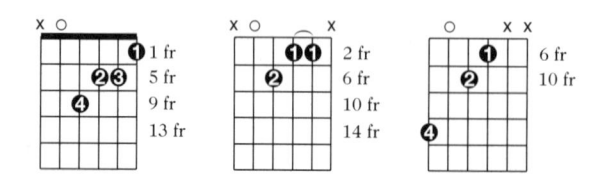

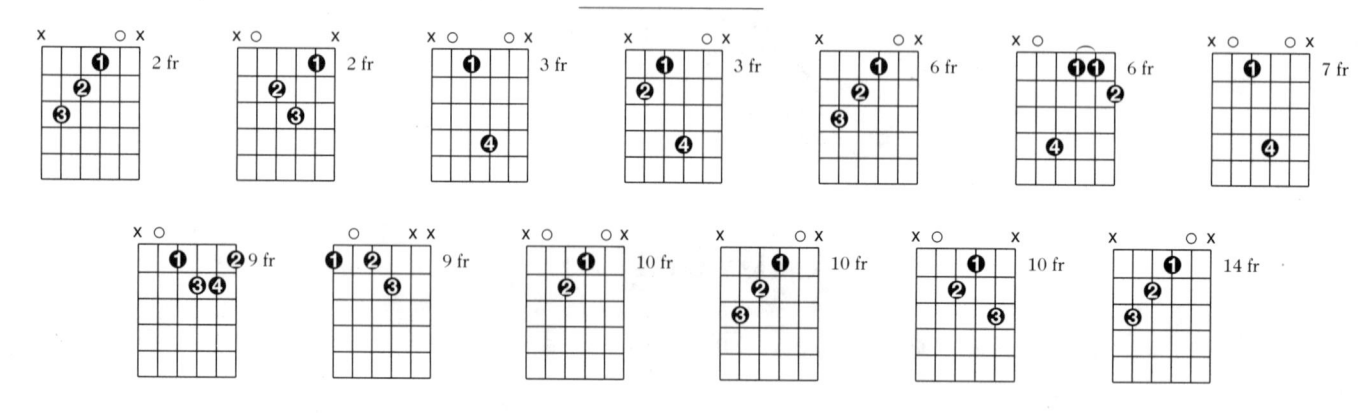

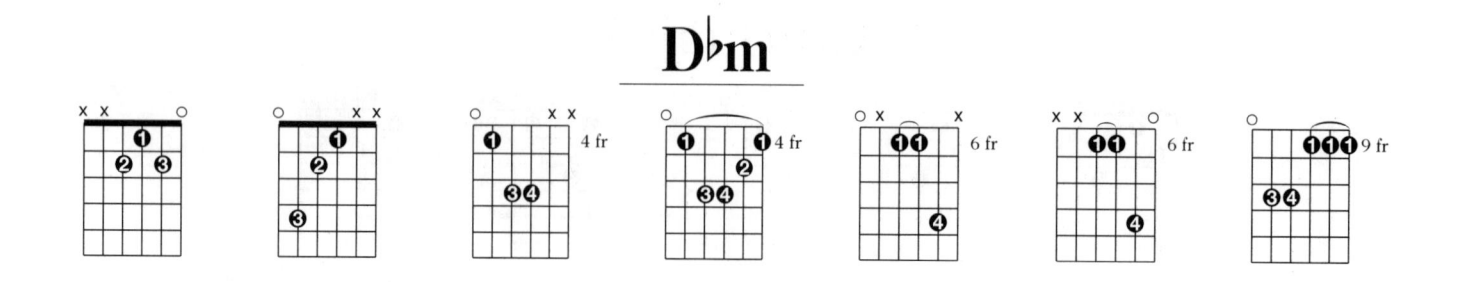

D♭°

D♭+

D♭+7

D♭+9

D♭m

D♭m (cont'd)

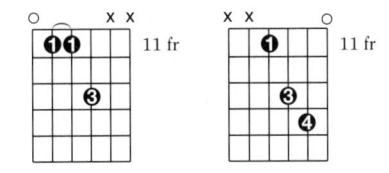

D♭m6

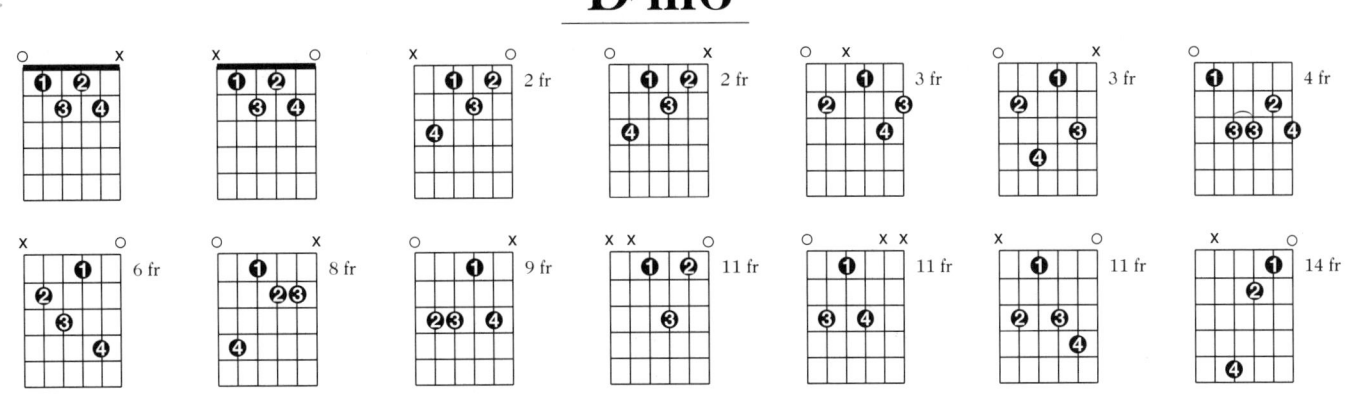

D♭m⁶⁄₉

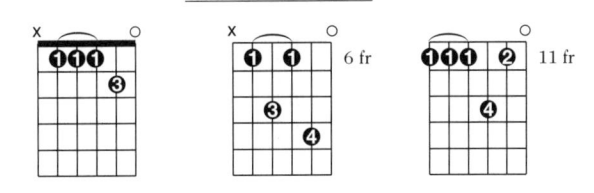

D♭m13

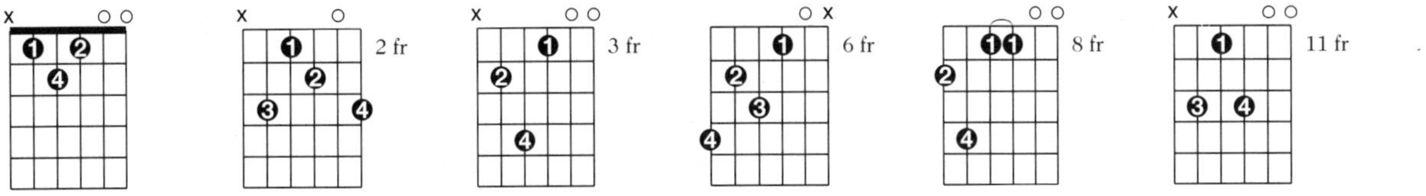

D♭m7

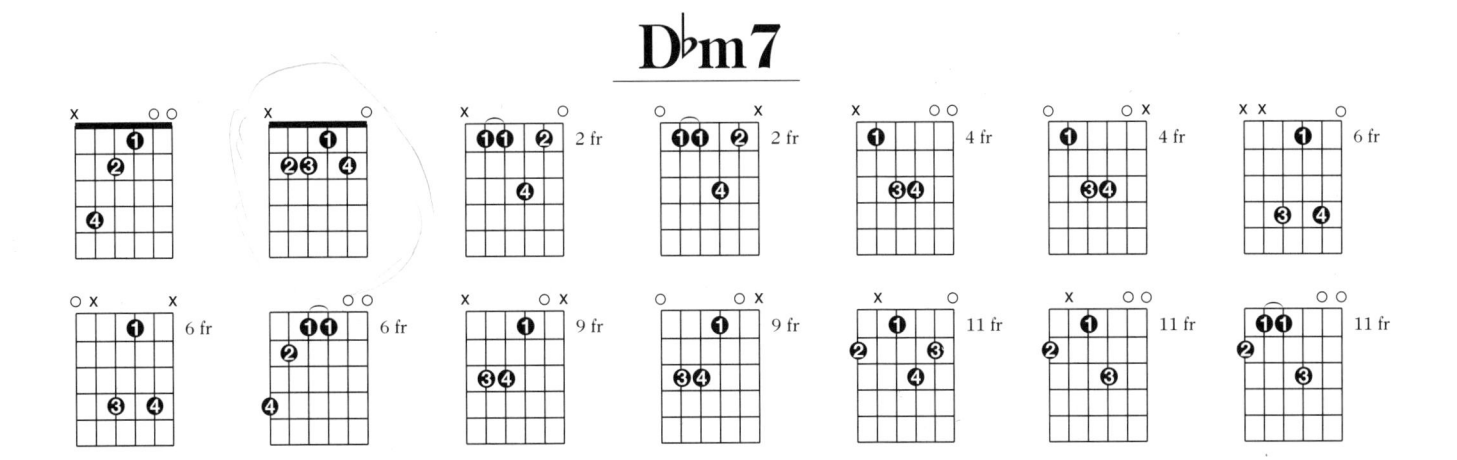

45

D♭

D♭m(add9)

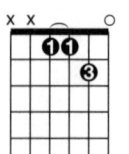

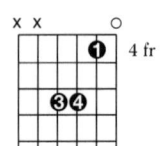

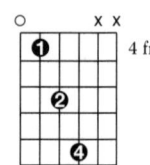

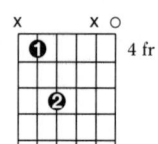

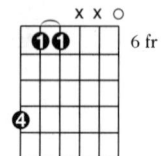

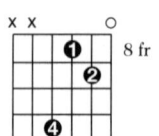

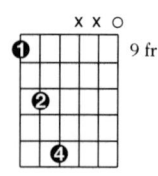

D♭m9

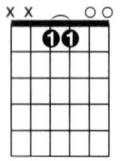

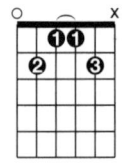

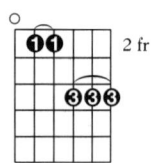

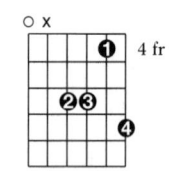

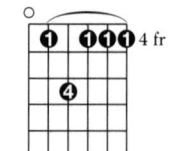

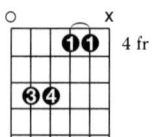

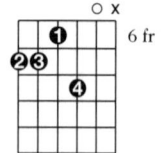

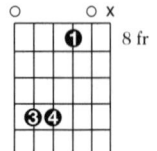

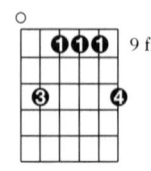

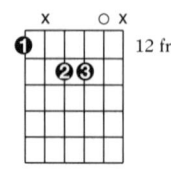

D♭m11

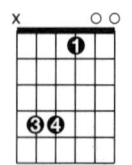

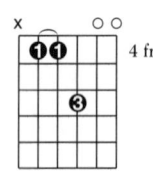

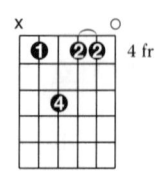

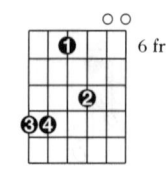

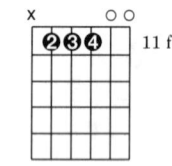

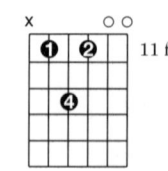

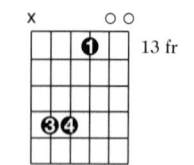

D♭m7♭5

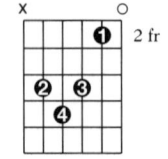

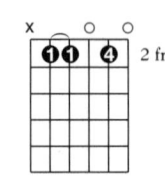

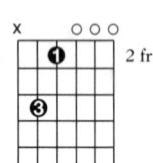

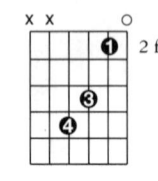

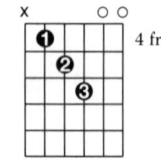

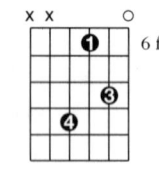

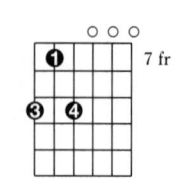

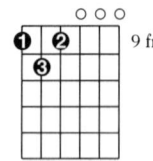

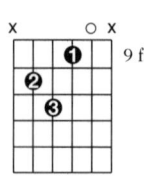

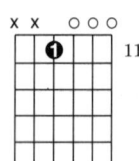

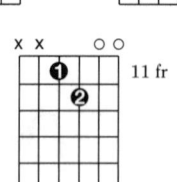

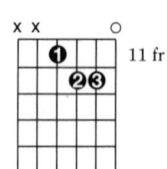

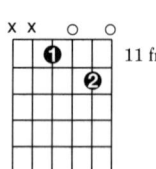

D♭m9♭5

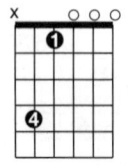

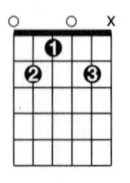

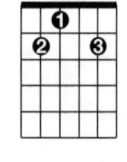

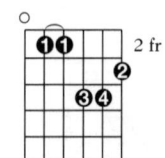

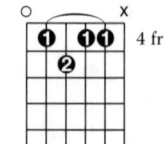

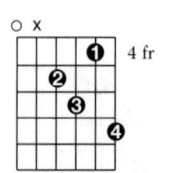

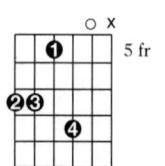

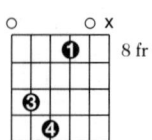

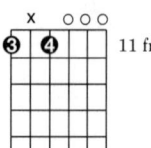

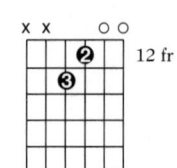

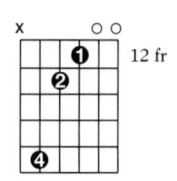

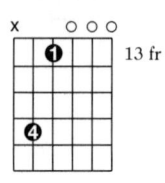

D♭m11♭5

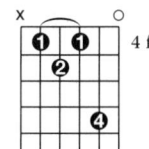

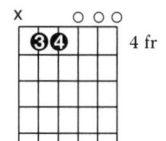

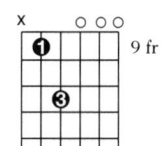

D♭7

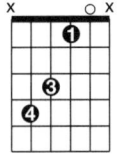

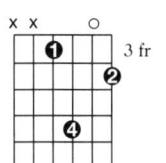

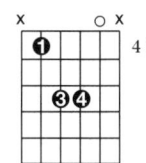

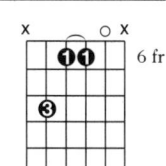

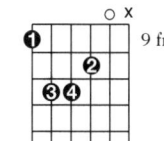

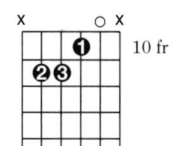

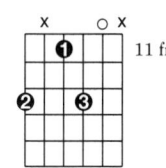

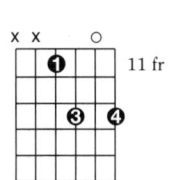

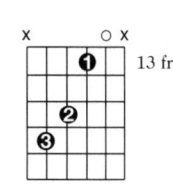

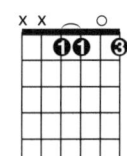

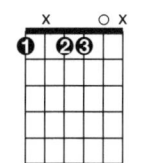

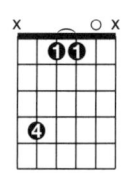

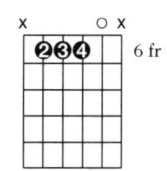

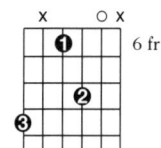

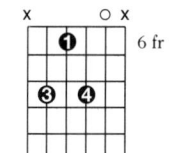

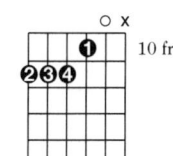

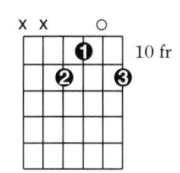

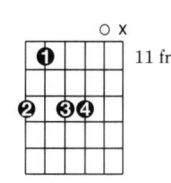

D♭9

D♭7sus4

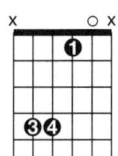

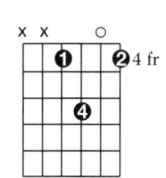

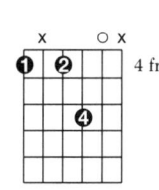

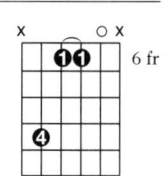

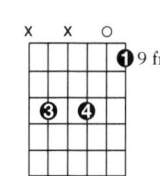

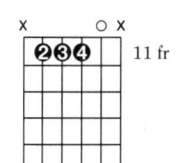

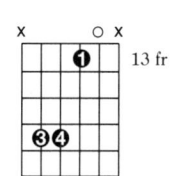

D♭11

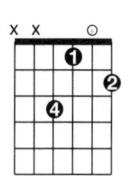

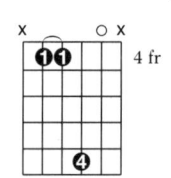

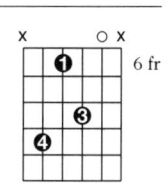

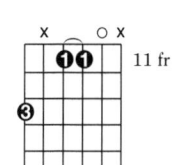

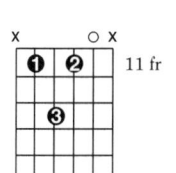

D♭7♭5

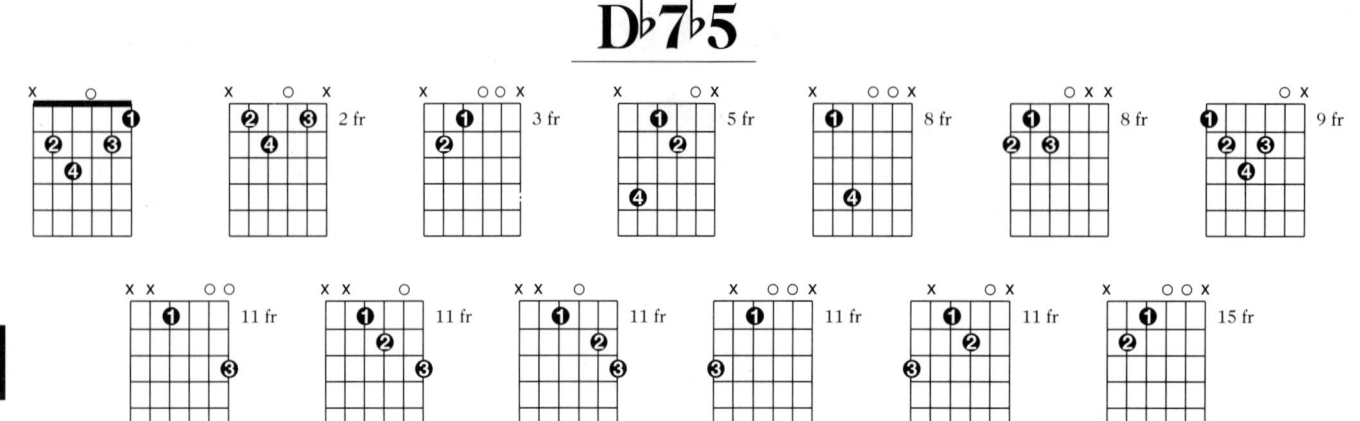

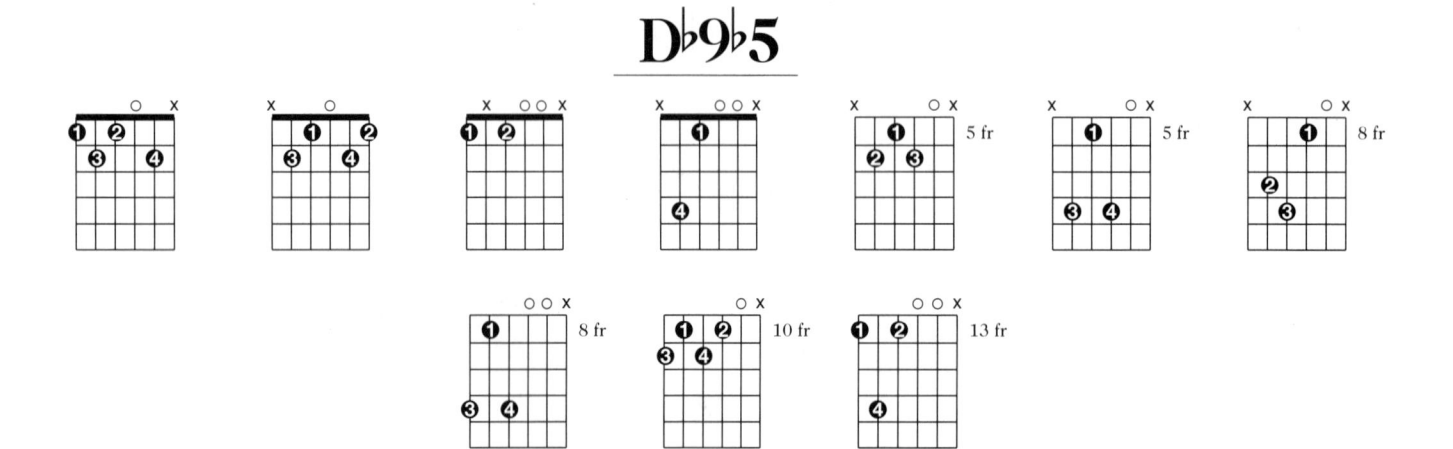

D♭9♭5

D♭9#11

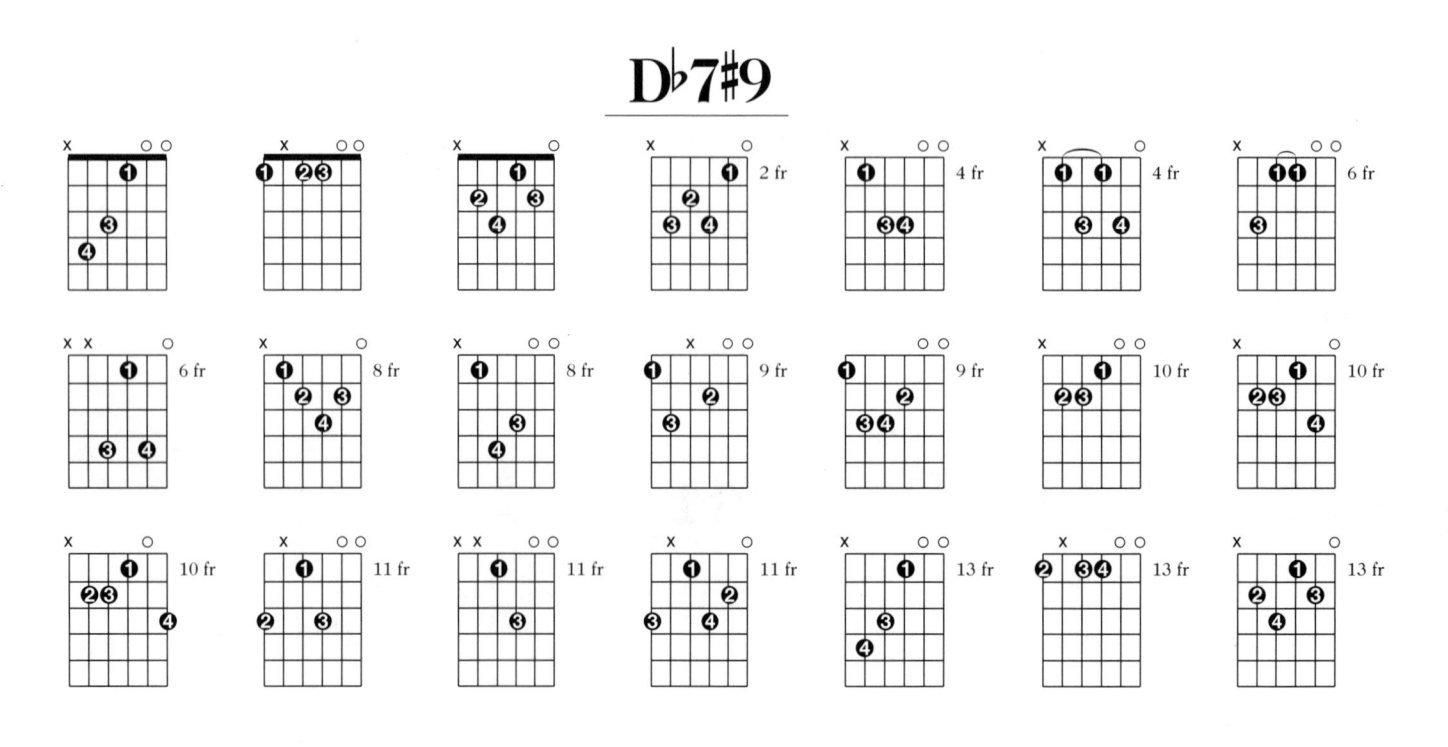

D♭7#9

D♭7♭9

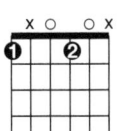

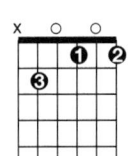

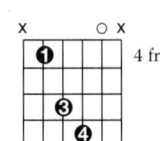

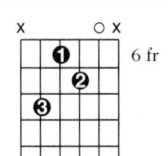

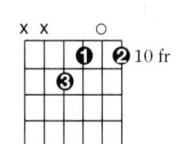

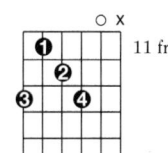

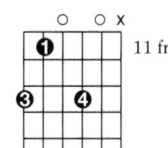

D♭m(maj7)

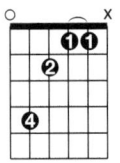

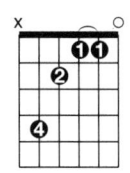

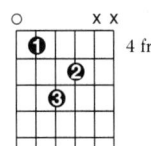

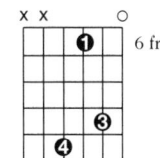

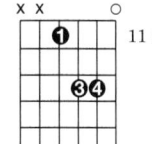

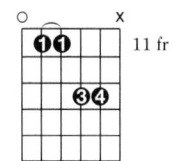

D♭m(maj9)

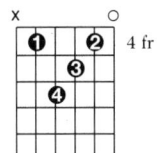

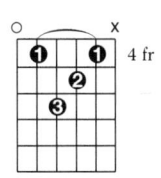

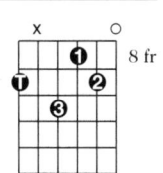

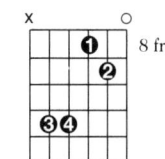

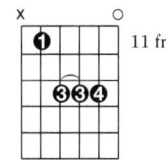

D♭+7♯9

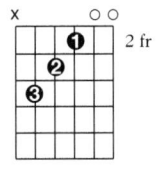

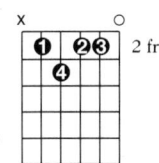

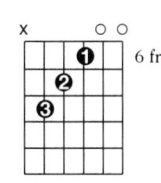

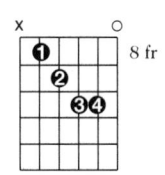

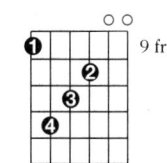

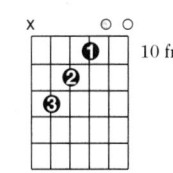

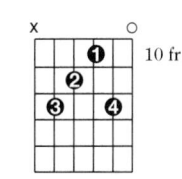

D♭m13♭5

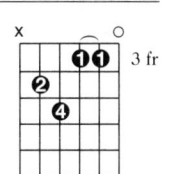

D♭7♭5(♯9)

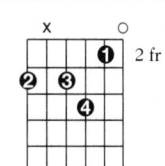

D♭m7♭5(♭9)

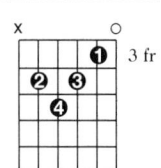

D

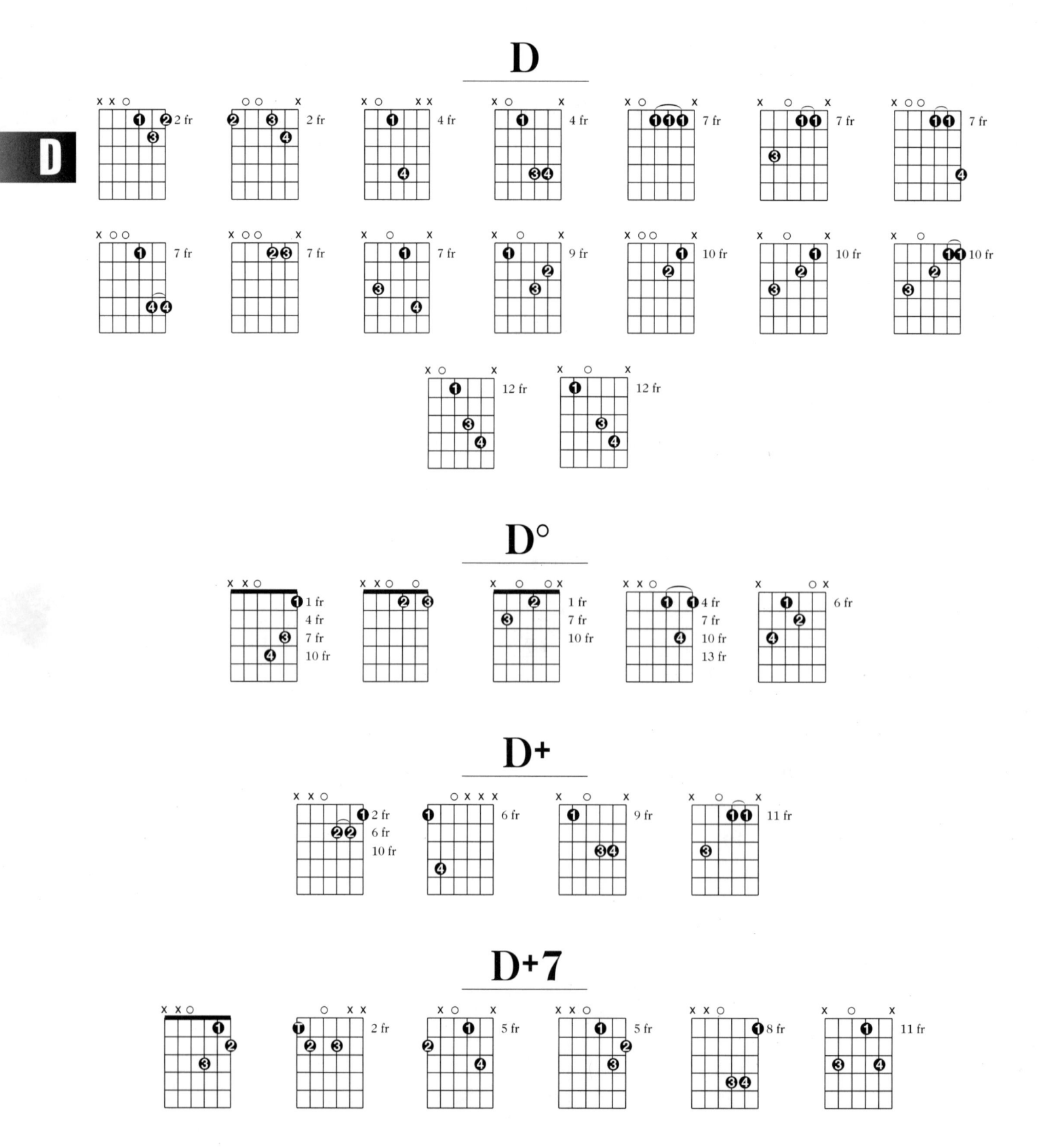

D

D°

D+

D+7

D+9

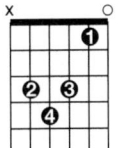

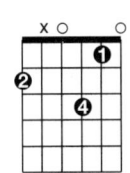

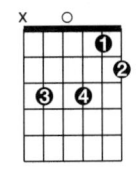

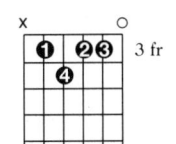

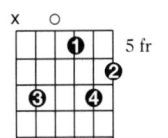

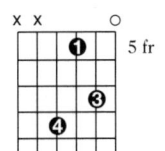

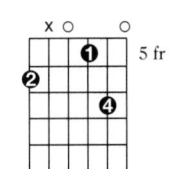

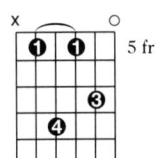

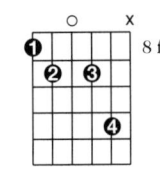

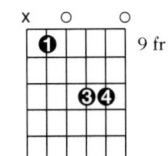

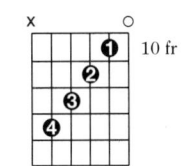

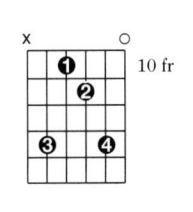

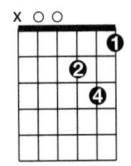

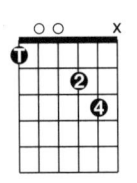

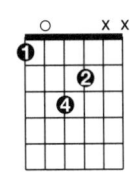

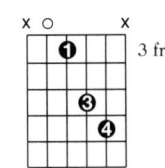

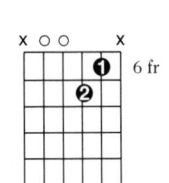

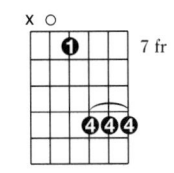

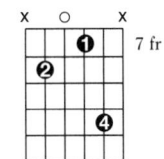

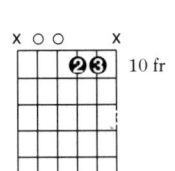

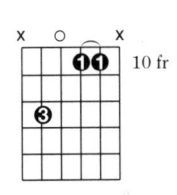

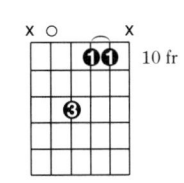

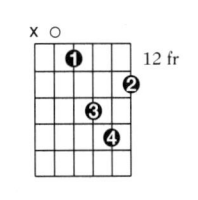

Dm

Dm6

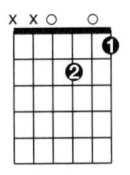

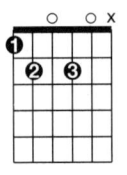

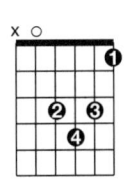

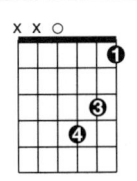

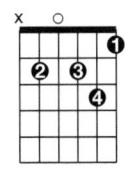

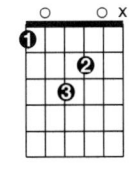

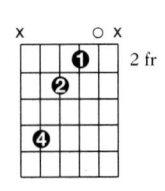

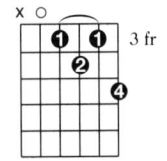

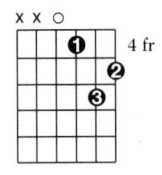

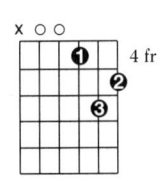

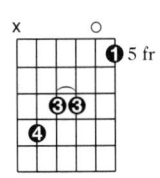

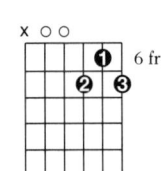

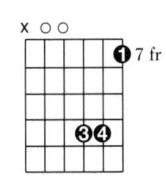

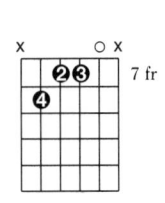

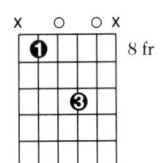

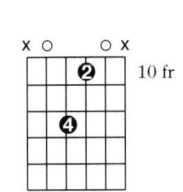

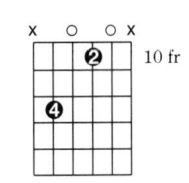

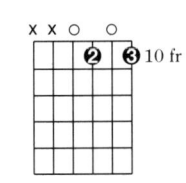

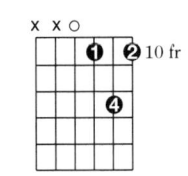

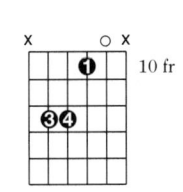

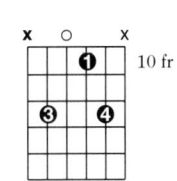

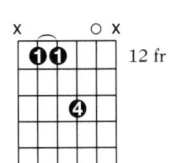

Dm6/9

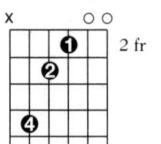

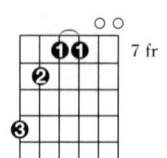

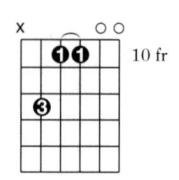

Dm13

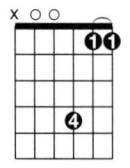

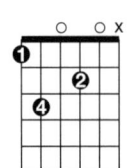

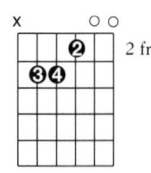

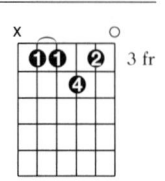

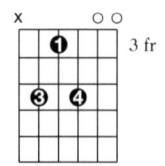

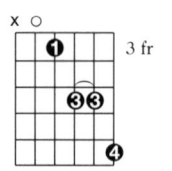

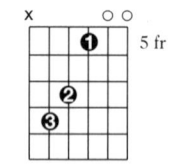

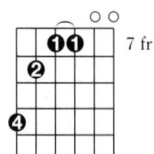

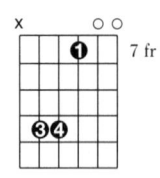

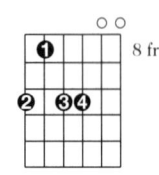

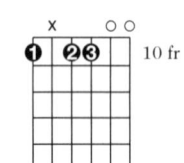

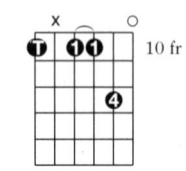

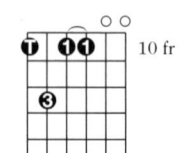

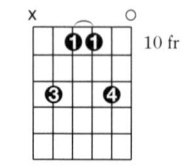

Dm7

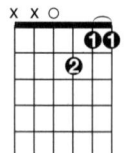

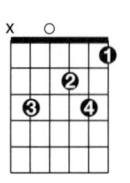

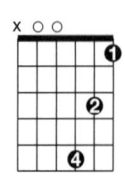

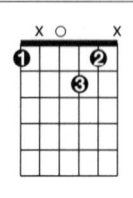

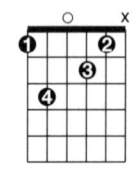

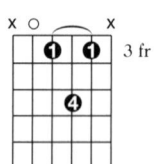

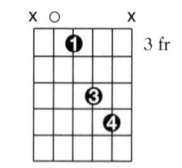

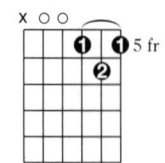

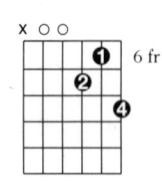

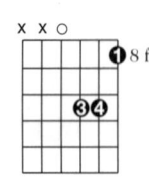

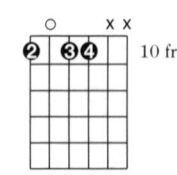

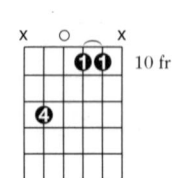

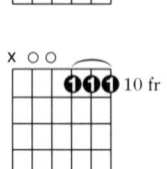

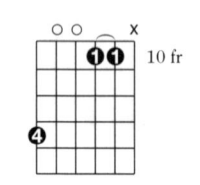

Dm(add9)

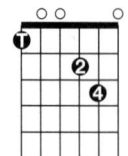

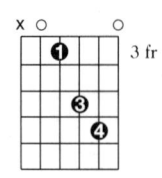

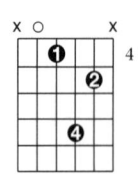

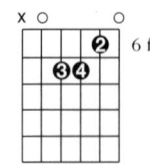

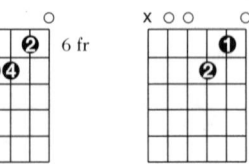

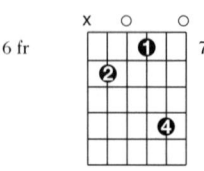

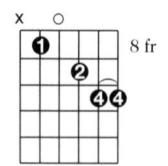

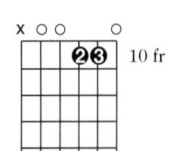

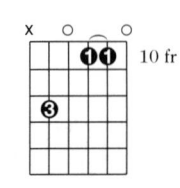

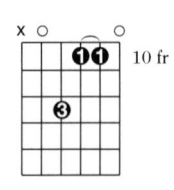

Dm9

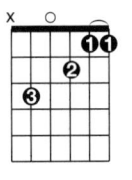

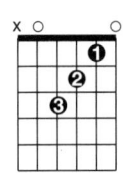

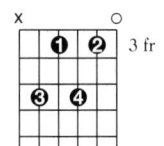

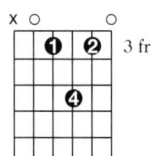

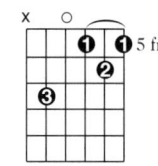

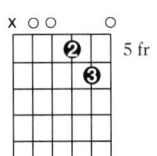

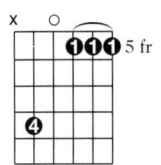

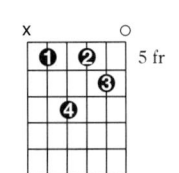

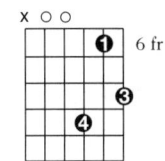

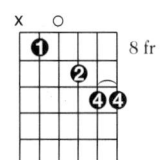

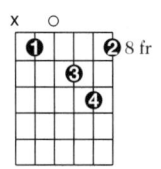

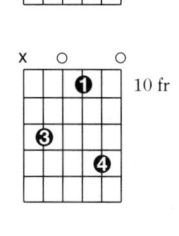

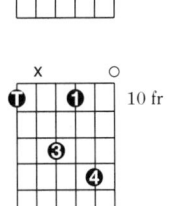

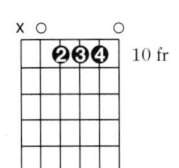

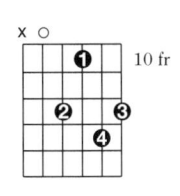

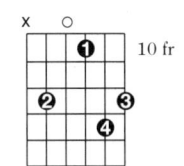

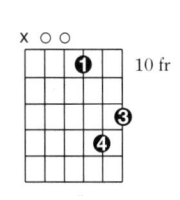

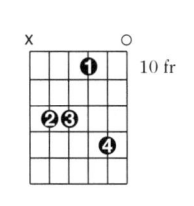

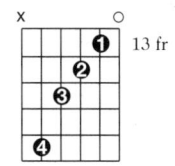

Dm11

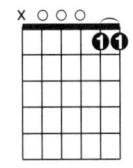

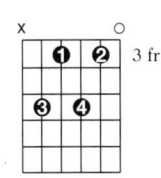

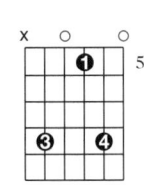

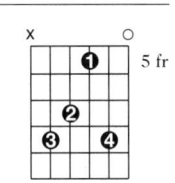

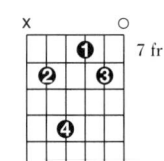

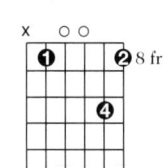

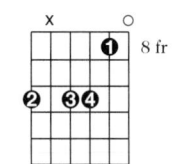

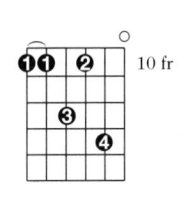

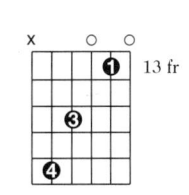

Dm7♭5

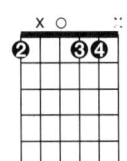

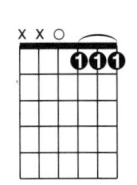

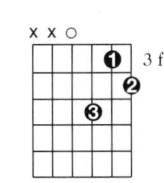

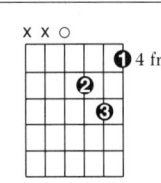

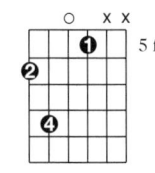

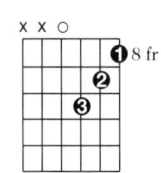

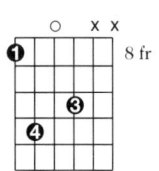

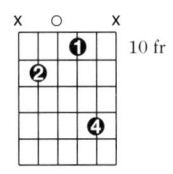

Dm9♭5

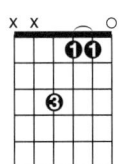

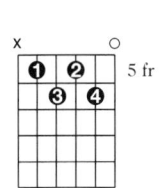

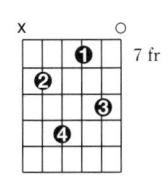

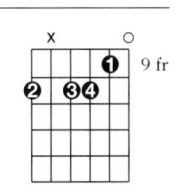

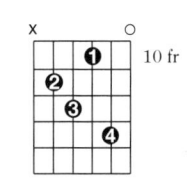

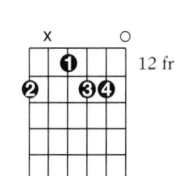

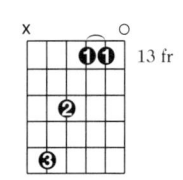

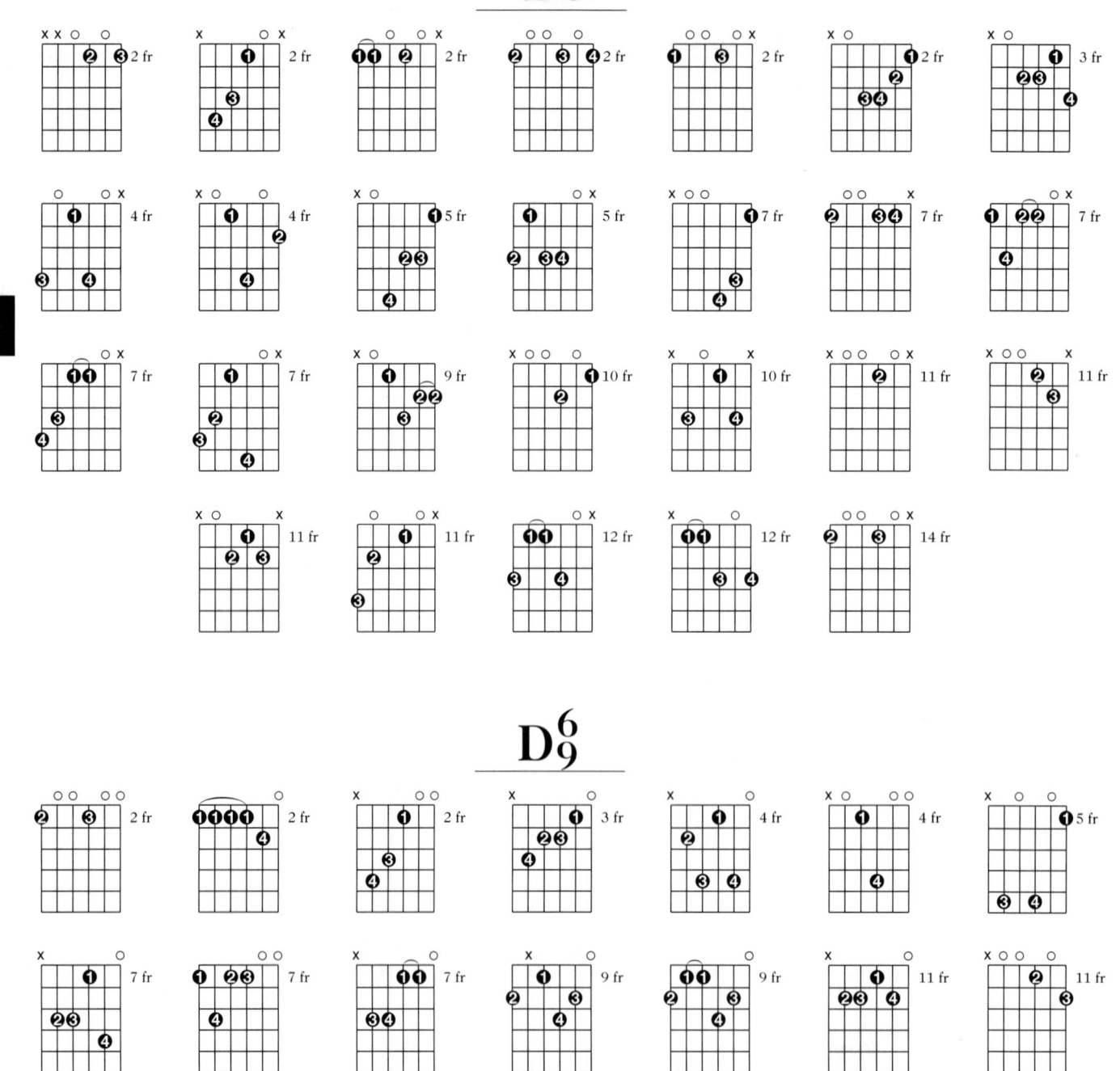

D6

D6/9

54

D13

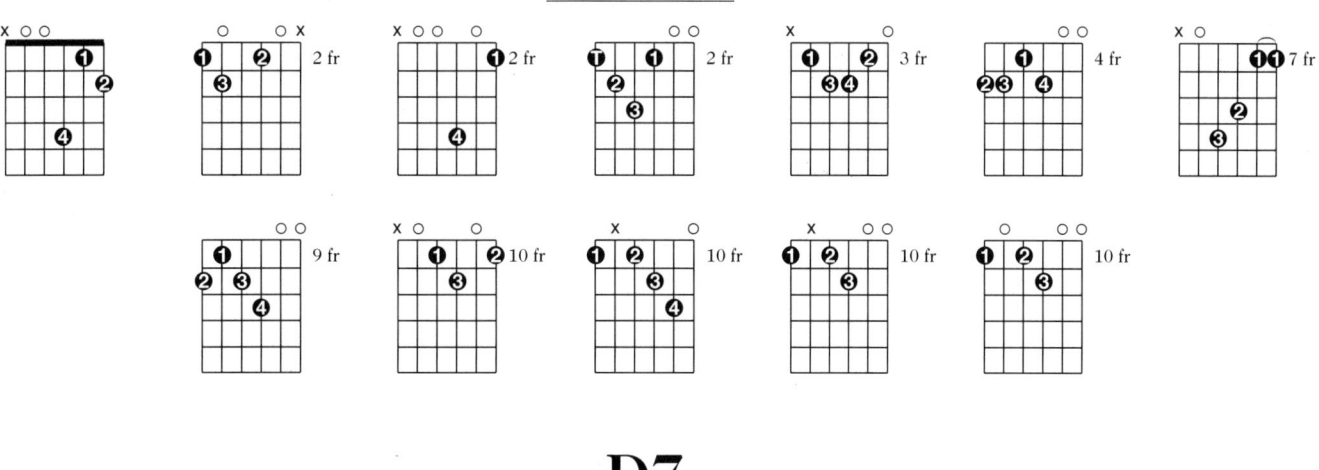

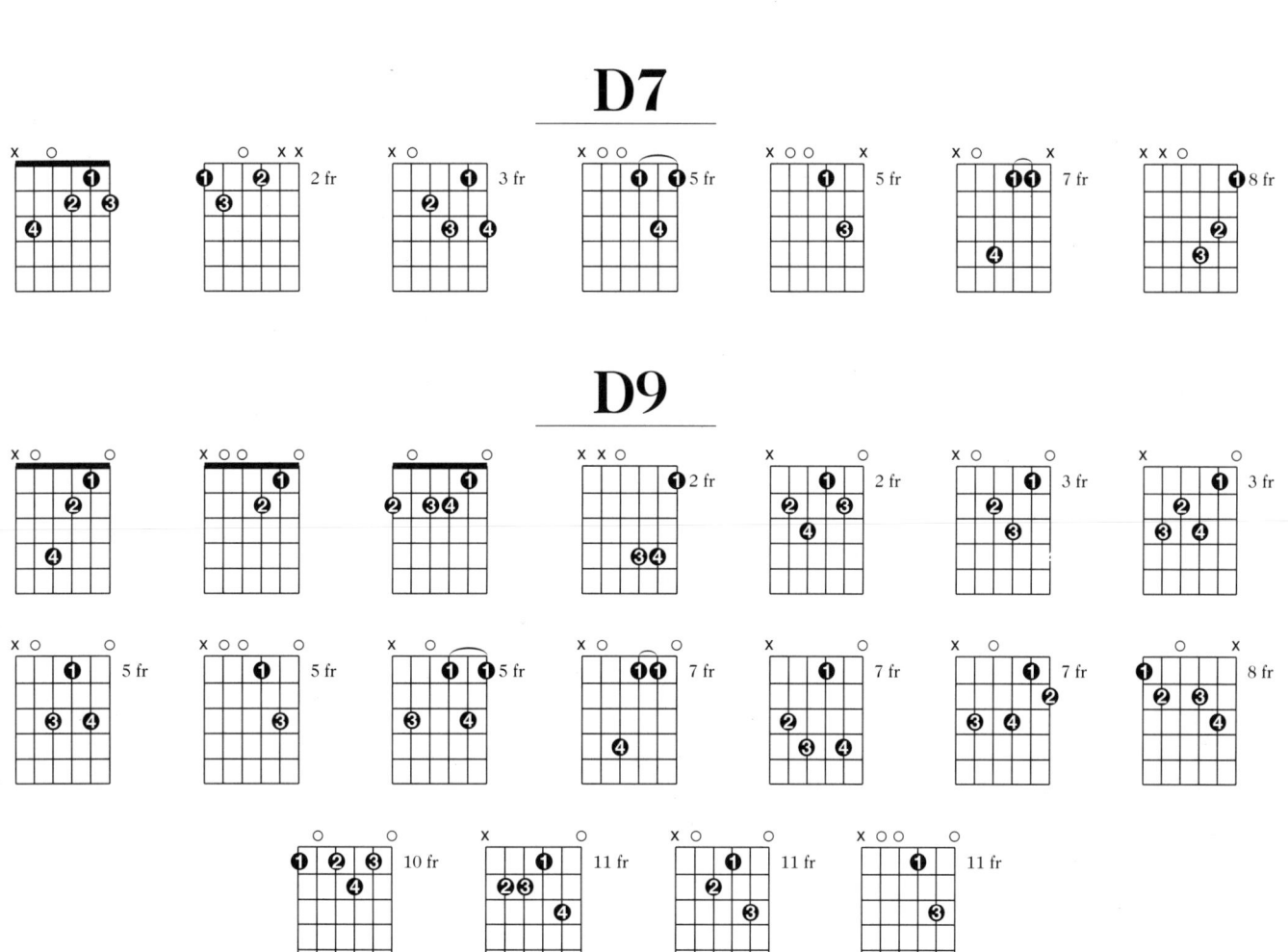

D7

D9

Dadd9

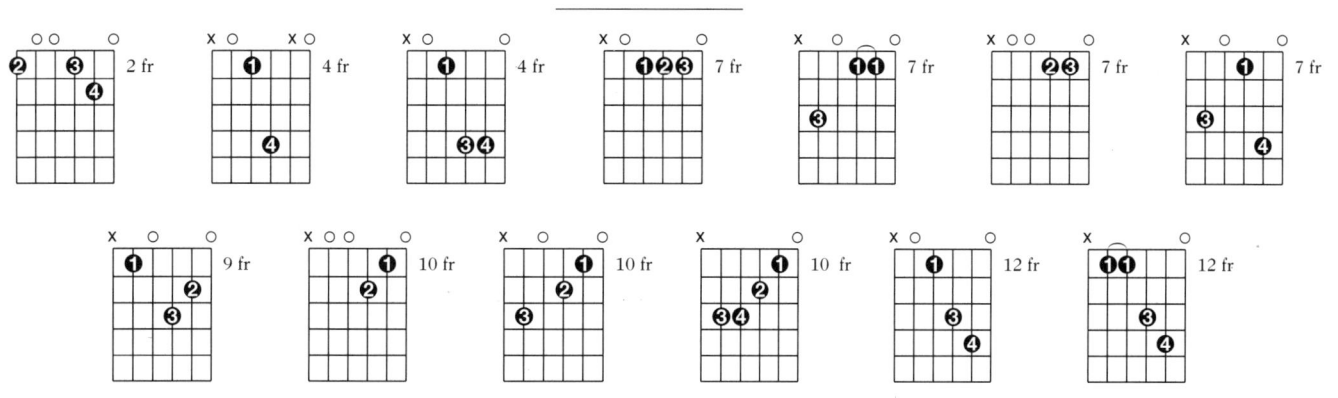

D

Dmaj7

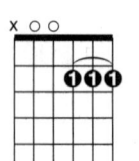

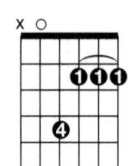

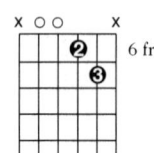

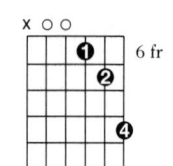

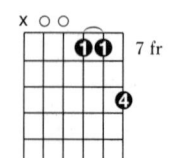

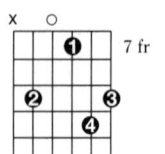

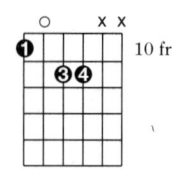

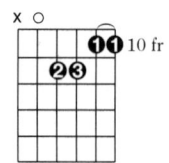

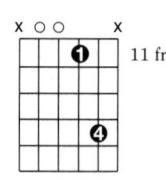

Dmaj9

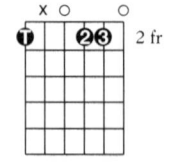

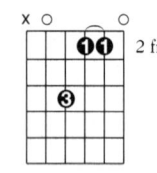

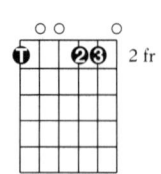

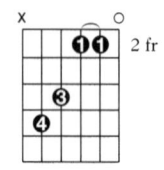

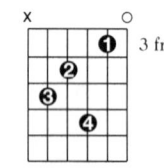

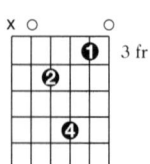

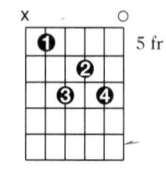

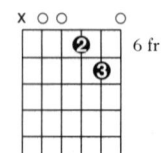

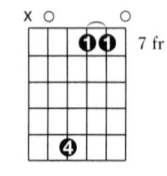

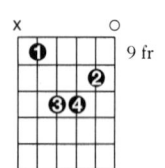

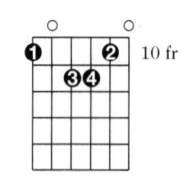

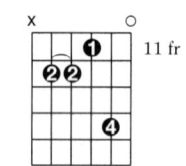

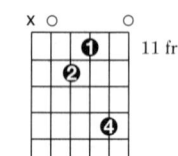

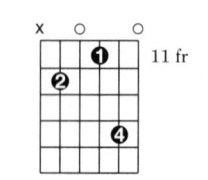

Dmaj13

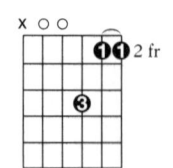

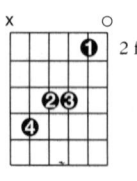

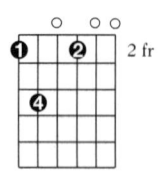

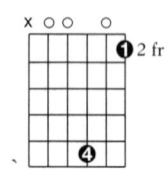

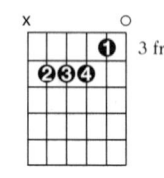

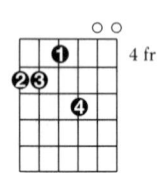

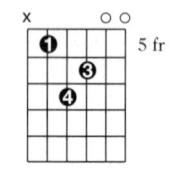

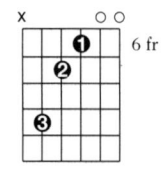

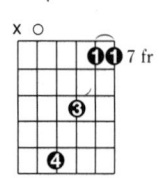

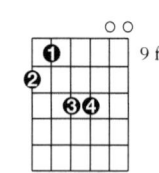

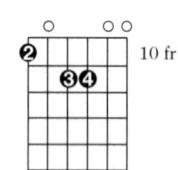

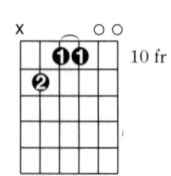

D7sus4

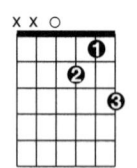

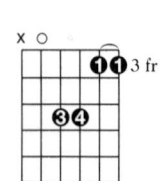

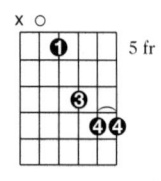

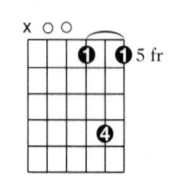

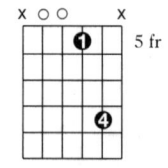

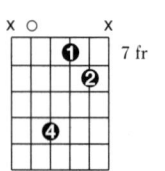

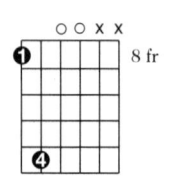

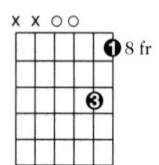

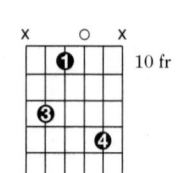

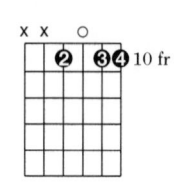

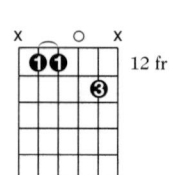

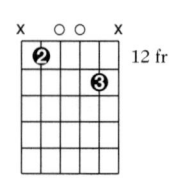

D11

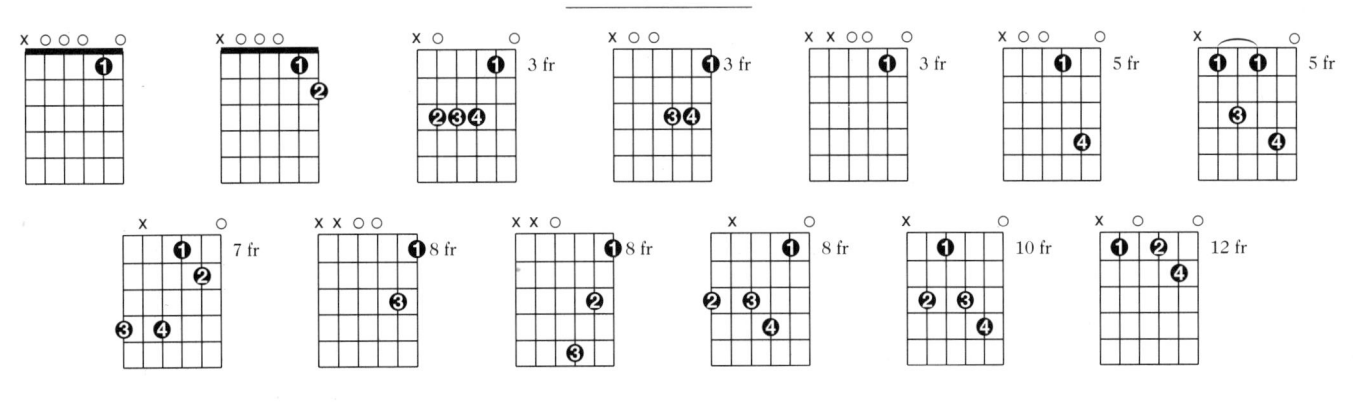

D7♭5

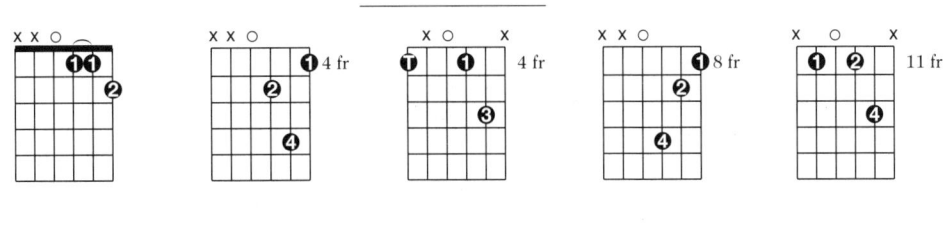

D9♭5

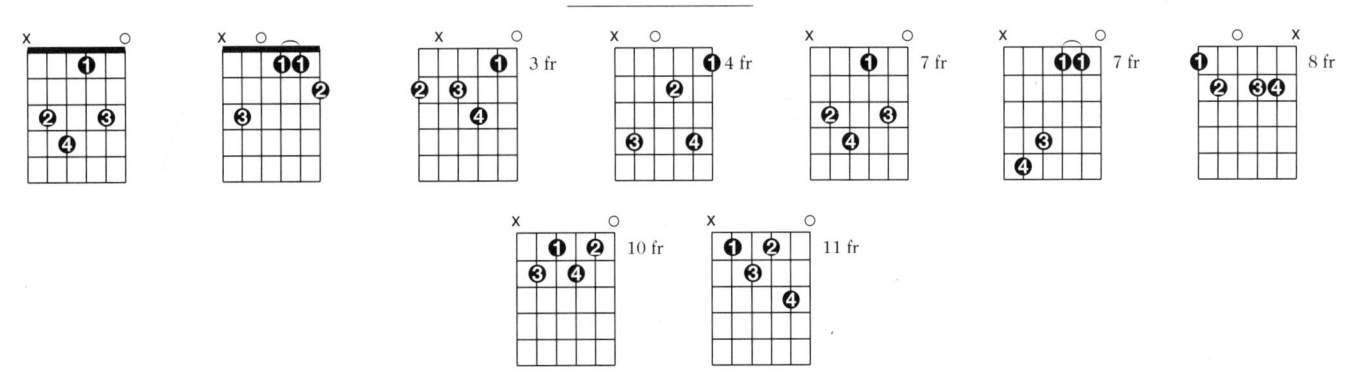

D9♯11

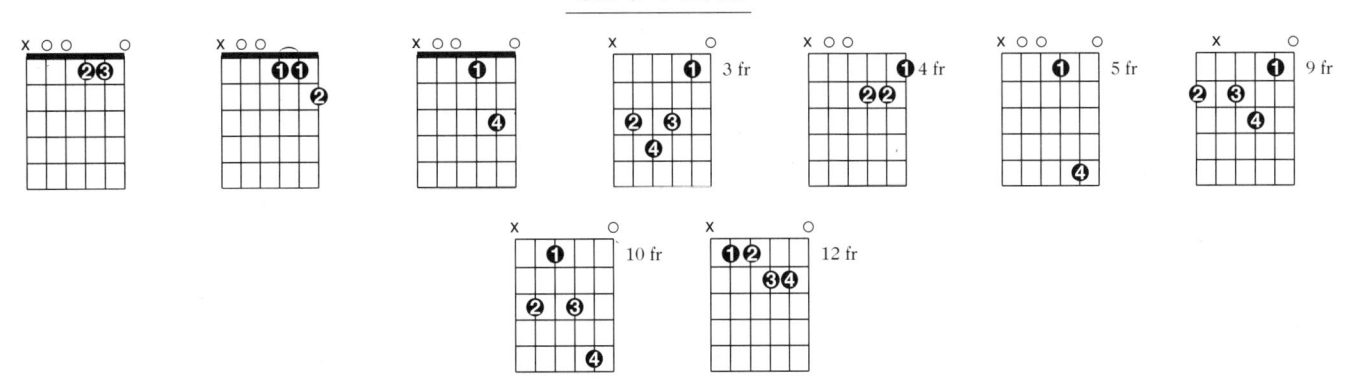

D7♯9

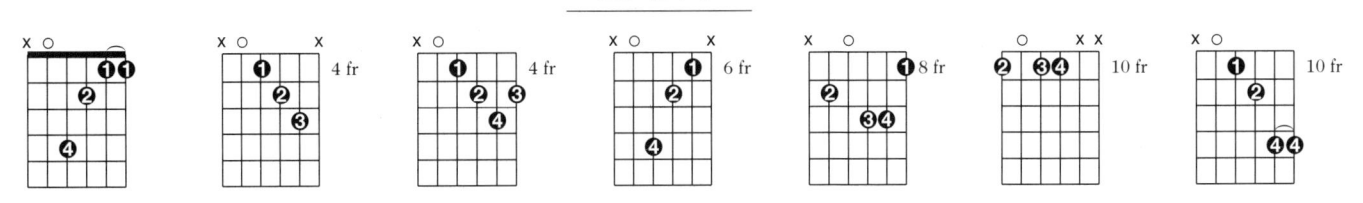

D7#9 (cont'd)

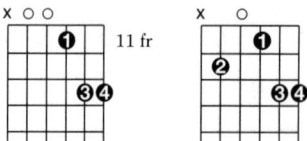

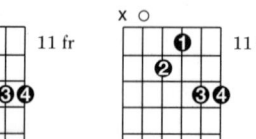

D7♭9

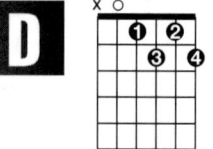

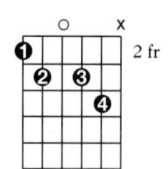

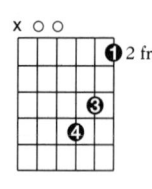

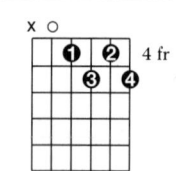

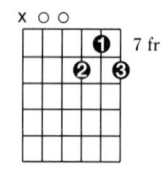

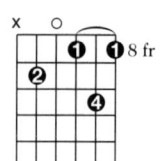

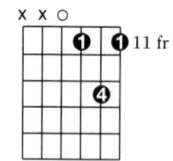

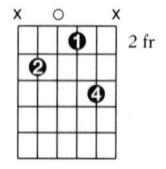

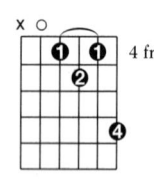

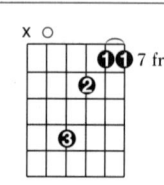

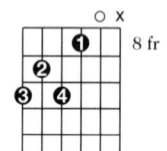

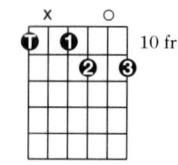

D13♭9

D13♭5(♭9)

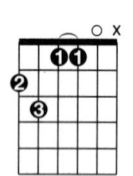

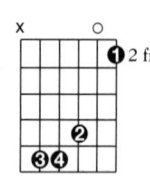

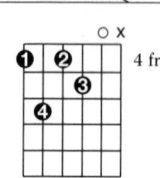

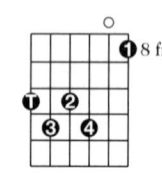

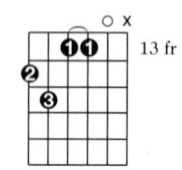

Dm(maj7)

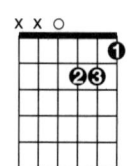

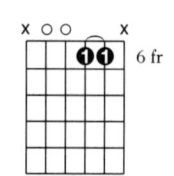

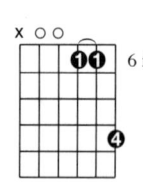

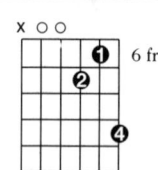

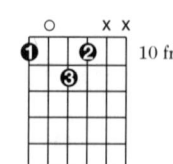

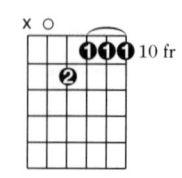

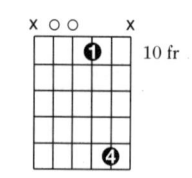

Dm(maj9)

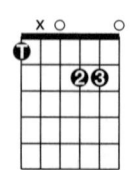

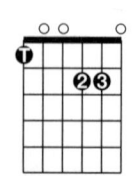

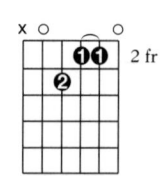

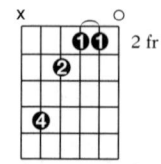

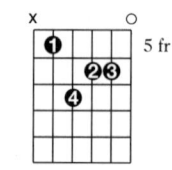

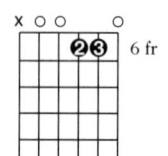

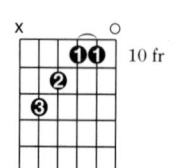

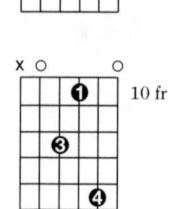

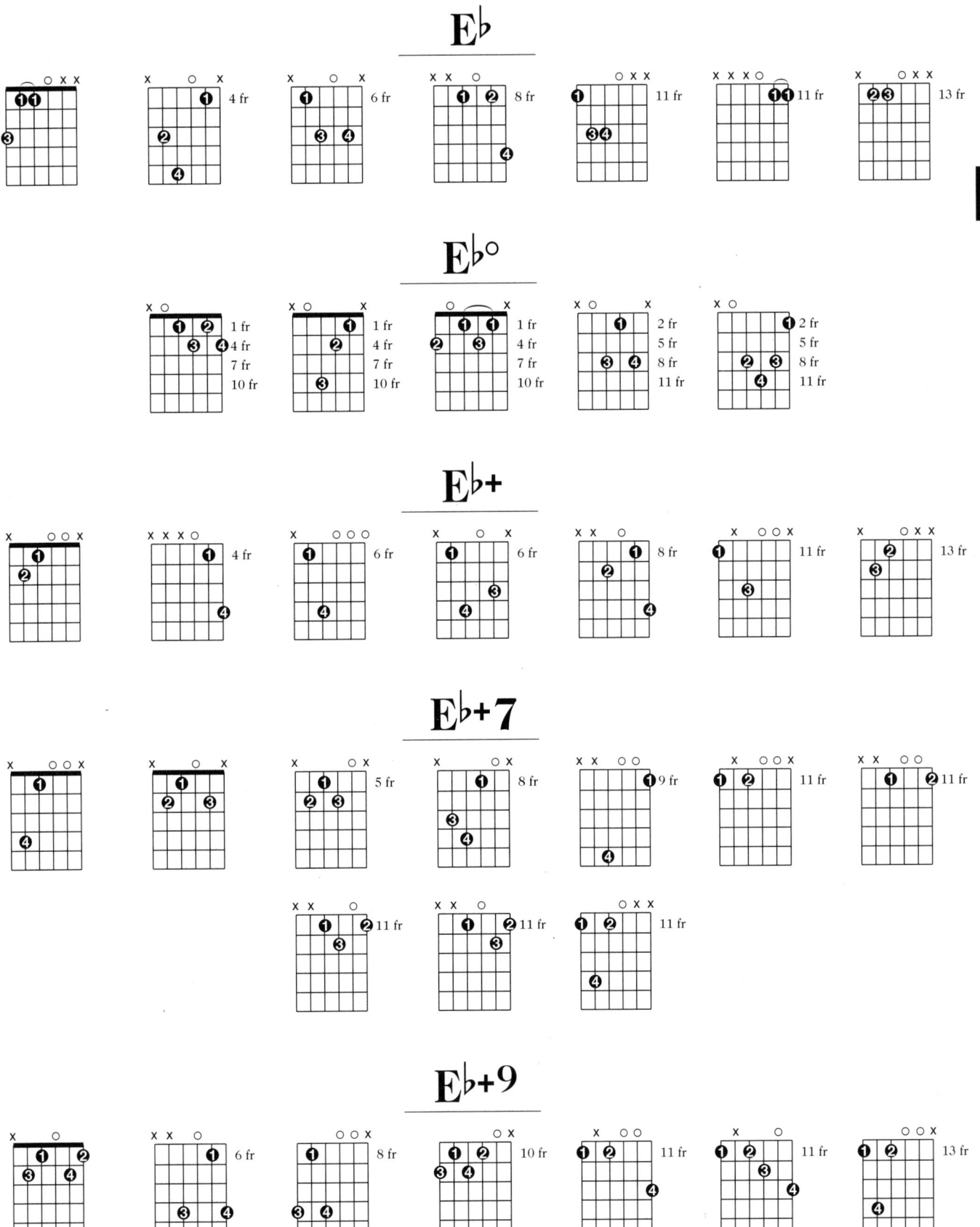

E♭

E♭

E♭°

E♭+

E♭+7

E♭+9

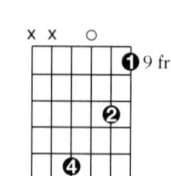

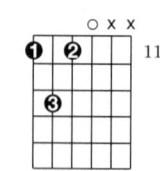

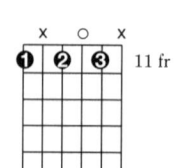

E♭m7♭5

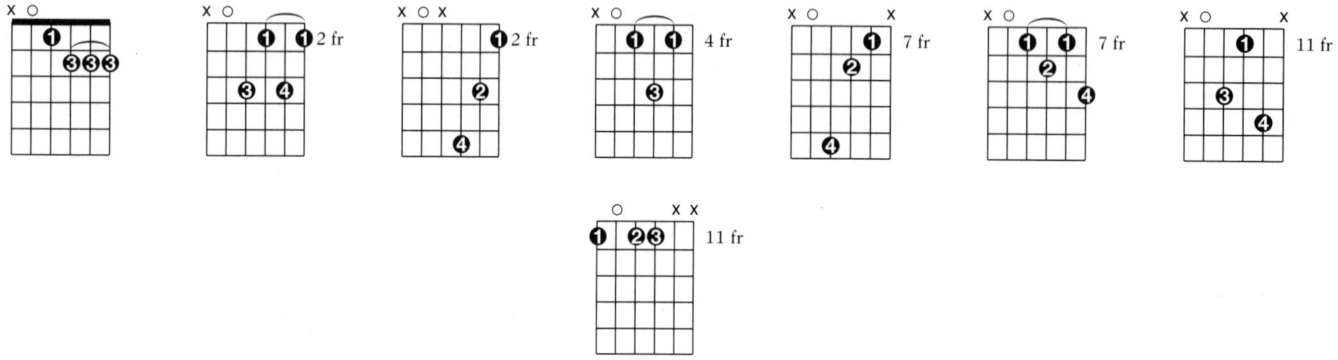

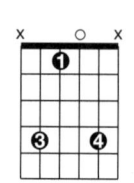

E♭6

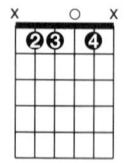

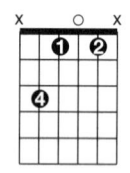

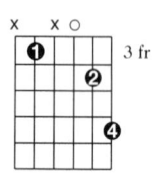

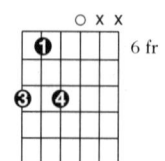

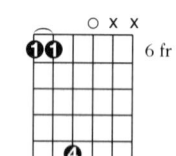

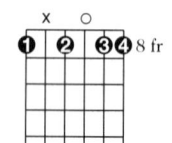

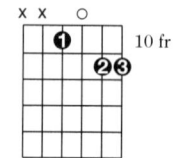

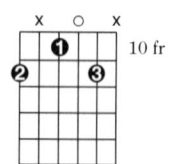

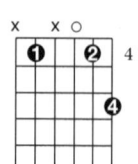

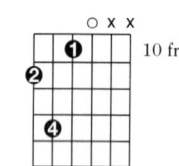

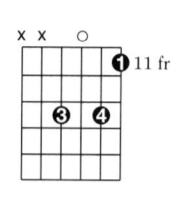

E♭6/9

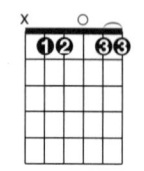

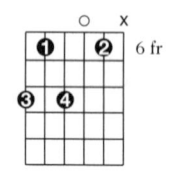

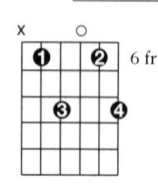

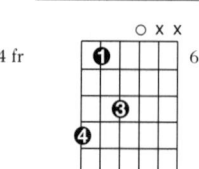

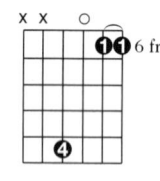

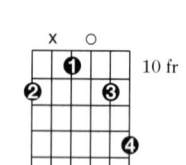

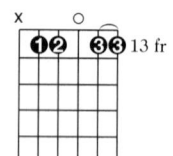

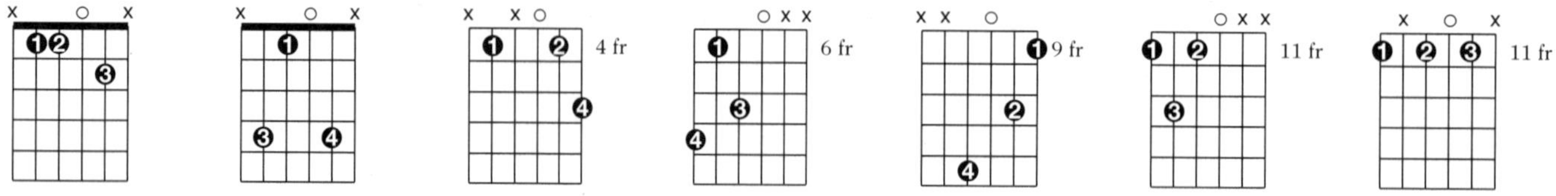

E♭7

E♭9

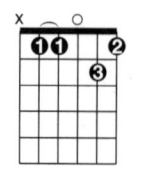

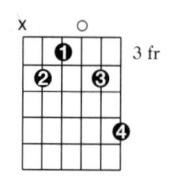

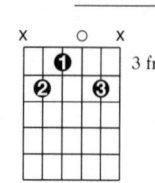

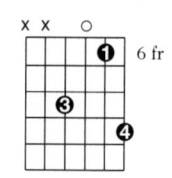

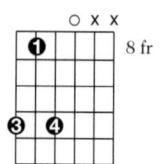

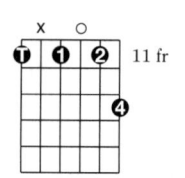

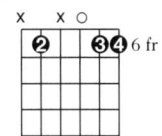

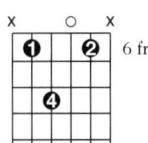

E♭add9

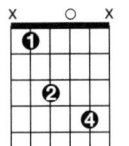

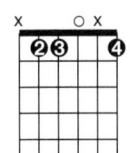

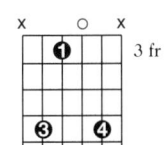

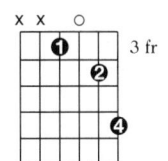

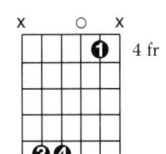

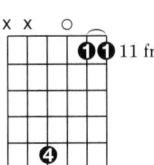

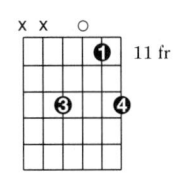

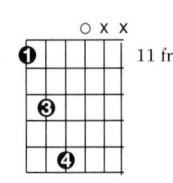

E♭maj7

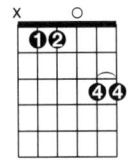

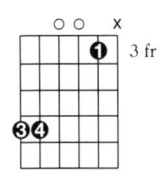

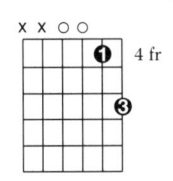

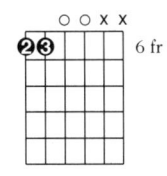

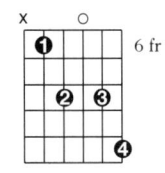

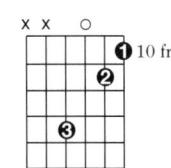

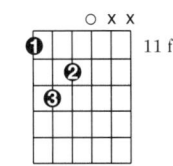

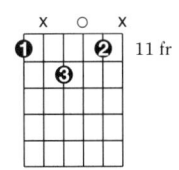

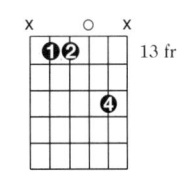

E♭maj9

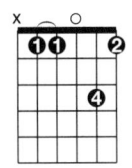

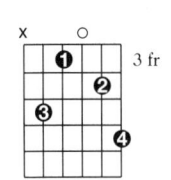

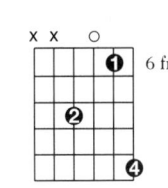

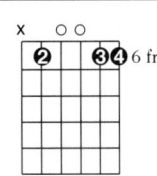

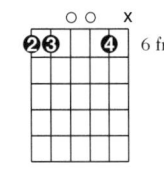

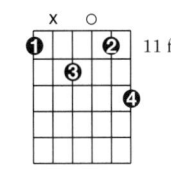

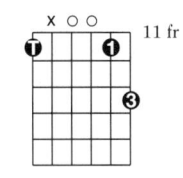

E♭maj13

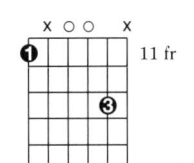

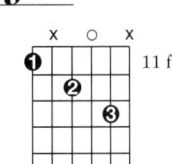

E♭11

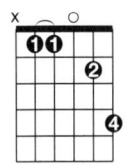

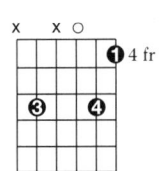

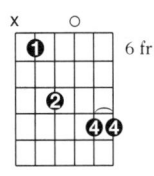

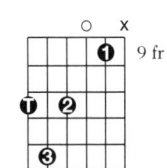

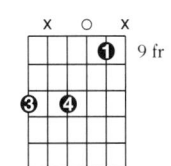

E♭7♭5

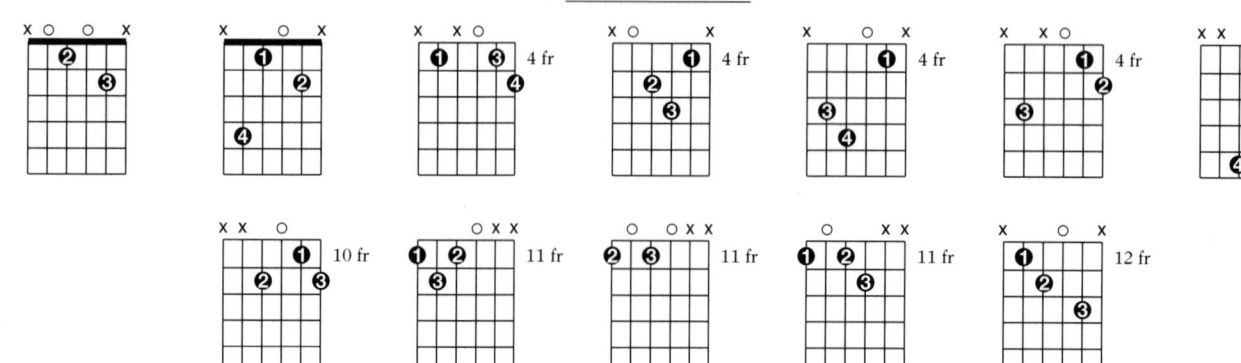

E♭9♭5

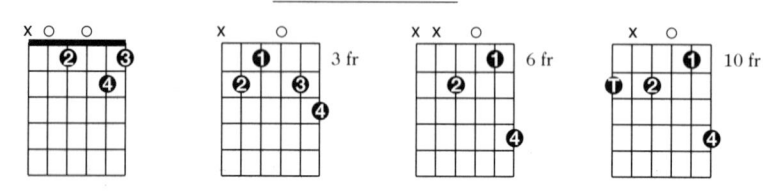

E♭7#11

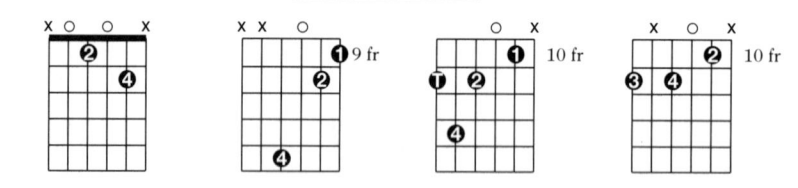

E♭7#9

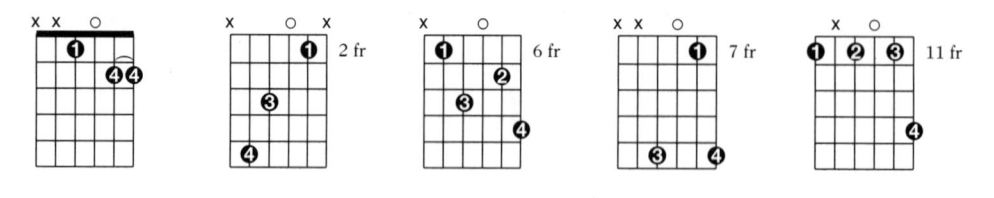

E♭7♭9

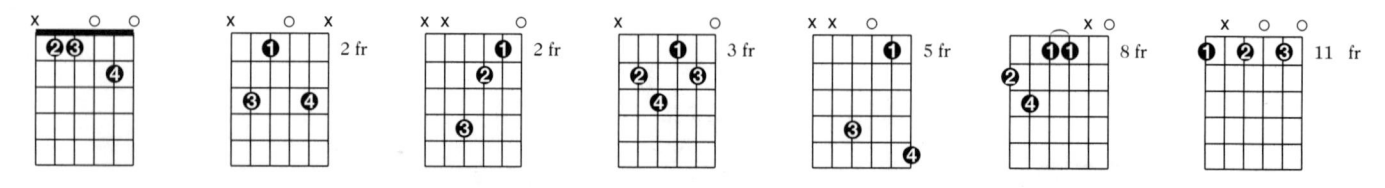

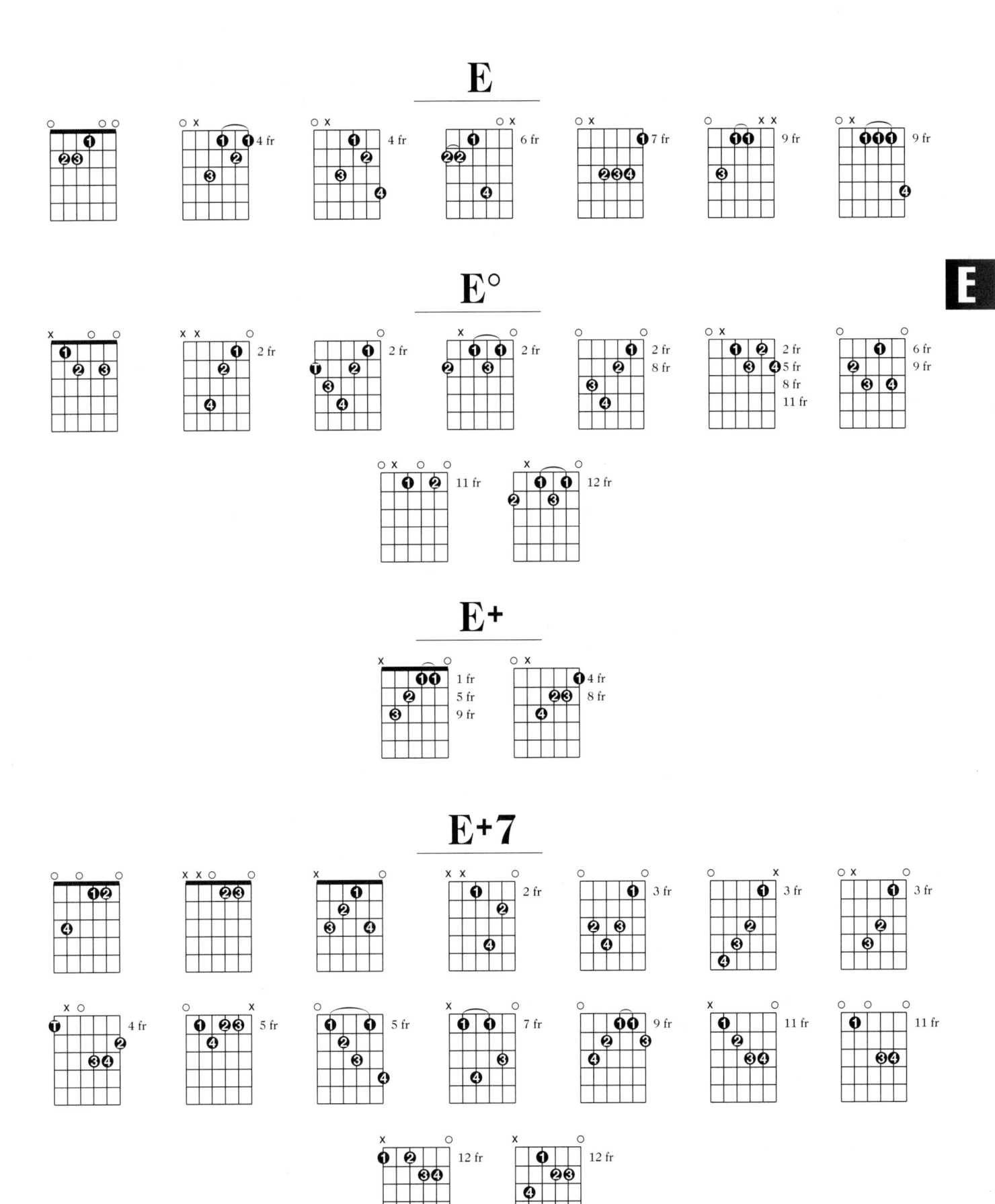

E

E

E°

E+

E+7

E+9

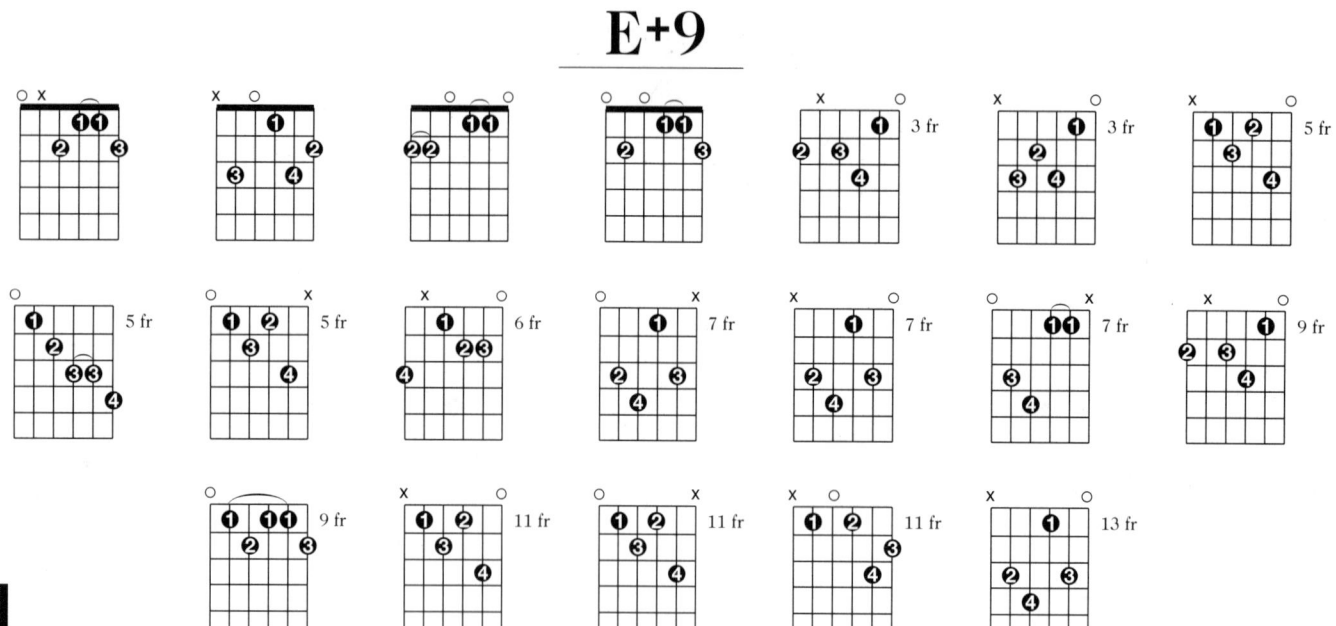

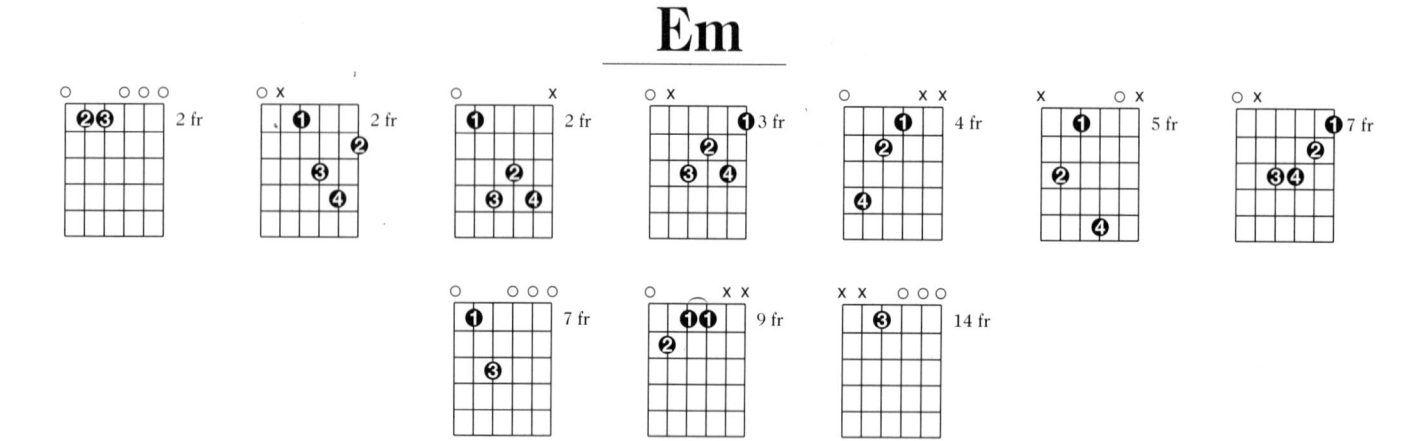

Em

Em6

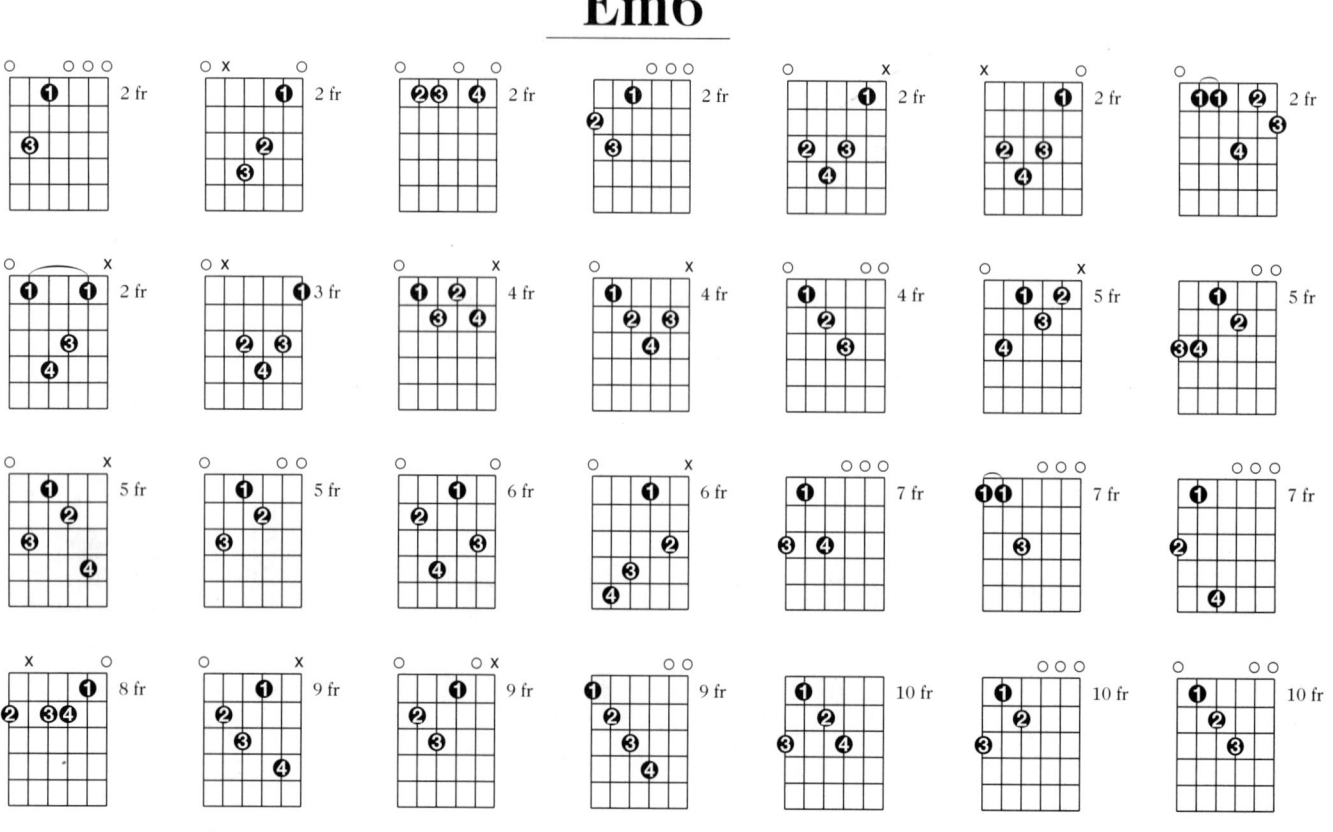

Em6 (cont'd)

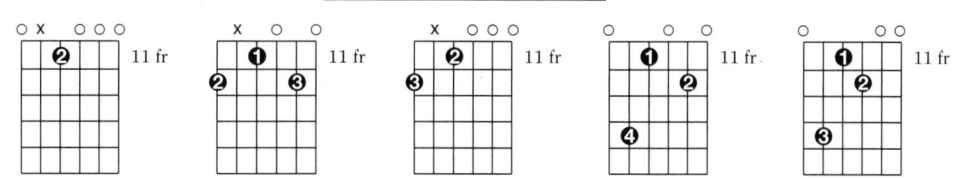

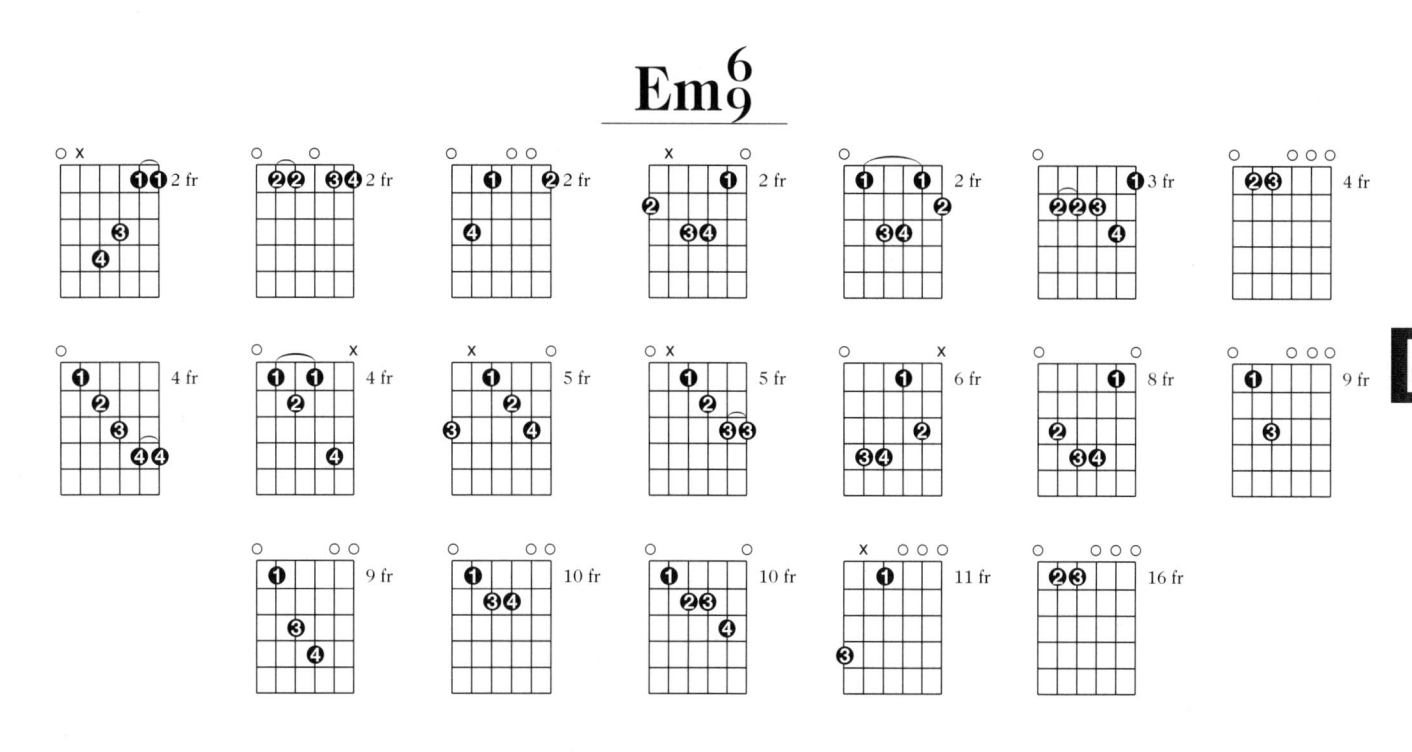

Em6/9

Em13

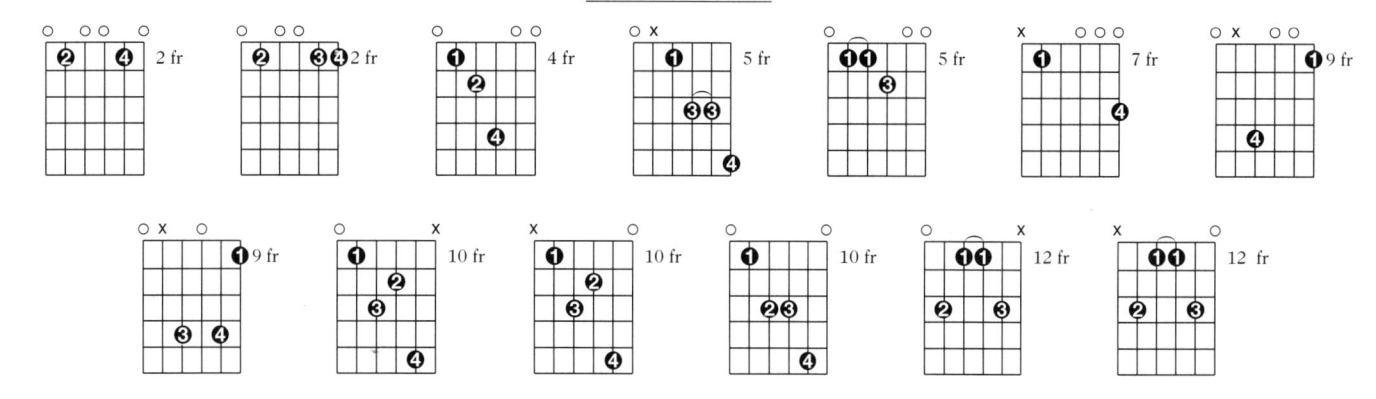

Em7

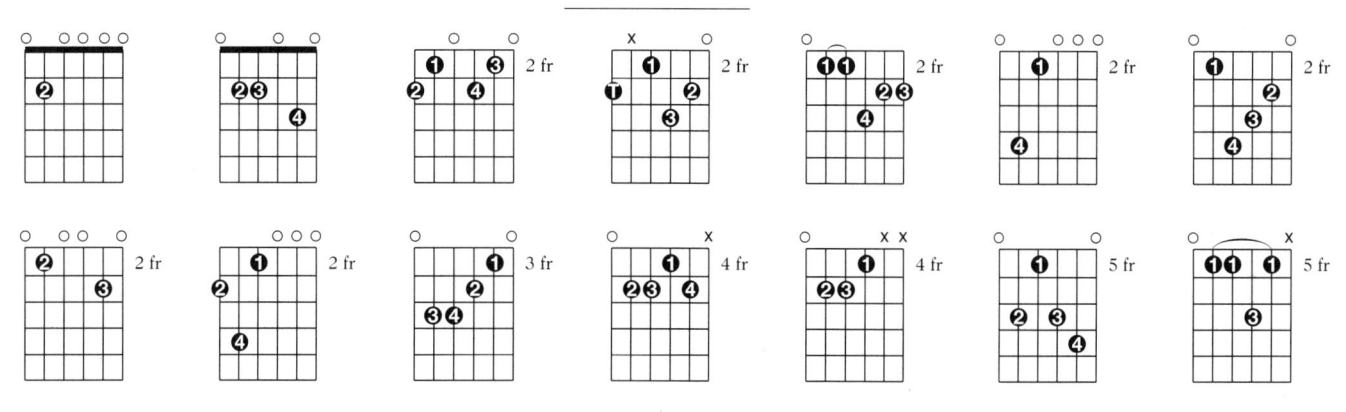

Em7 (cont'd)

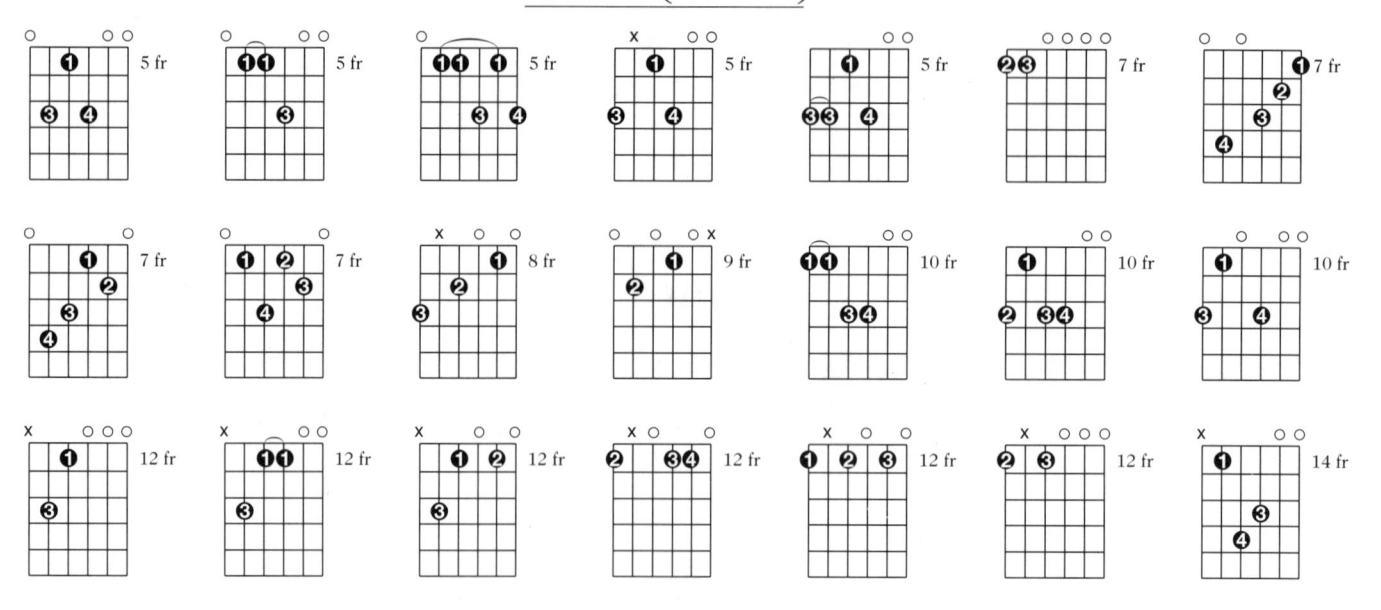

Em(add9)

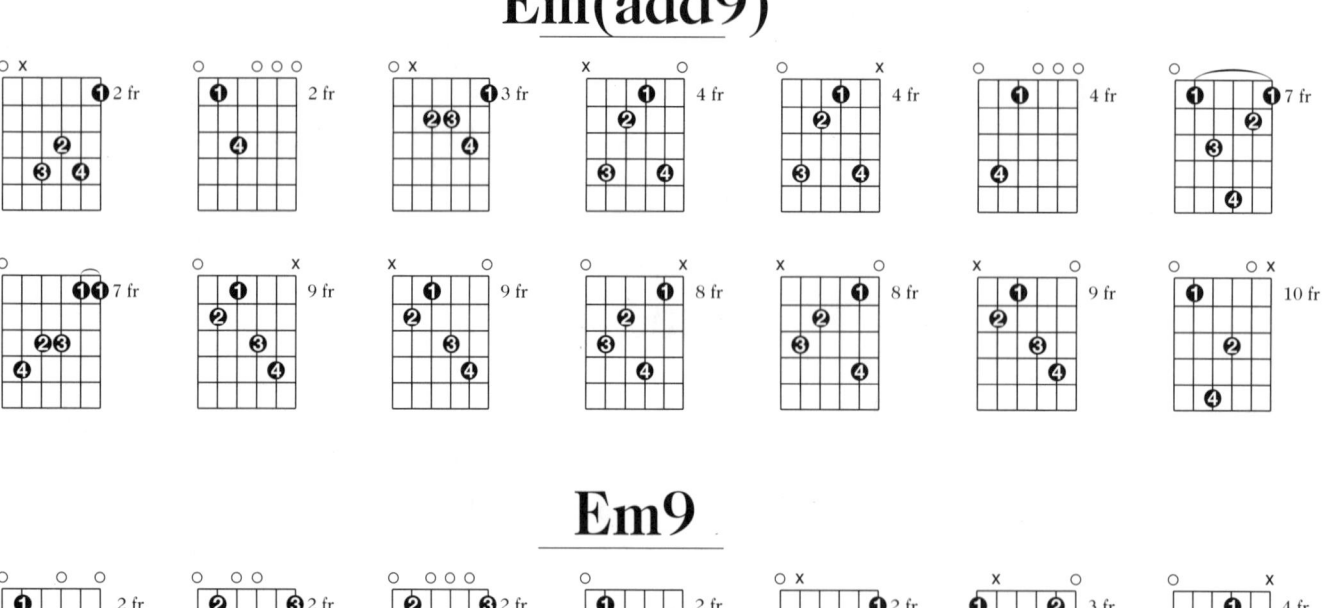

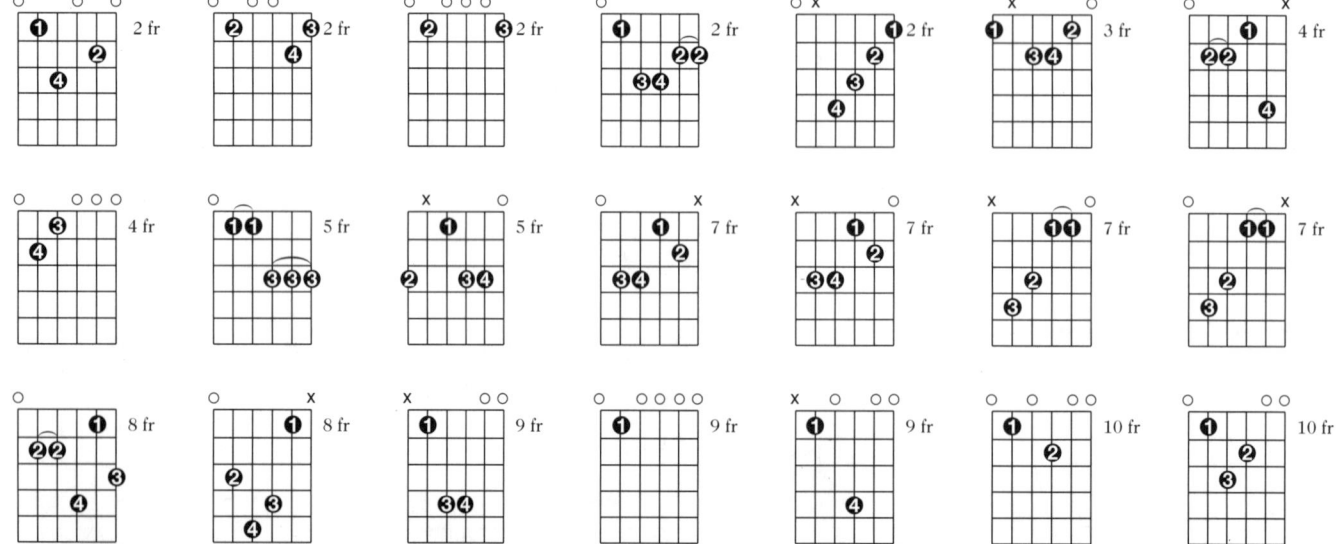

Em9

Em9 (cont'd)

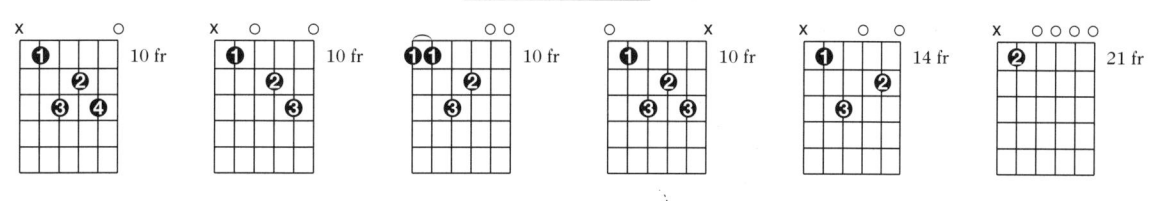

Em11

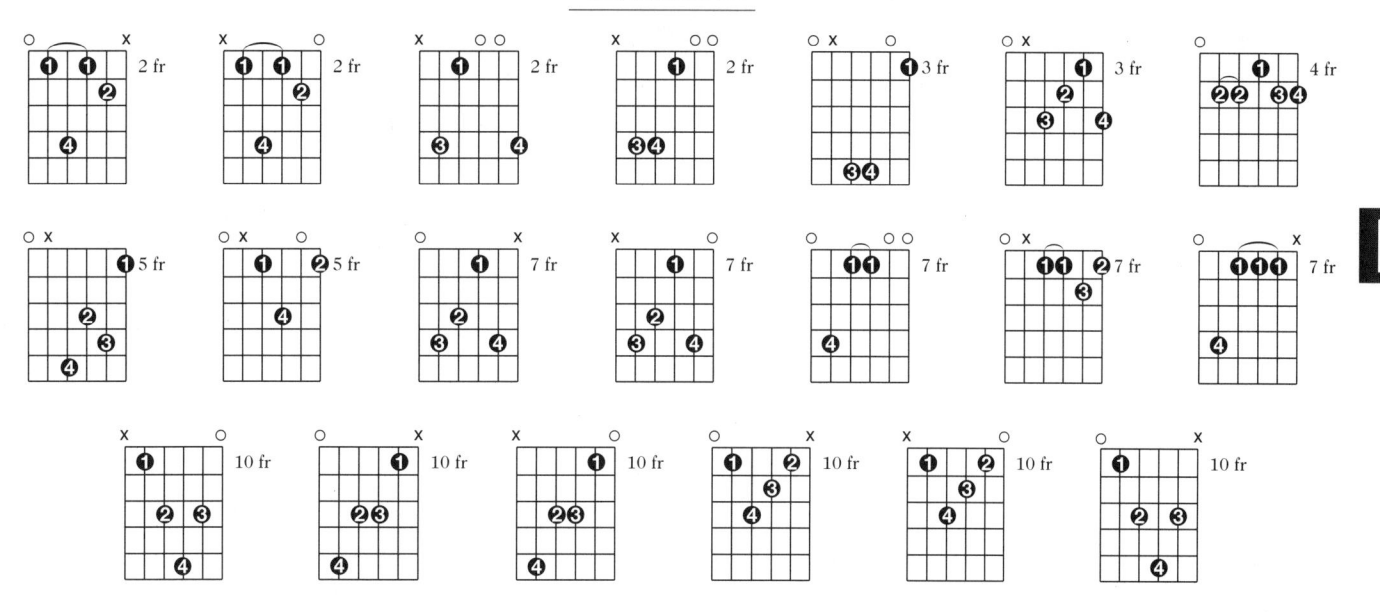

Em7♭5

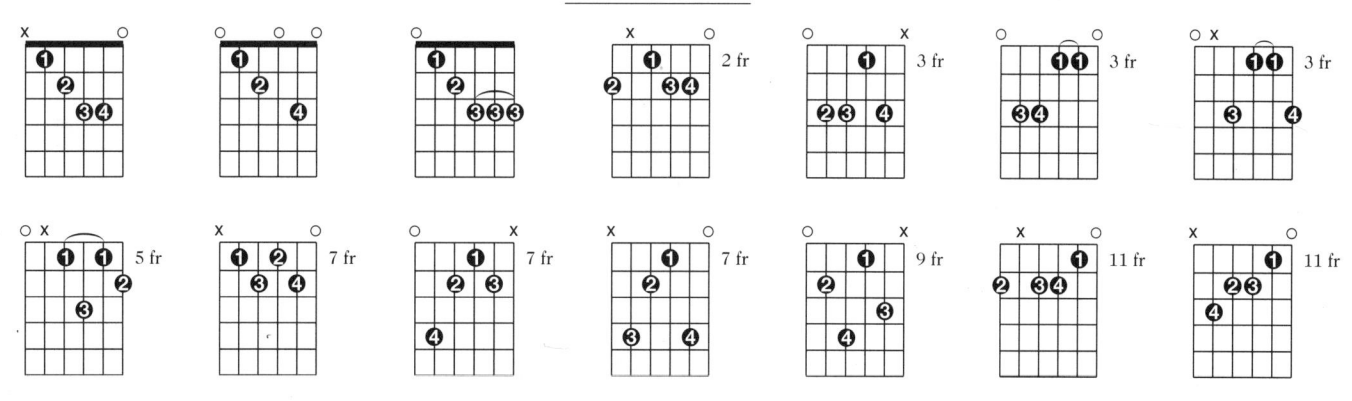

Em9♭5

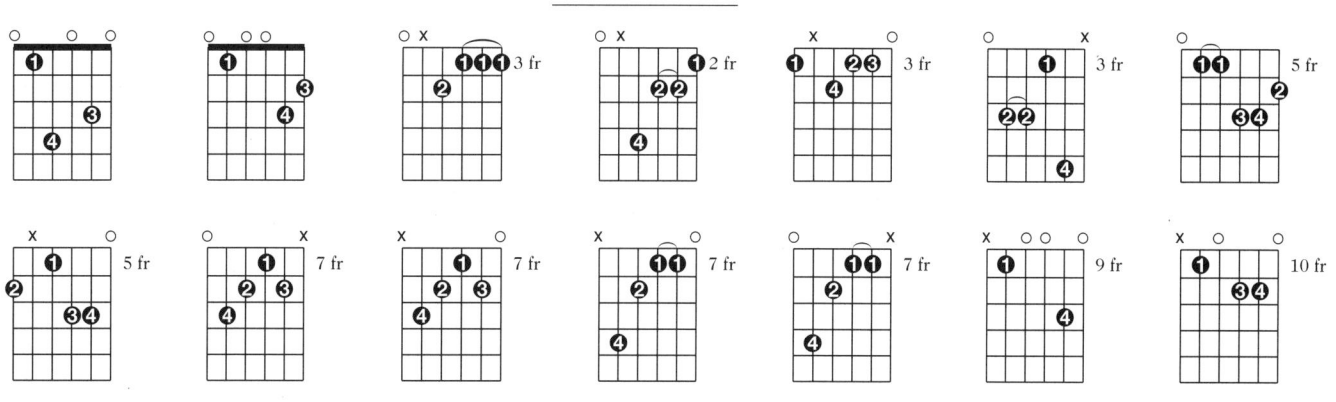

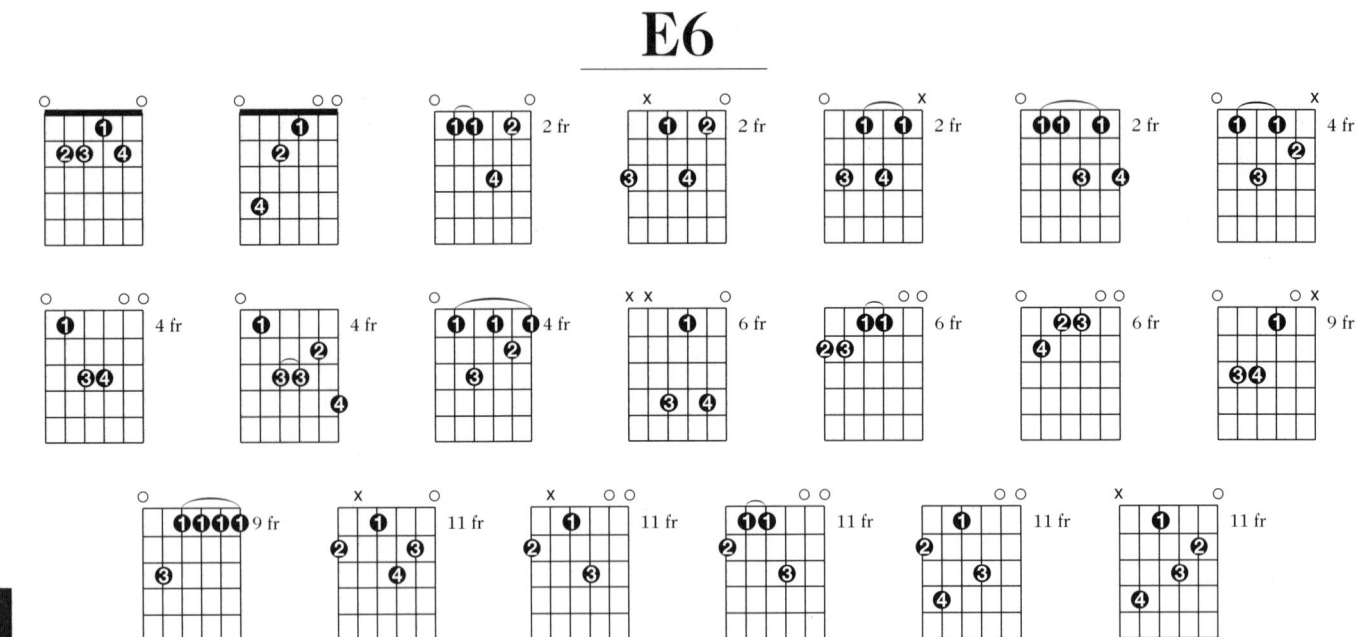

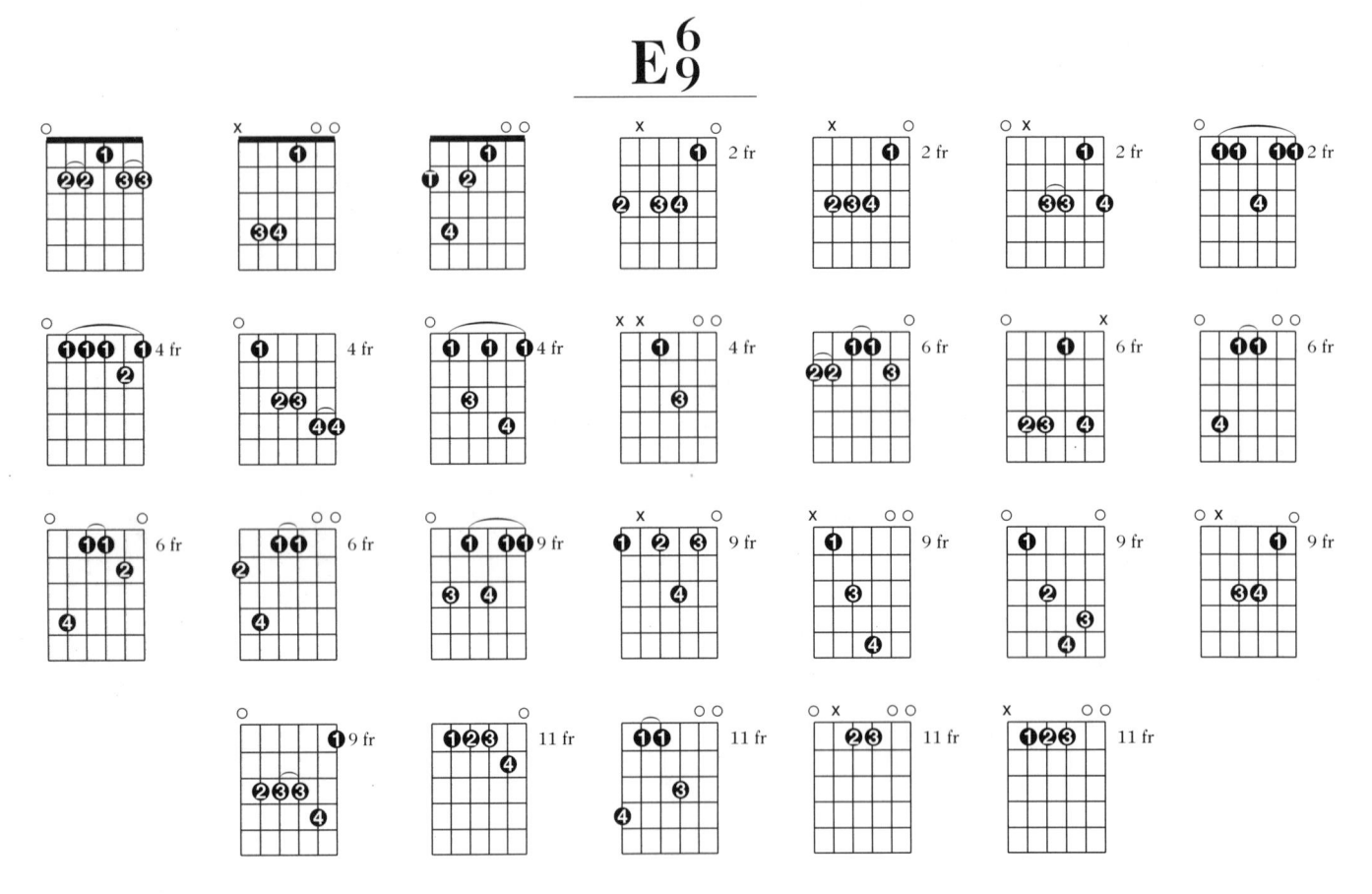

E6

E6/9

E13

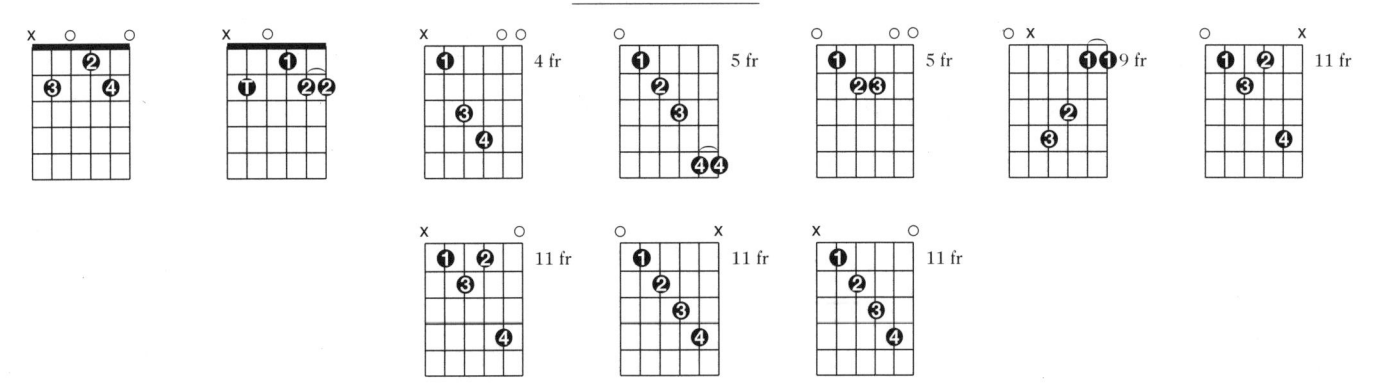

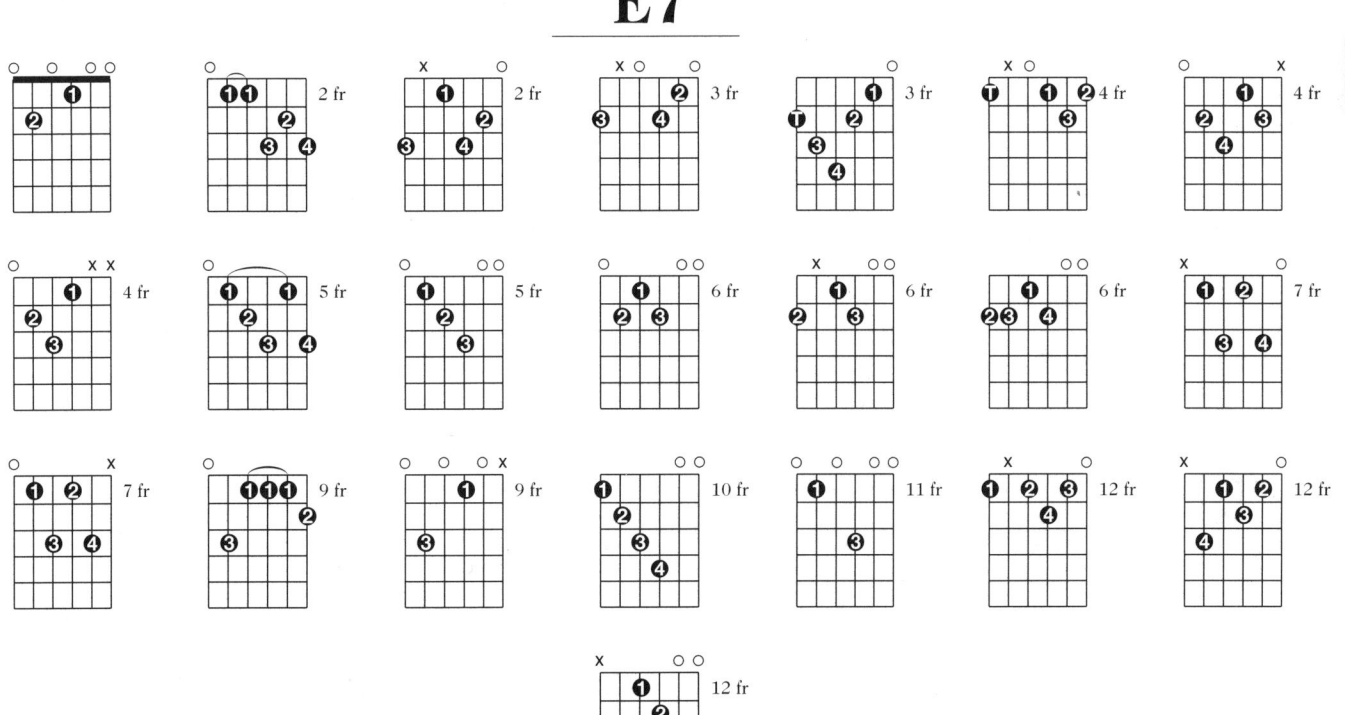

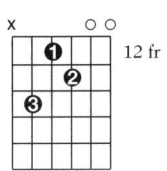

E7

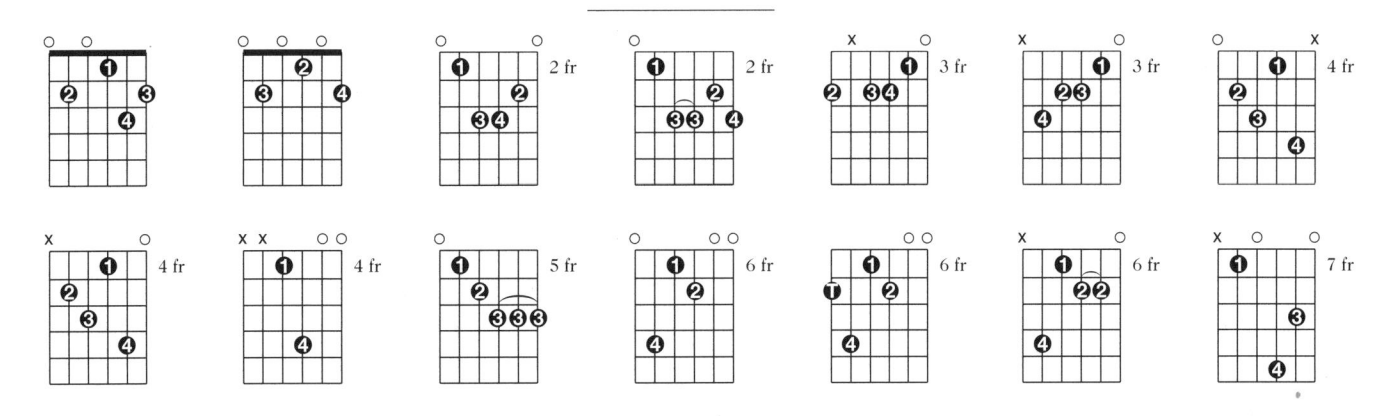

E9

E9 (cont'd)

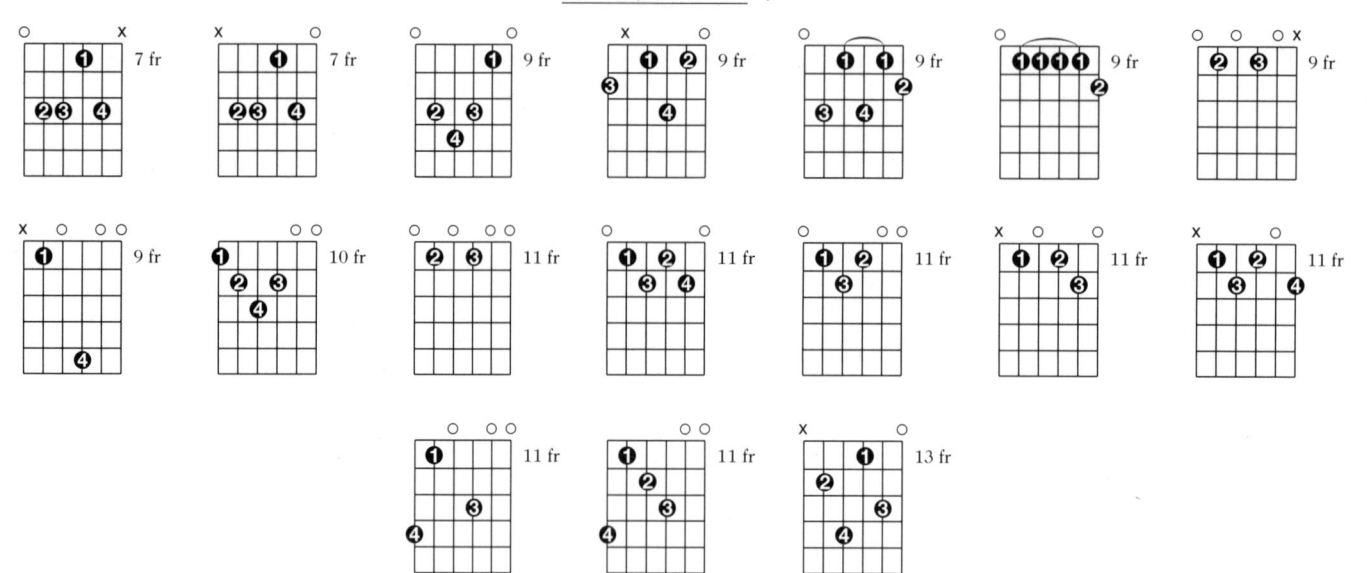

Eadd9

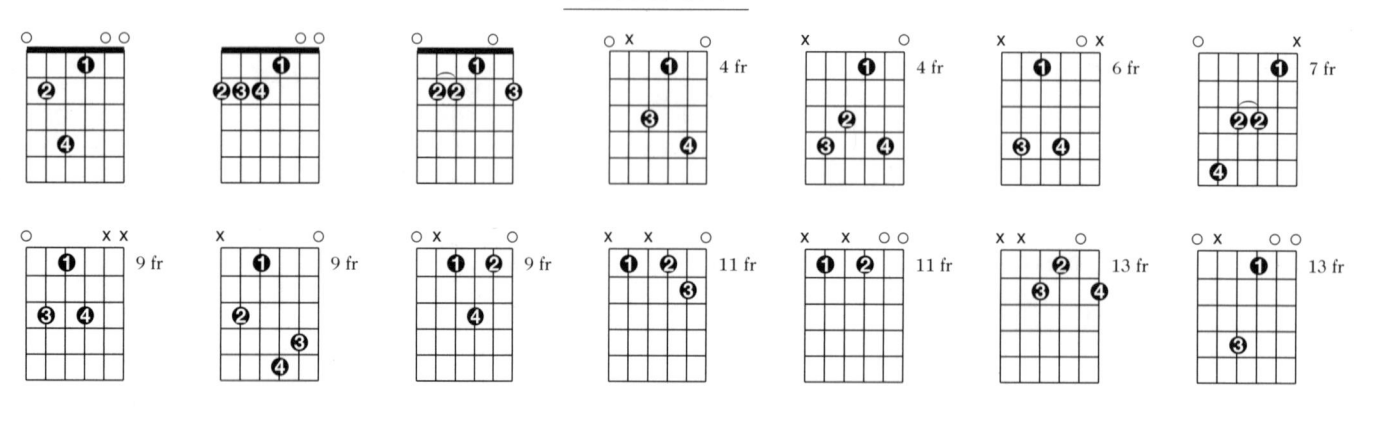

Emaj7

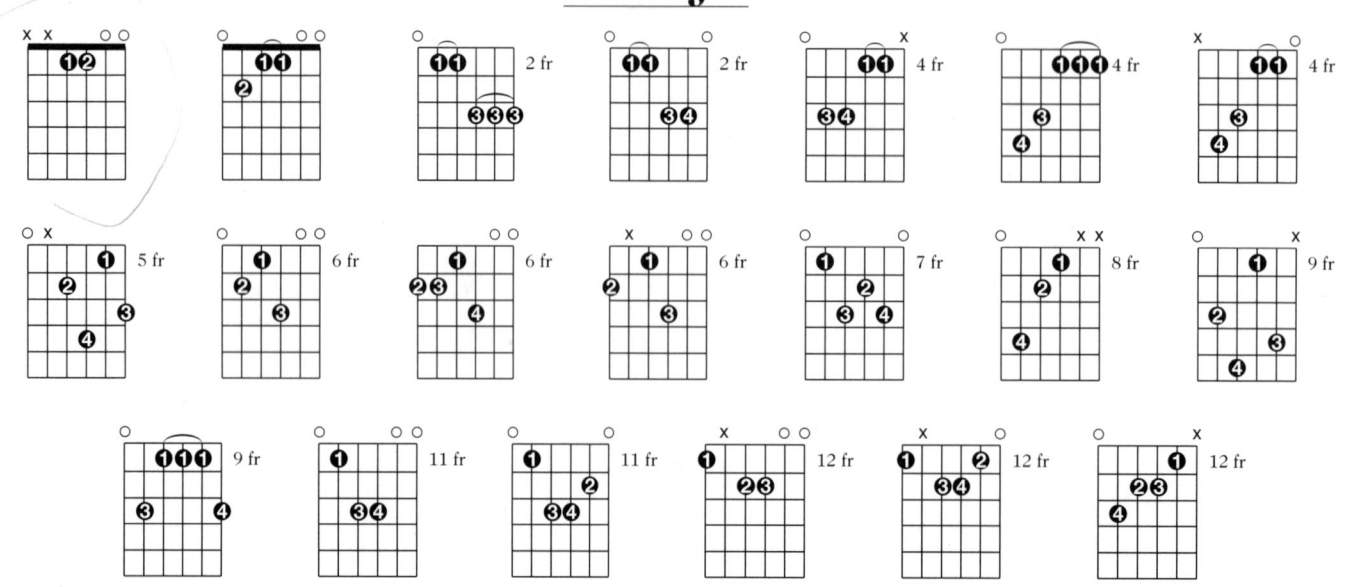

Emaj9

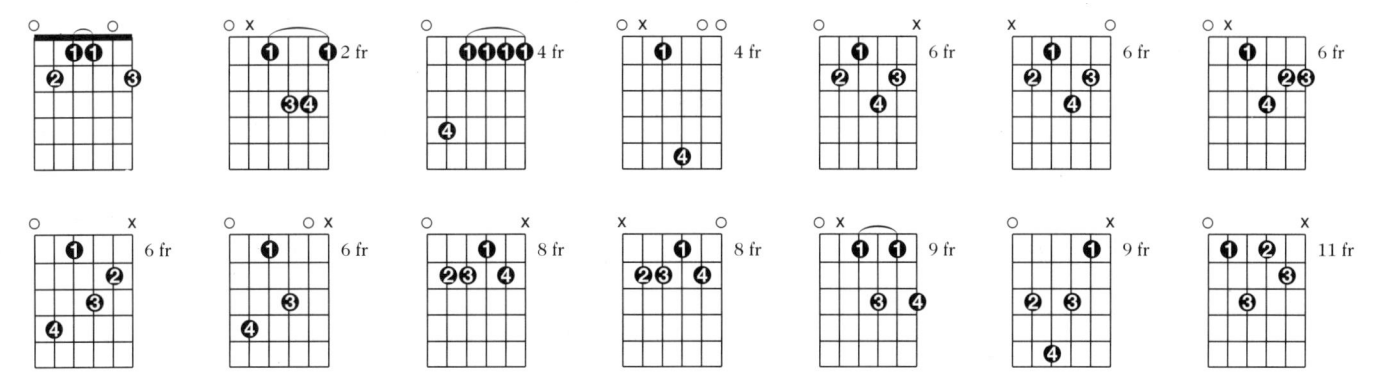

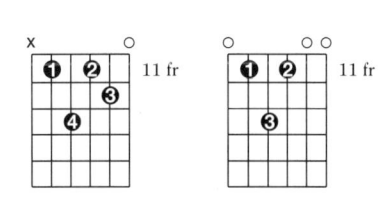

Emaj13

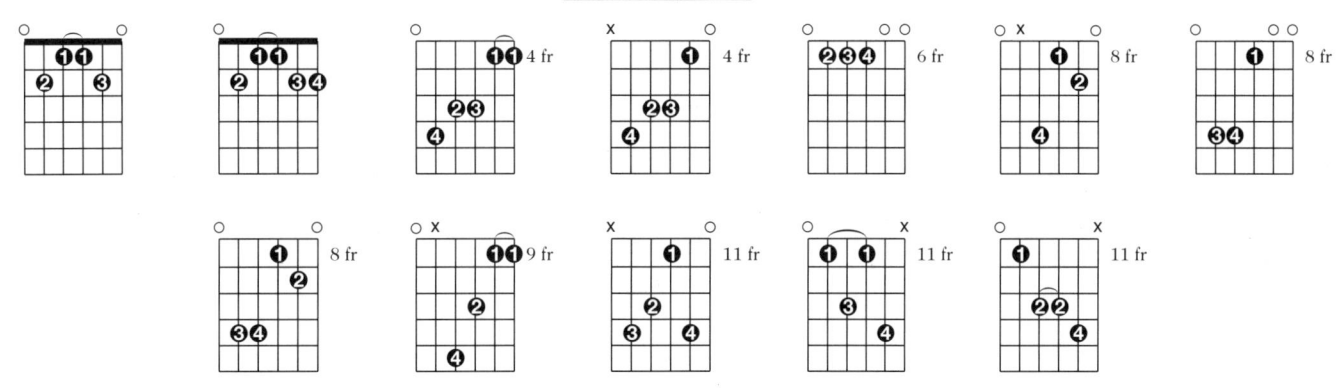

E7sus4

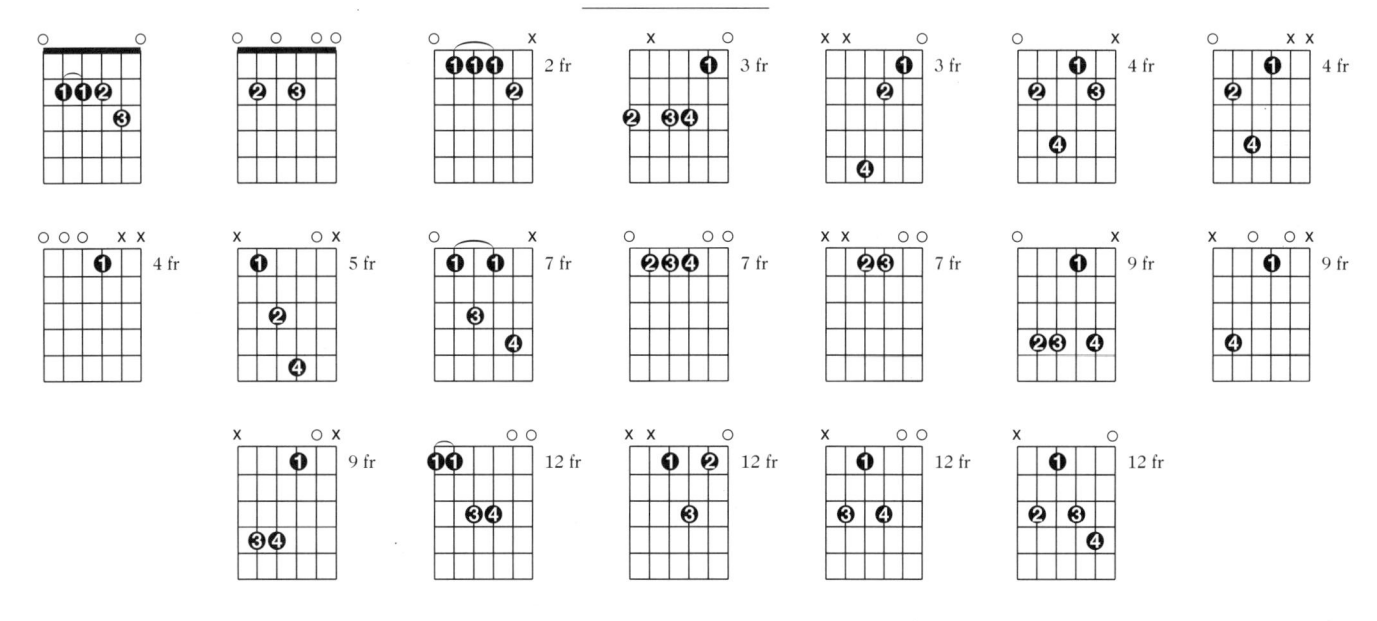

E11

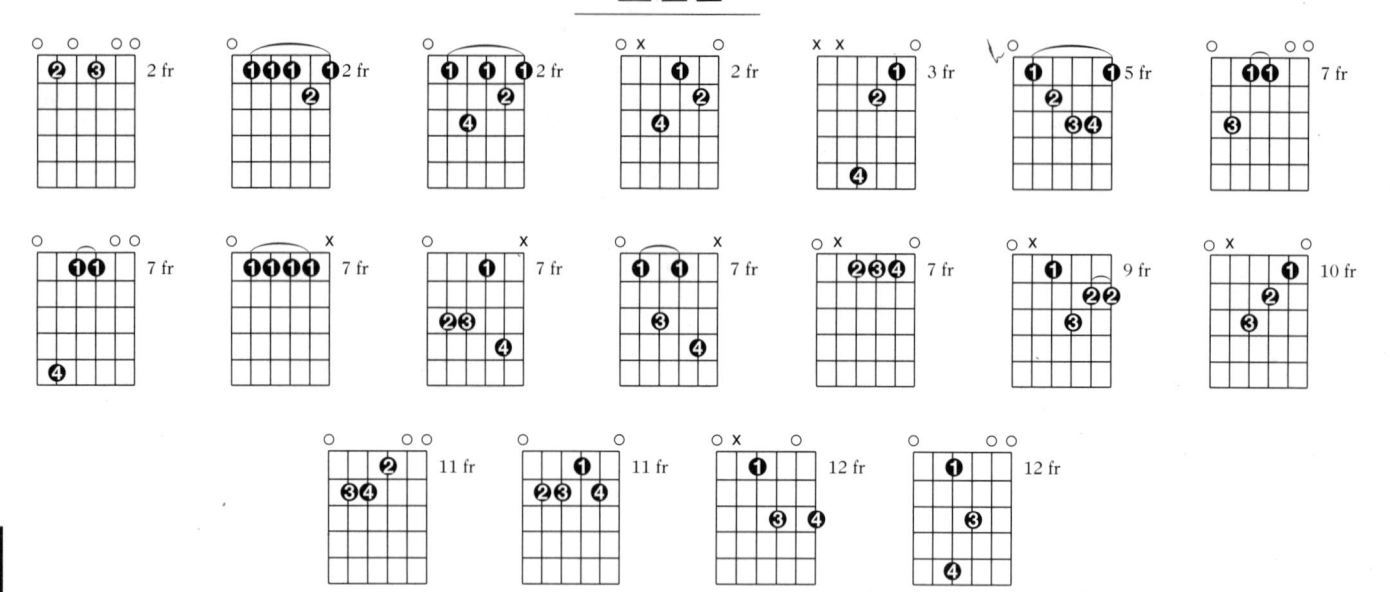

E7♭5

E9♭5

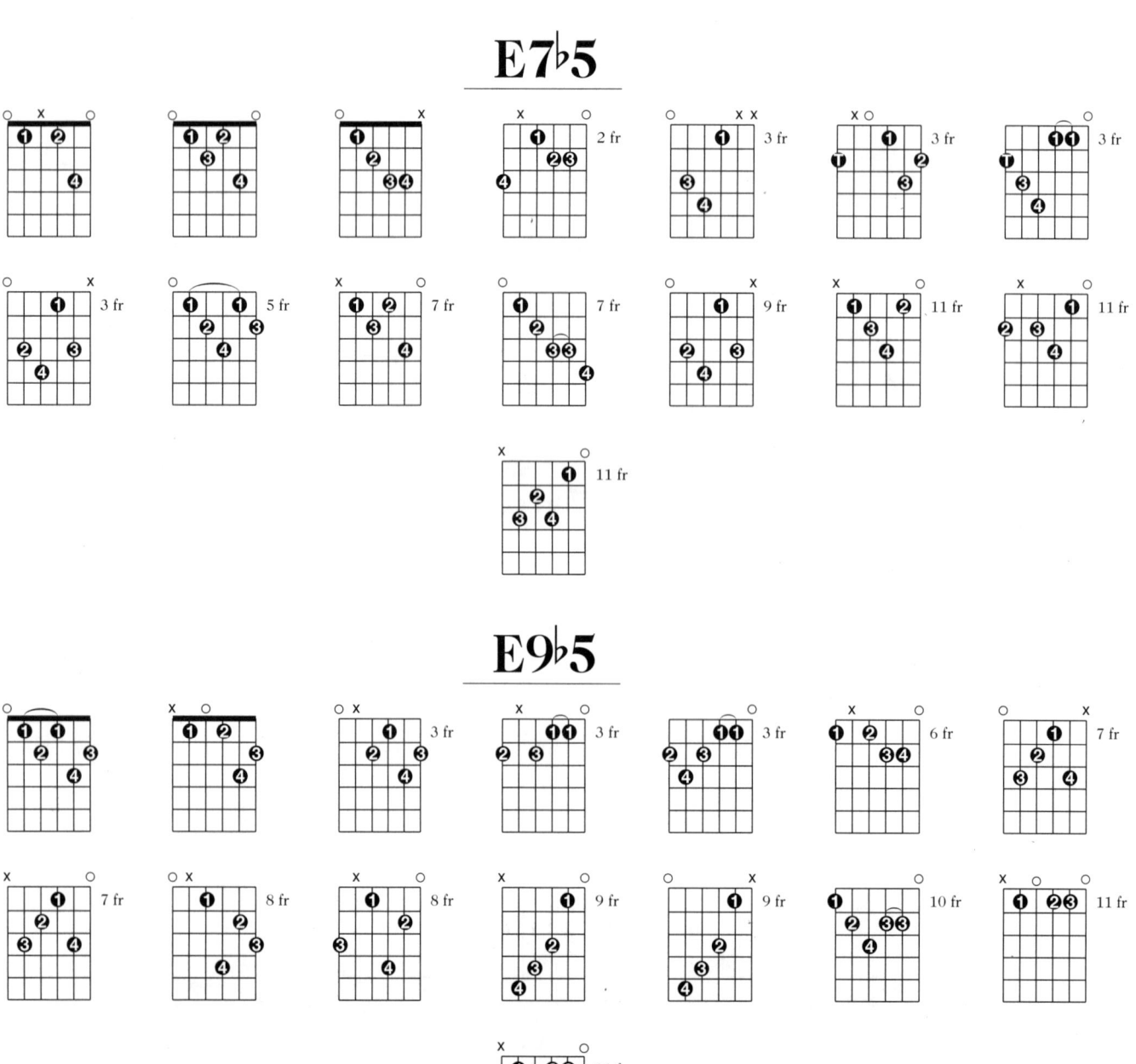

E9#11

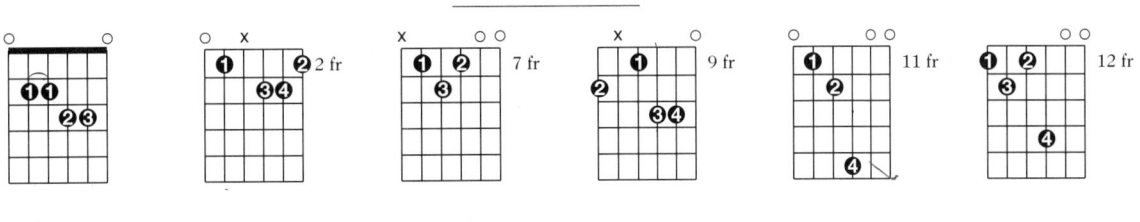

E7#9

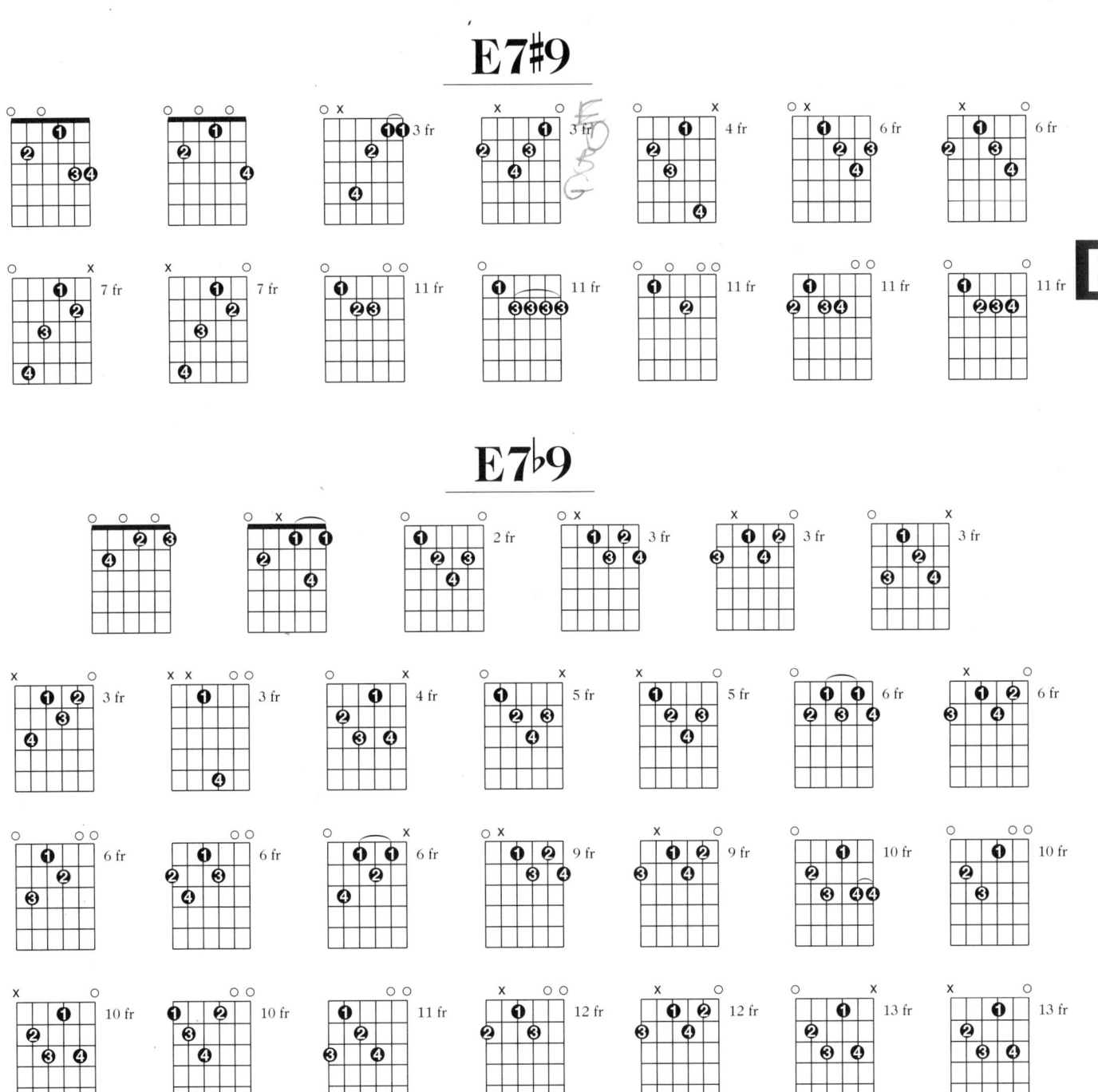

E7♭9

E13♭9

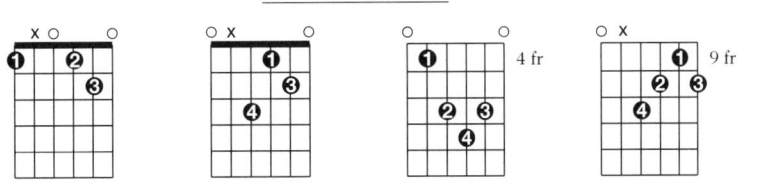

Em(maj7)

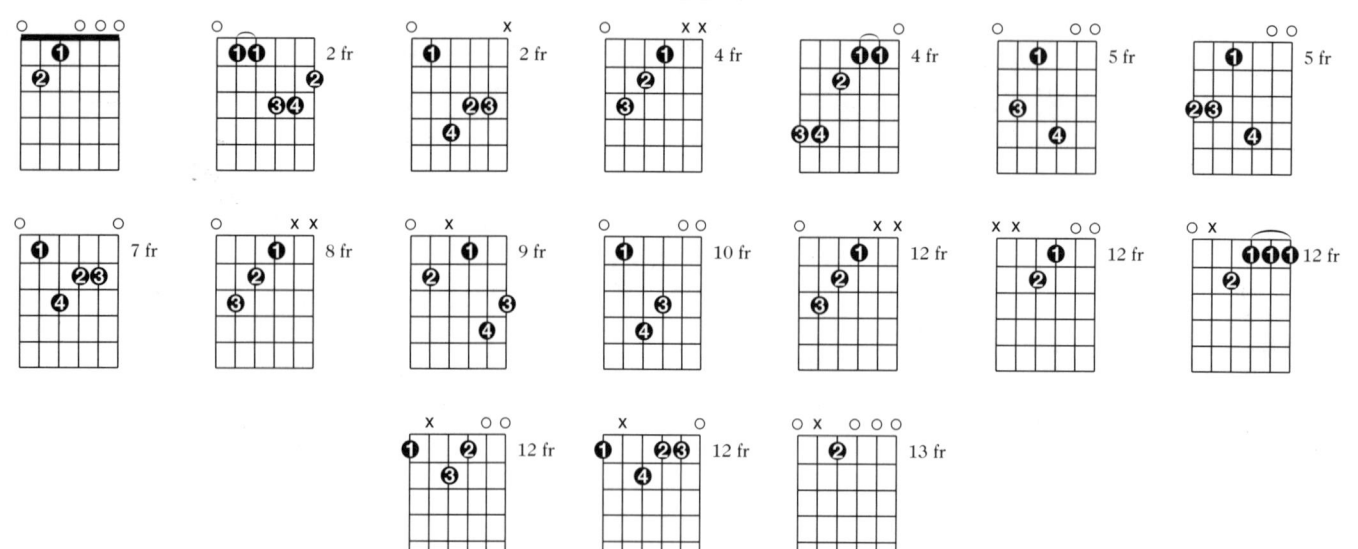

Em(maj9)

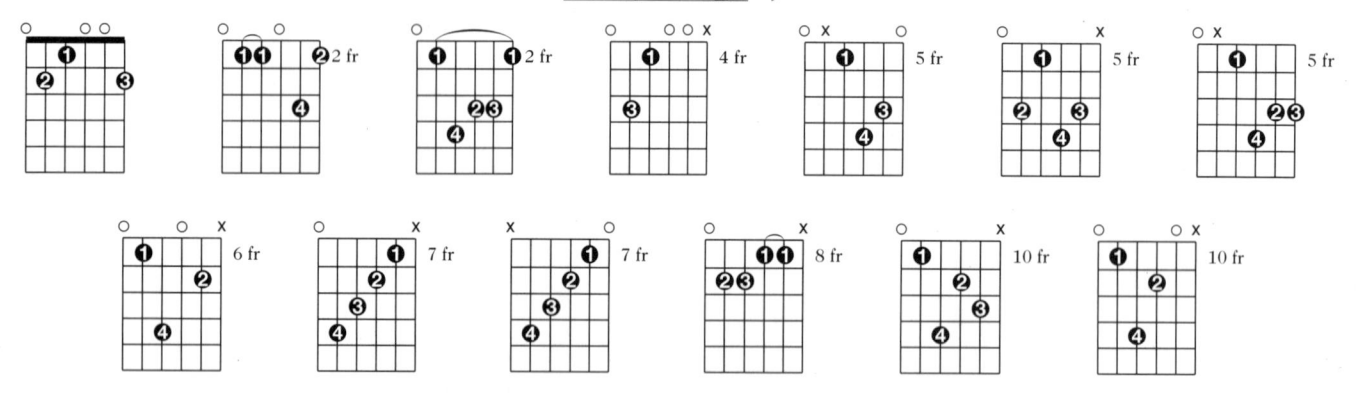

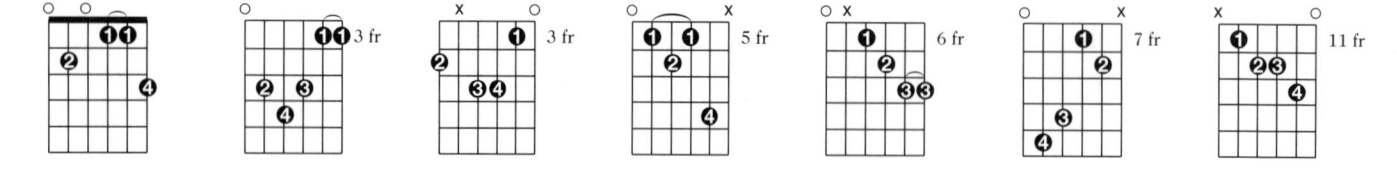

E+7♯9

E+add♯9

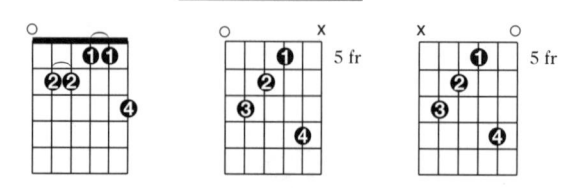

F

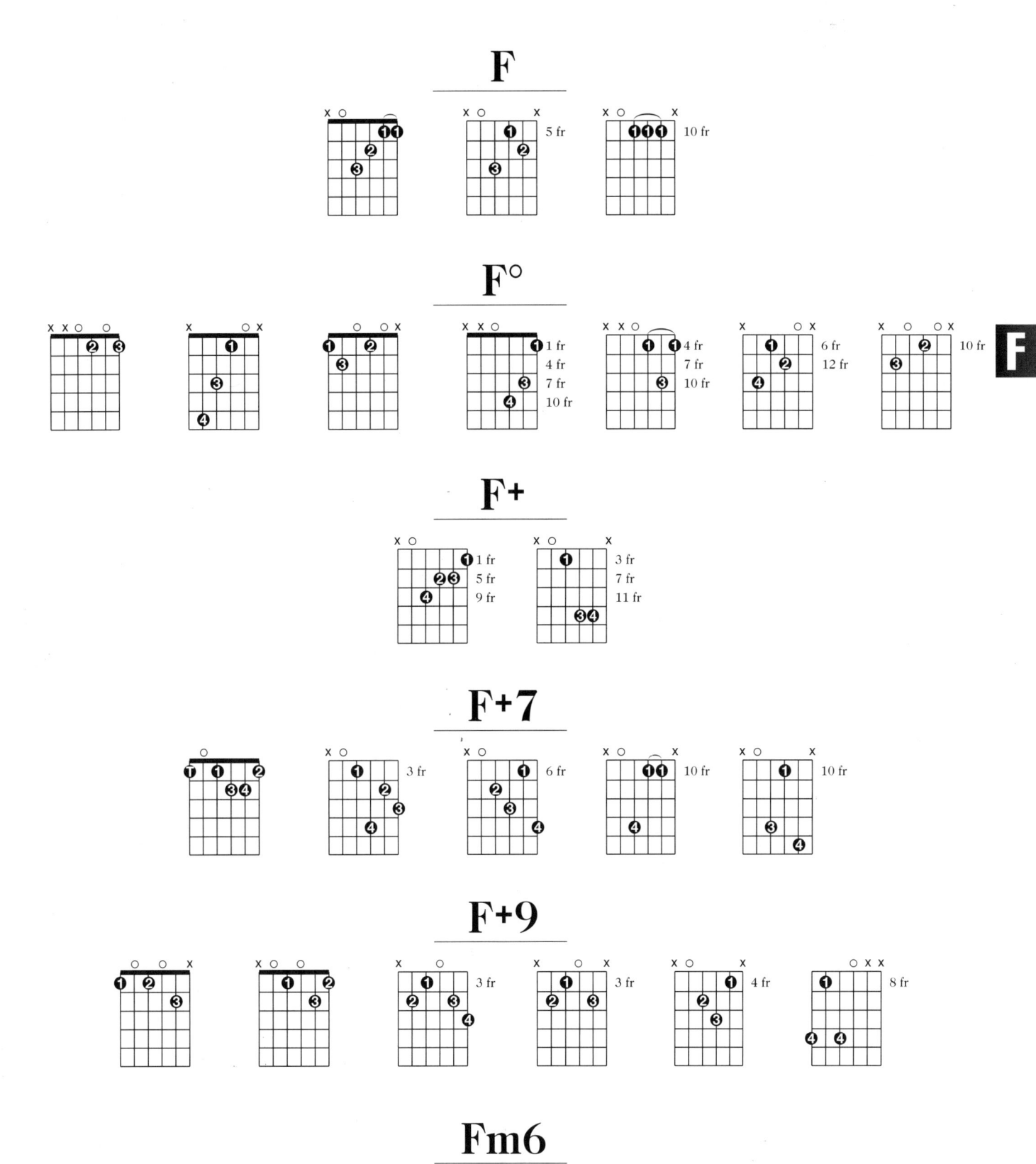

F

F°

F+

F+7

F+9

Fm6

Fm6/9

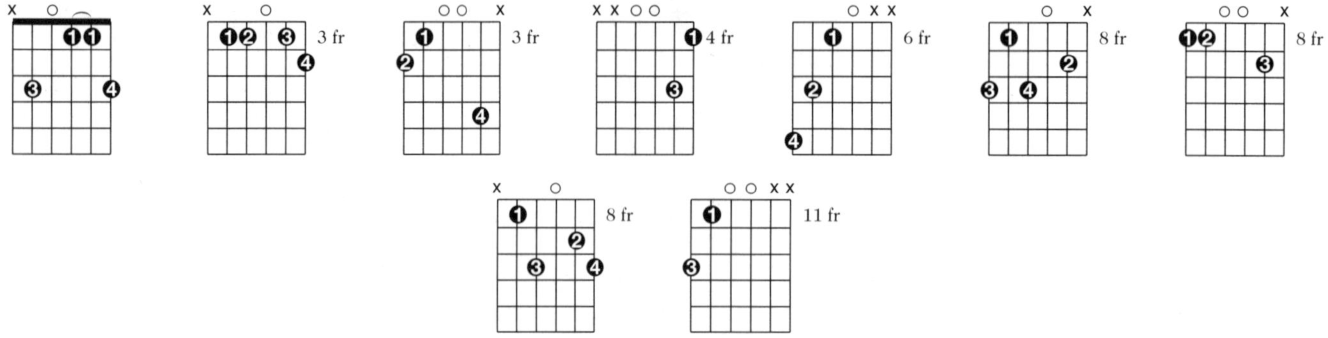

Fm13

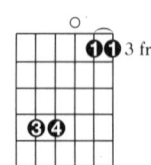

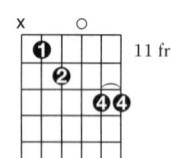

Fm(add9)

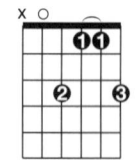

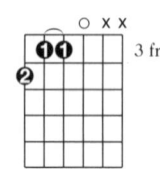

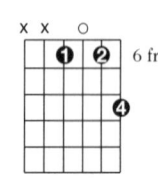

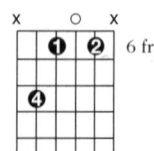

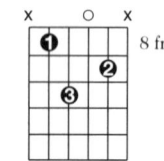

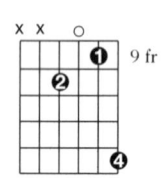

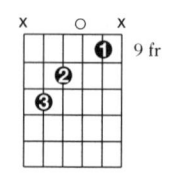

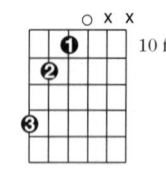

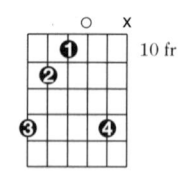

Fm9

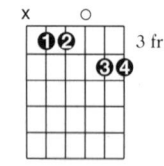

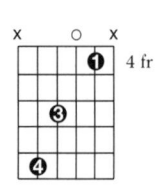

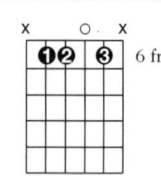

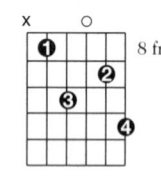

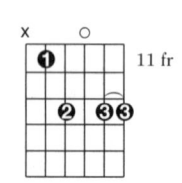

Fm11

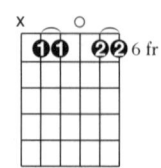

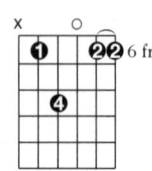

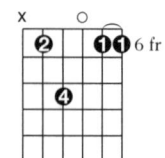

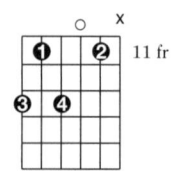

Fm7♭5

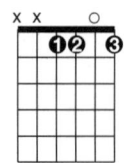

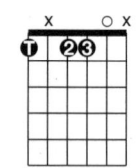

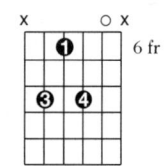

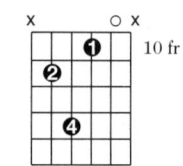

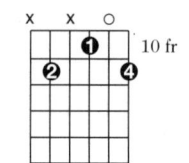

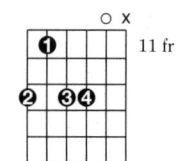

Fm9♭5

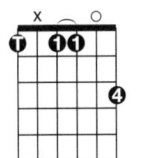

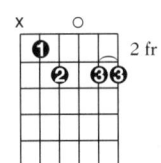

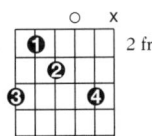

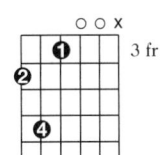

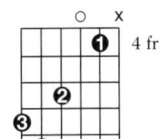

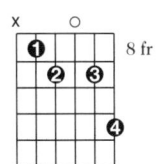

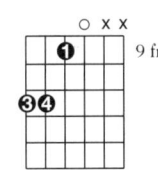

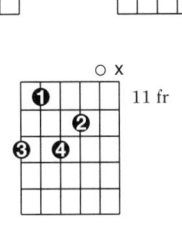

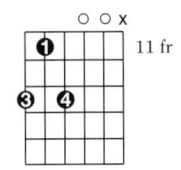

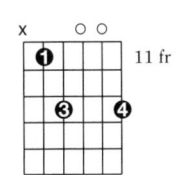

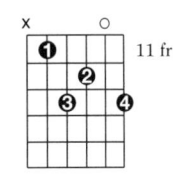

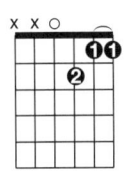

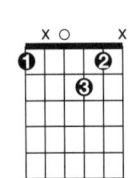

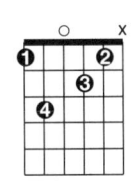

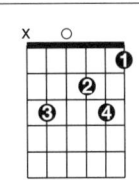

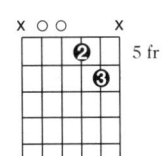

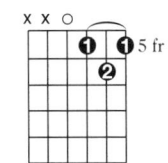

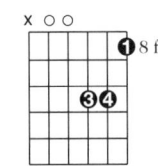

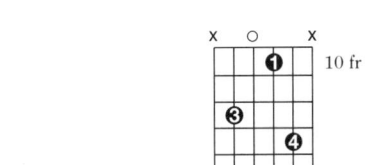

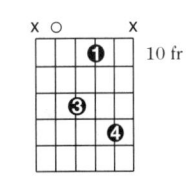

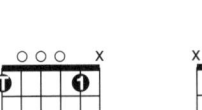

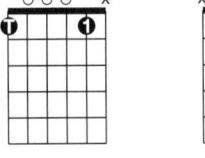

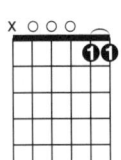

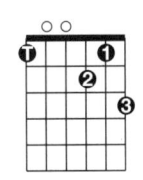

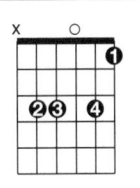

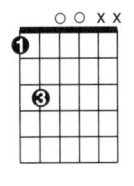

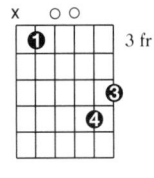

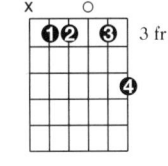

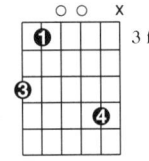

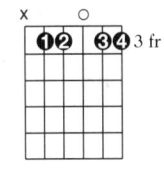

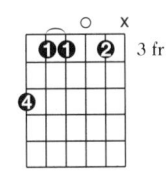

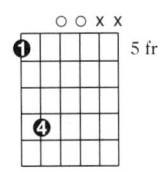

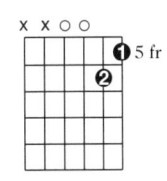

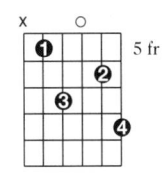

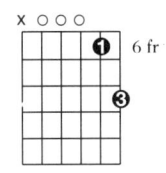

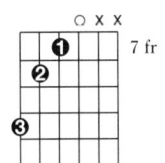

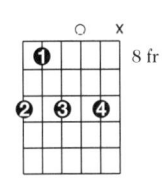

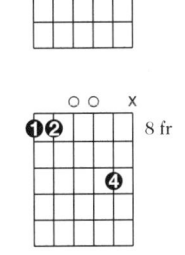

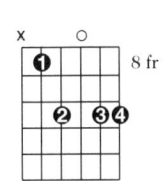

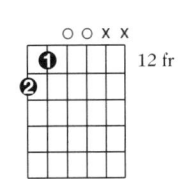

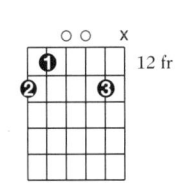

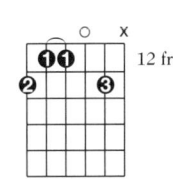

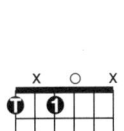

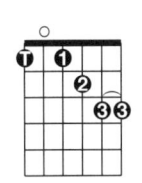

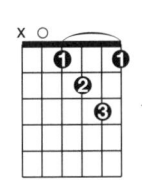

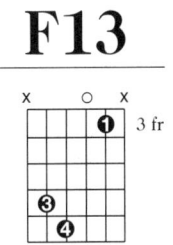

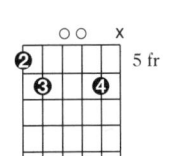

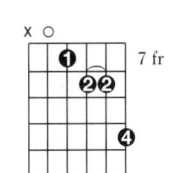

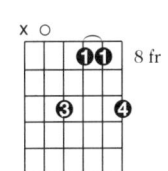

F6

F⁶⁹

F13

F7

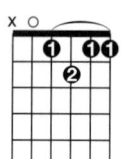

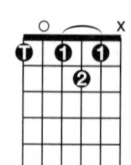

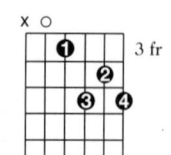

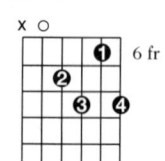

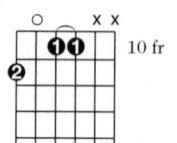

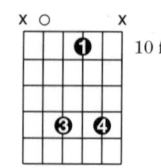

F9

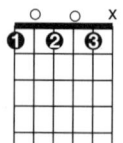

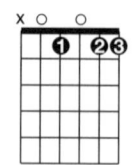

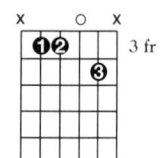

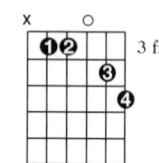

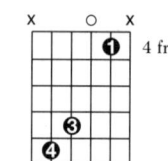

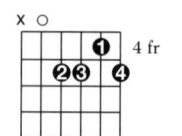

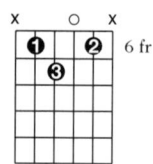

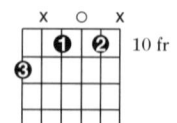

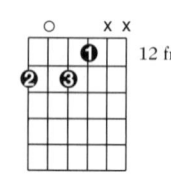

Fadd9

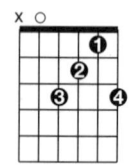

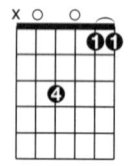

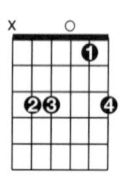

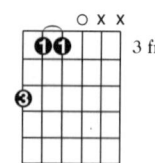

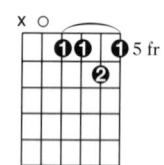

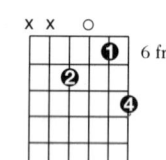

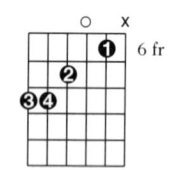

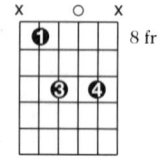

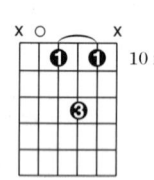

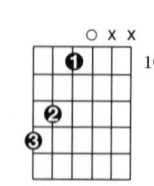

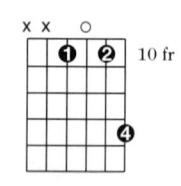

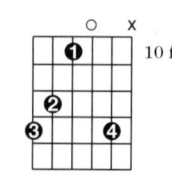

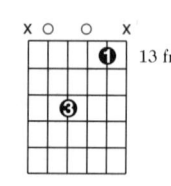

Fmaj7

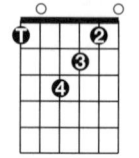

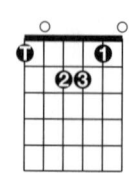

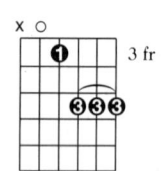

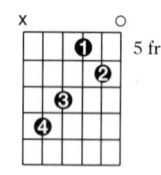

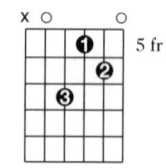

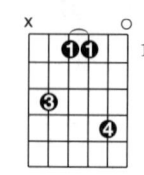

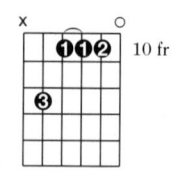

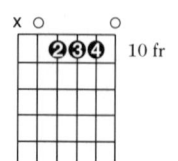

Fmaj9

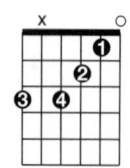

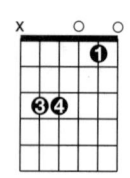

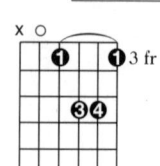

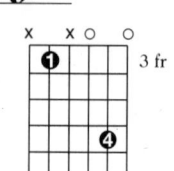

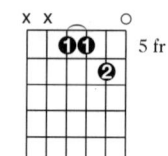

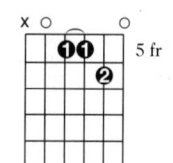

Fmaj9 (cont'd)

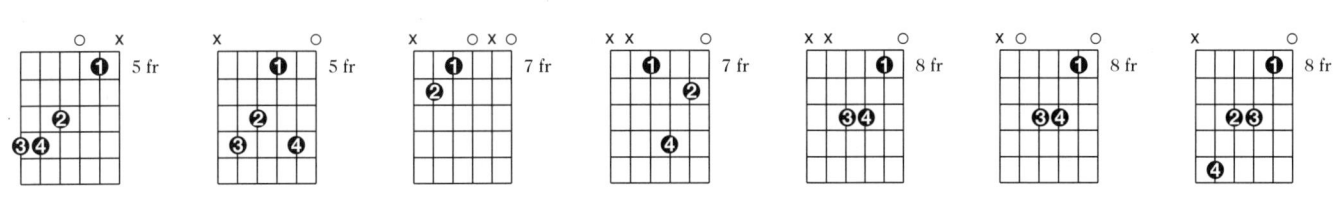

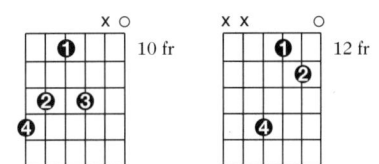

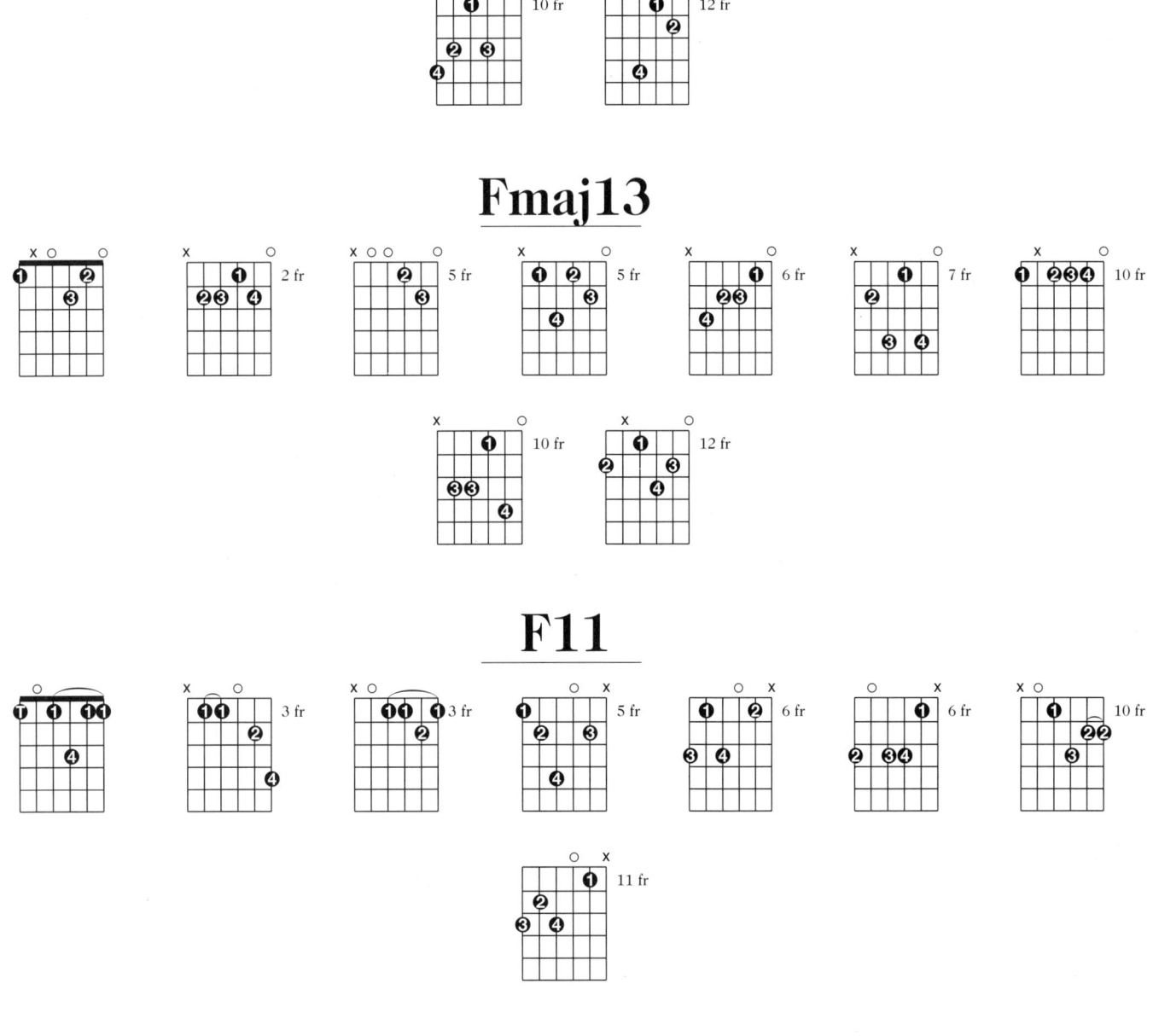

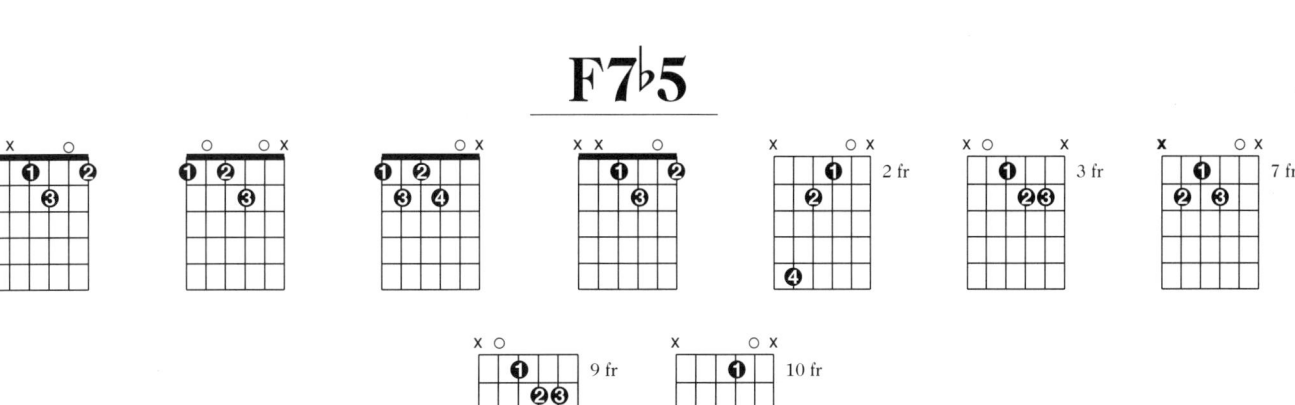

Fmaj13

F11

F7♭5

F9♭5

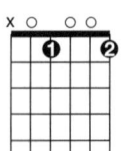

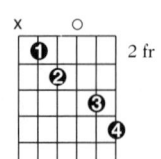

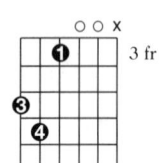

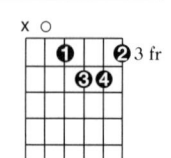

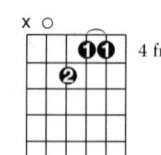

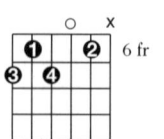

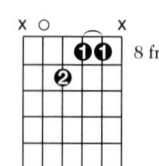

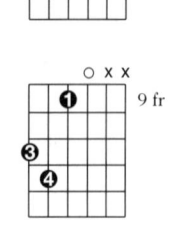

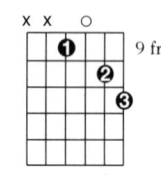

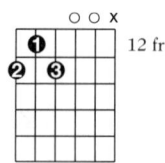

F9♯11

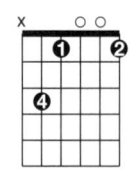

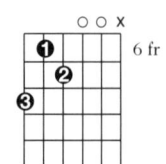

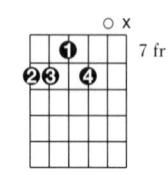

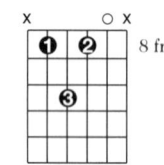

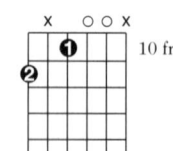

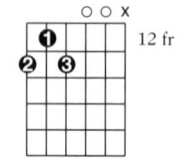

F7♯9

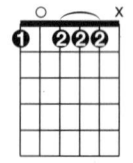

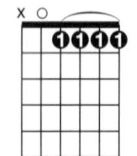

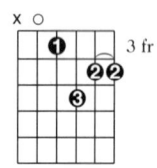

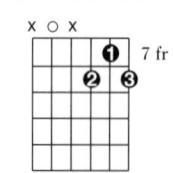

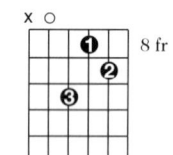

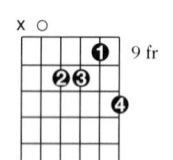

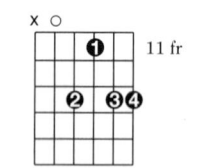

F7♭9

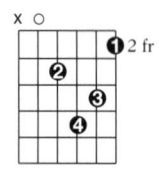

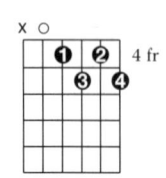

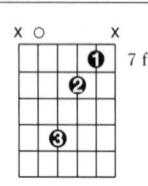

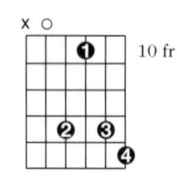

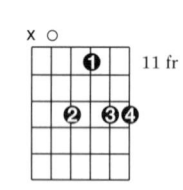

F13♭9

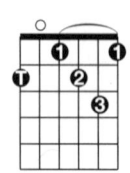

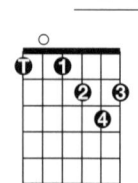

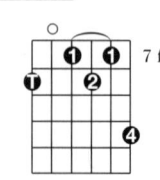

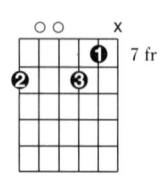

F13♭5 (♭9)

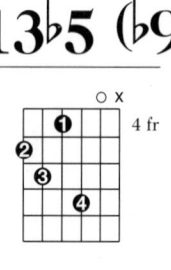

Fm(maj7)

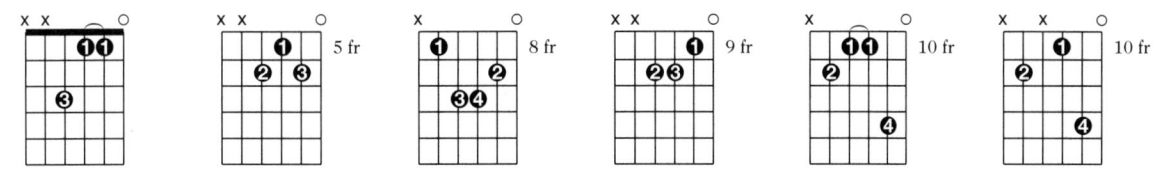

Fm(maj9)

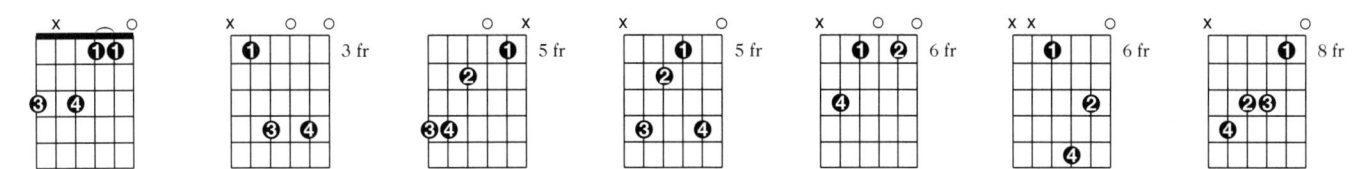

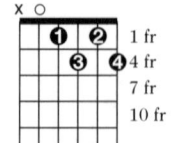

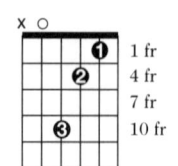

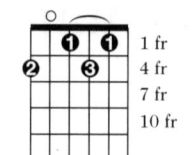

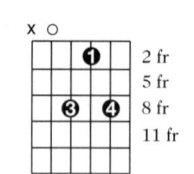

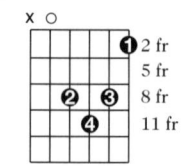

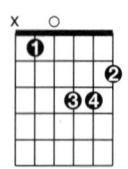

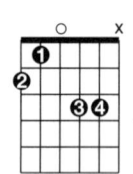

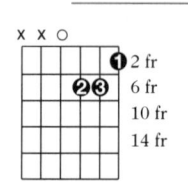

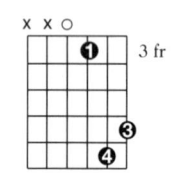

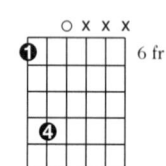

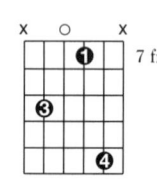

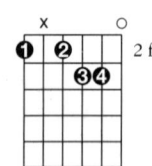

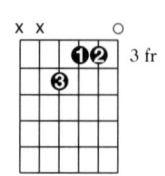

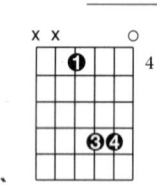

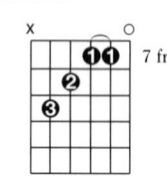

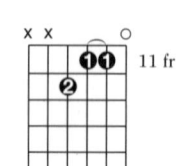

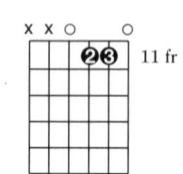

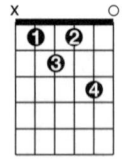

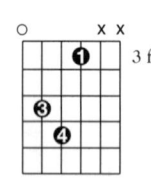

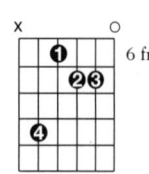

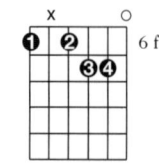

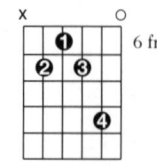

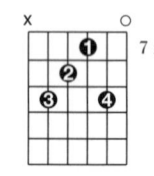

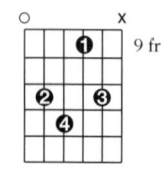

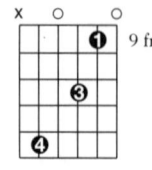

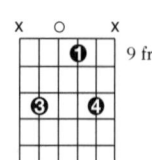

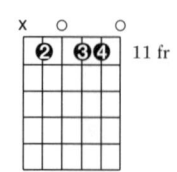

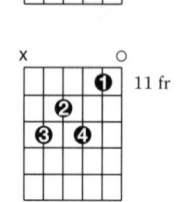

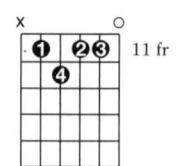

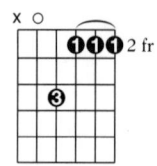

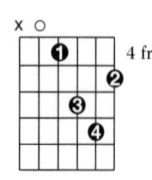

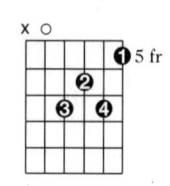

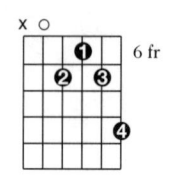

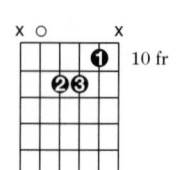

G♭

G♭°

G♭+

G♭+7

G♭+9

G♭m

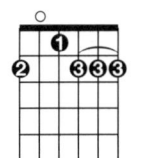

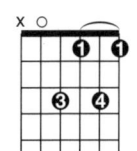

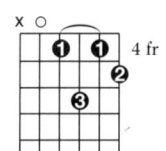

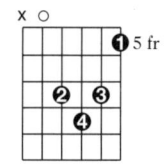

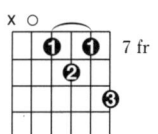

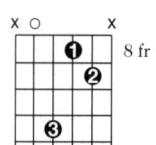

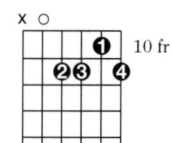

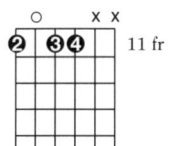

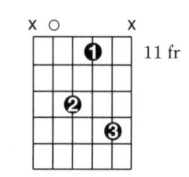

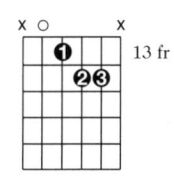

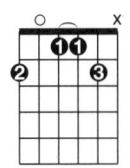

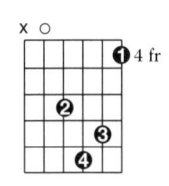

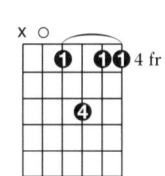

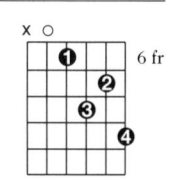

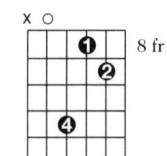

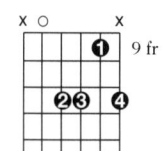

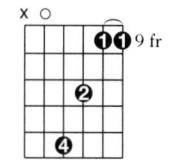

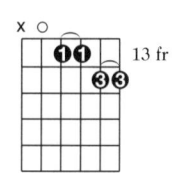

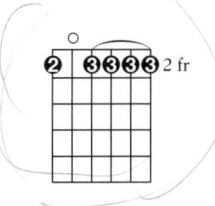

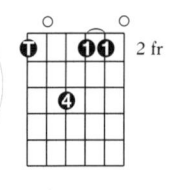

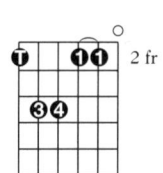

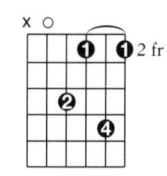

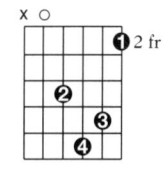

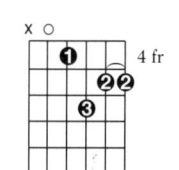

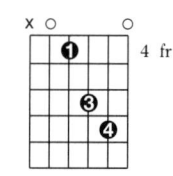

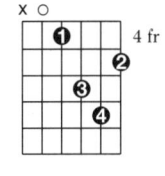

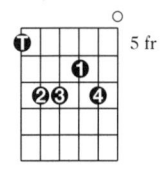

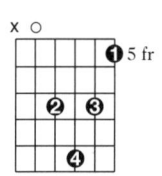

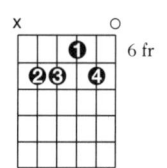

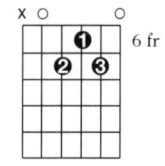

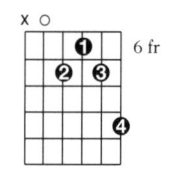

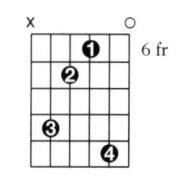

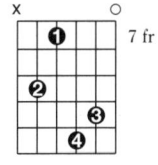

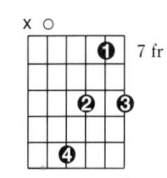

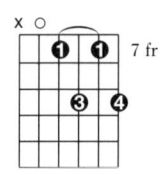

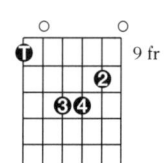

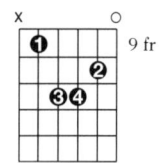

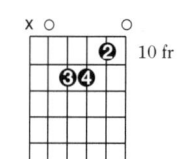

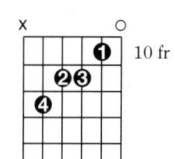

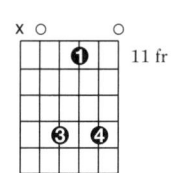

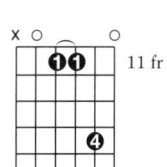

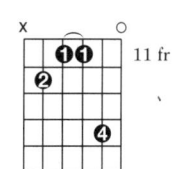

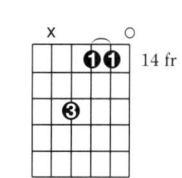

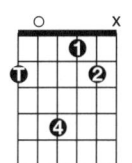

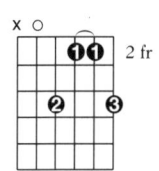

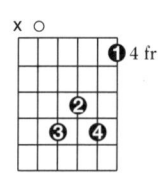

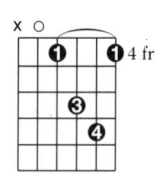

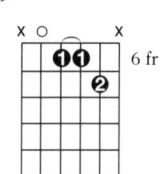

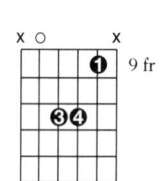

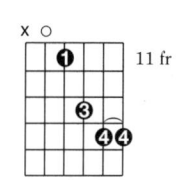

G♭m6

G♭m⁶⁄₉

G♭m7

G♭m(add9)

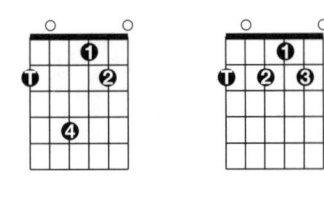

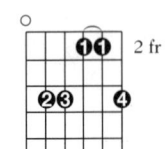

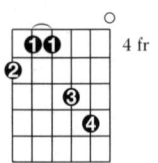

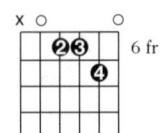

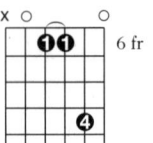

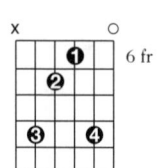

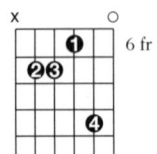

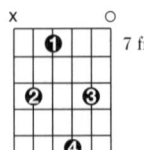

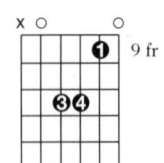

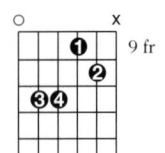

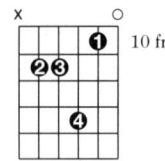

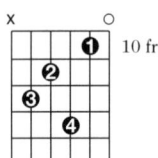

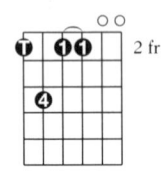

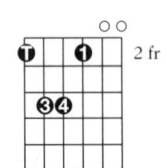

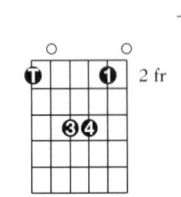

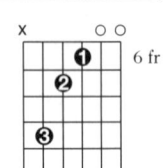

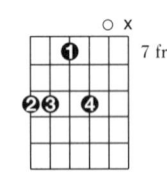

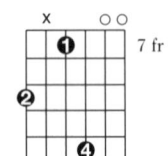

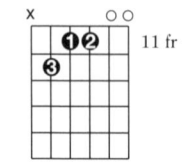

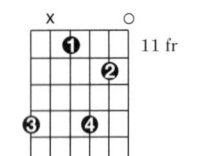

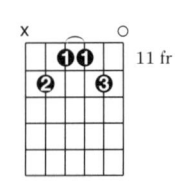

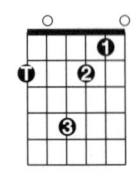

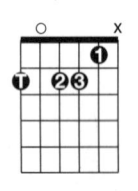

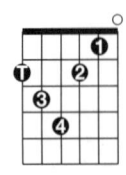

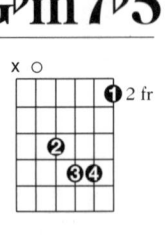

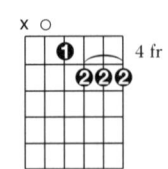

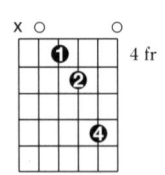

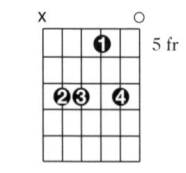

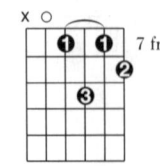

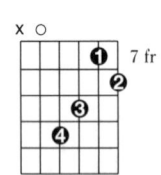

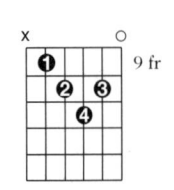

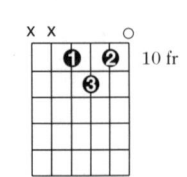

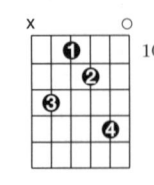

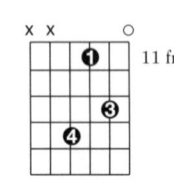

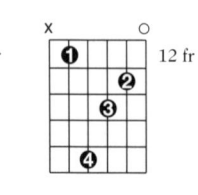

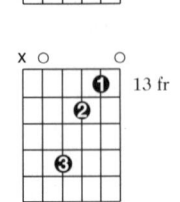

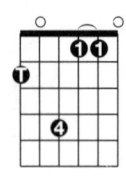

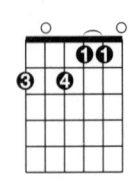

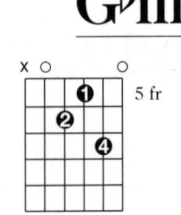

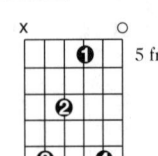

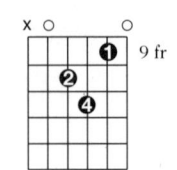

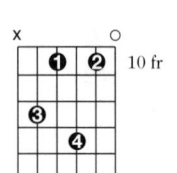

G♭m9

G♭m11

G♭m7♭5

G♭m9♭5

G♭m11♭5

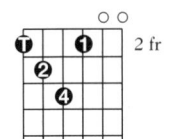

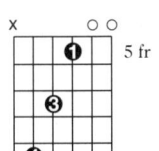

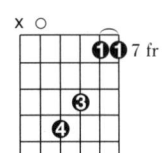

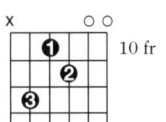

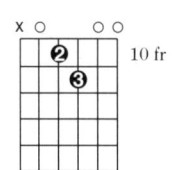

G♭13

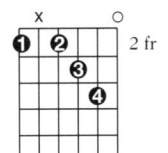

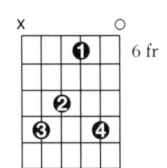

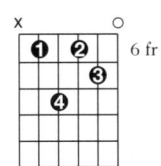

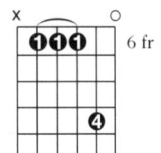

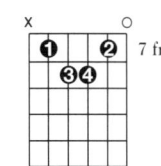

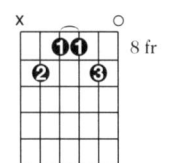

G♭7

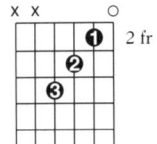

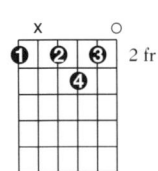

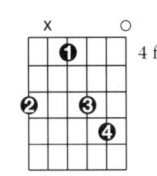

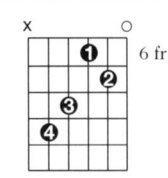

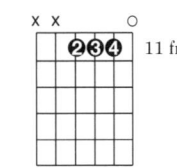

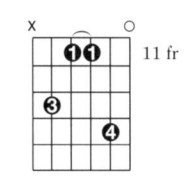

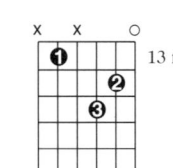

G♭9

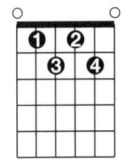

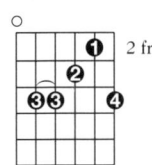

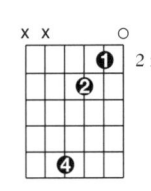

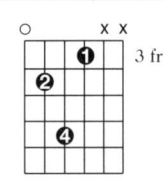

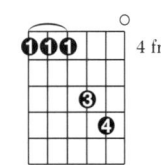

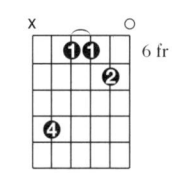

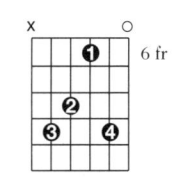

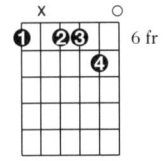

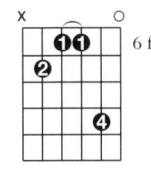

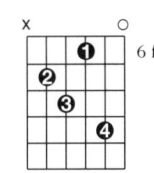

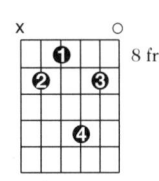

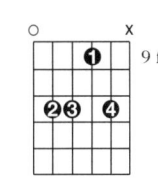

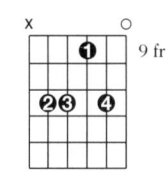

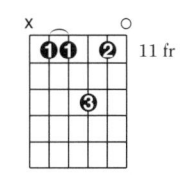

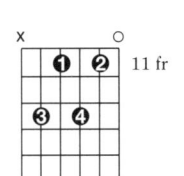

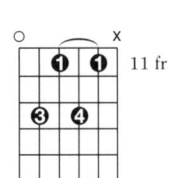

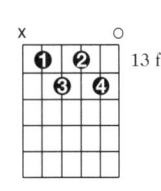

G♭7sus4

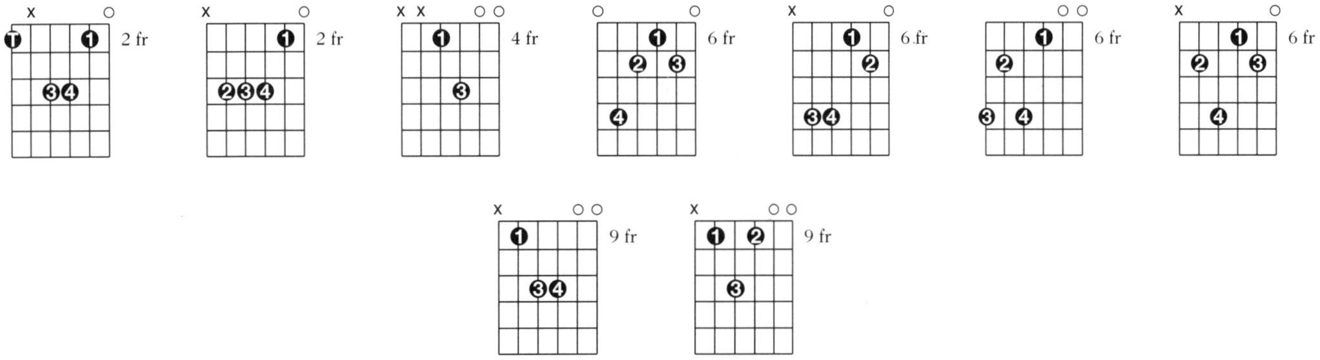

G♭11

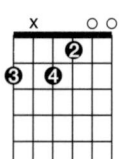

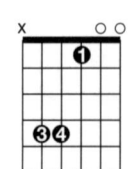

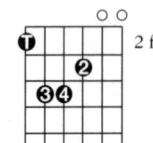

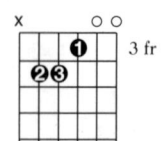

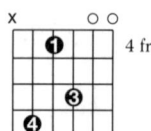

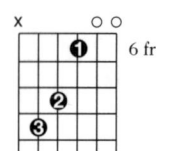

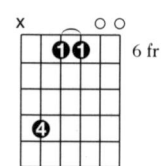

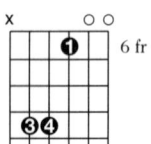

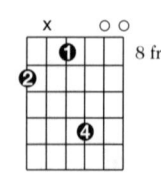

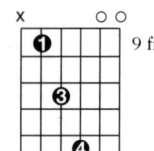

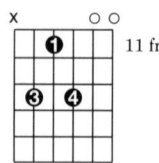

G♭7♭5

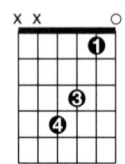

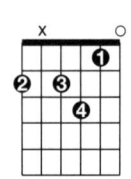

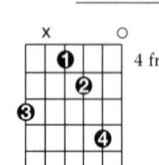

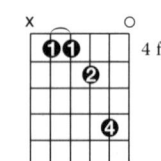

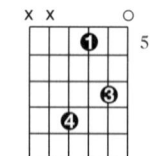

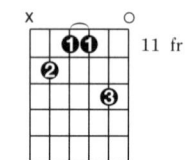

G♭9♭5

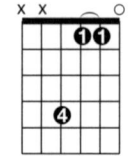

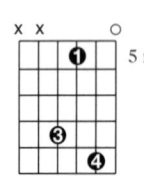

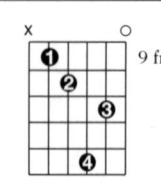

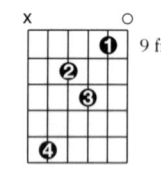

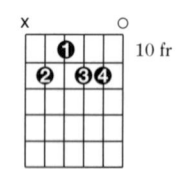

G♭7#9

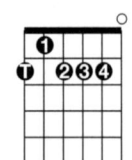

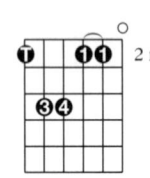

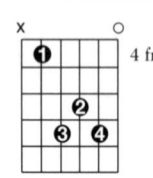

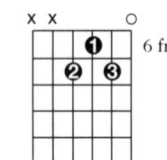

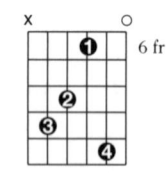

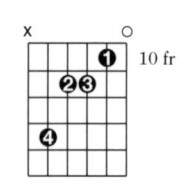

G♭7♭9

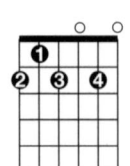

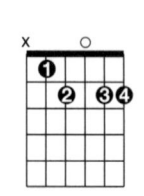

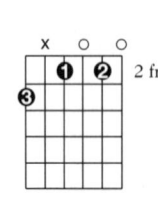

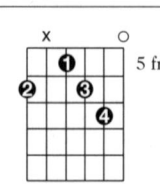

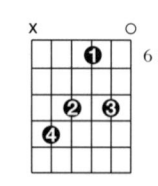

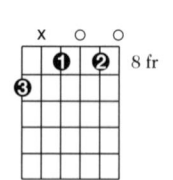

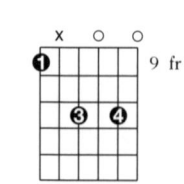

G♭11♭9

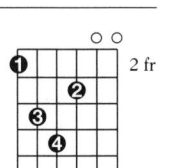

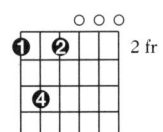

G♭13♭9

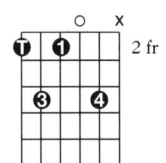

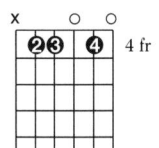

G♭13♭5(♭9)

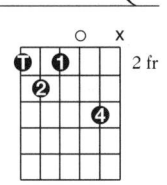

G♭7♭9(♭13)

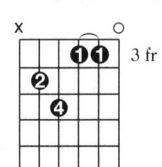

G♭m(maj7)

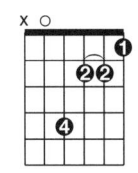

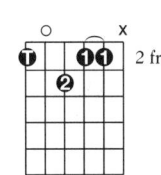

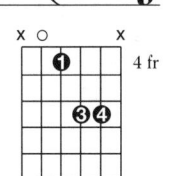

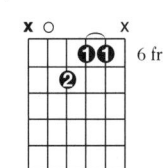

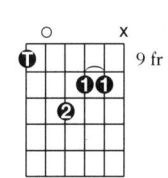

G♭m(maj9)

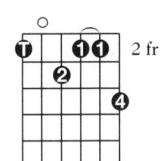

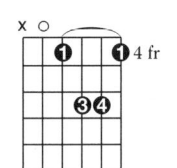

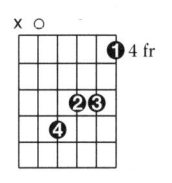

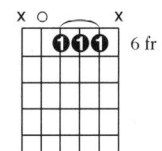

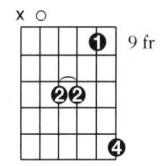

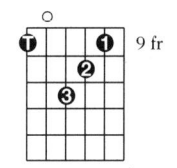

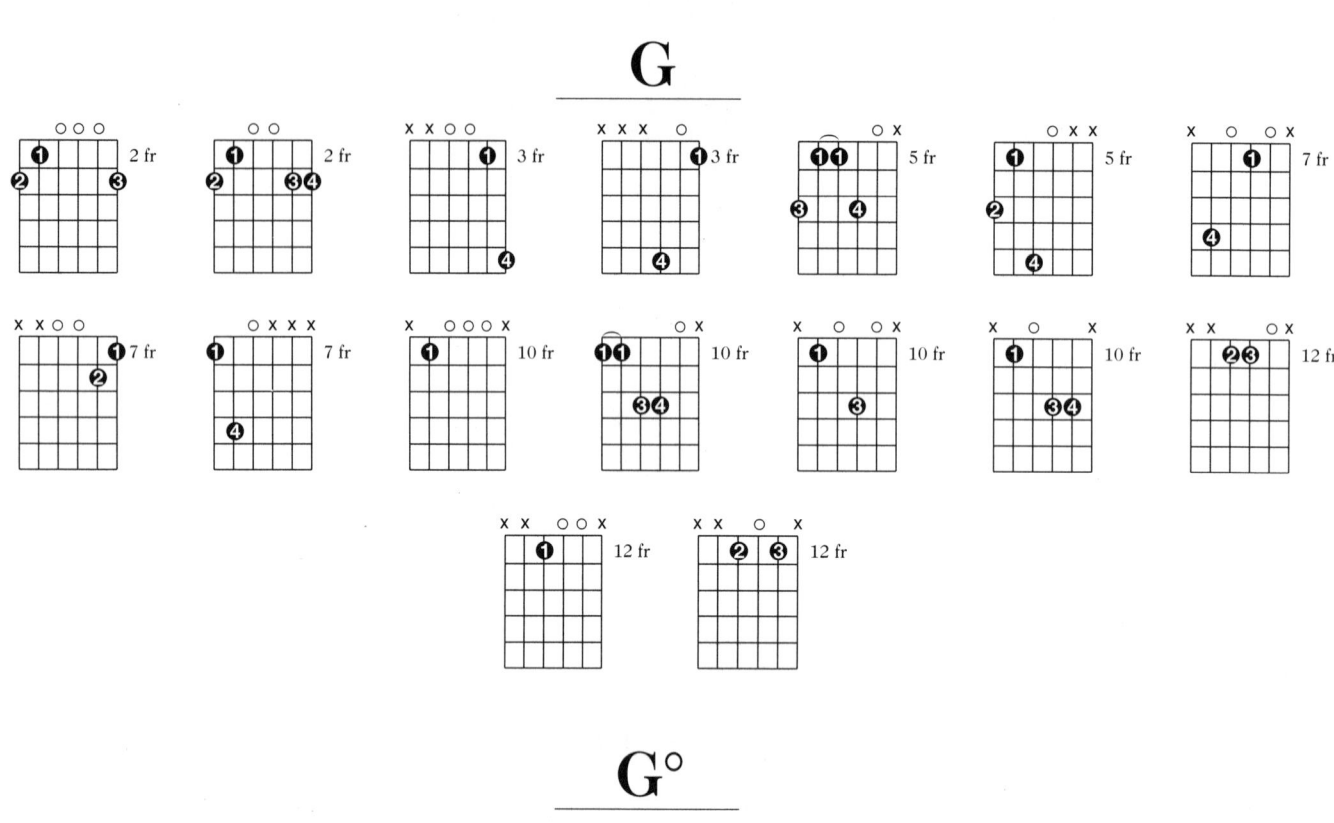

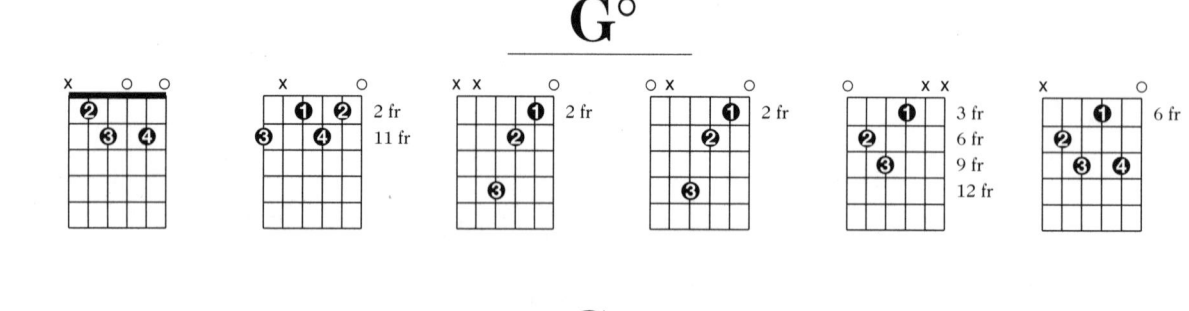

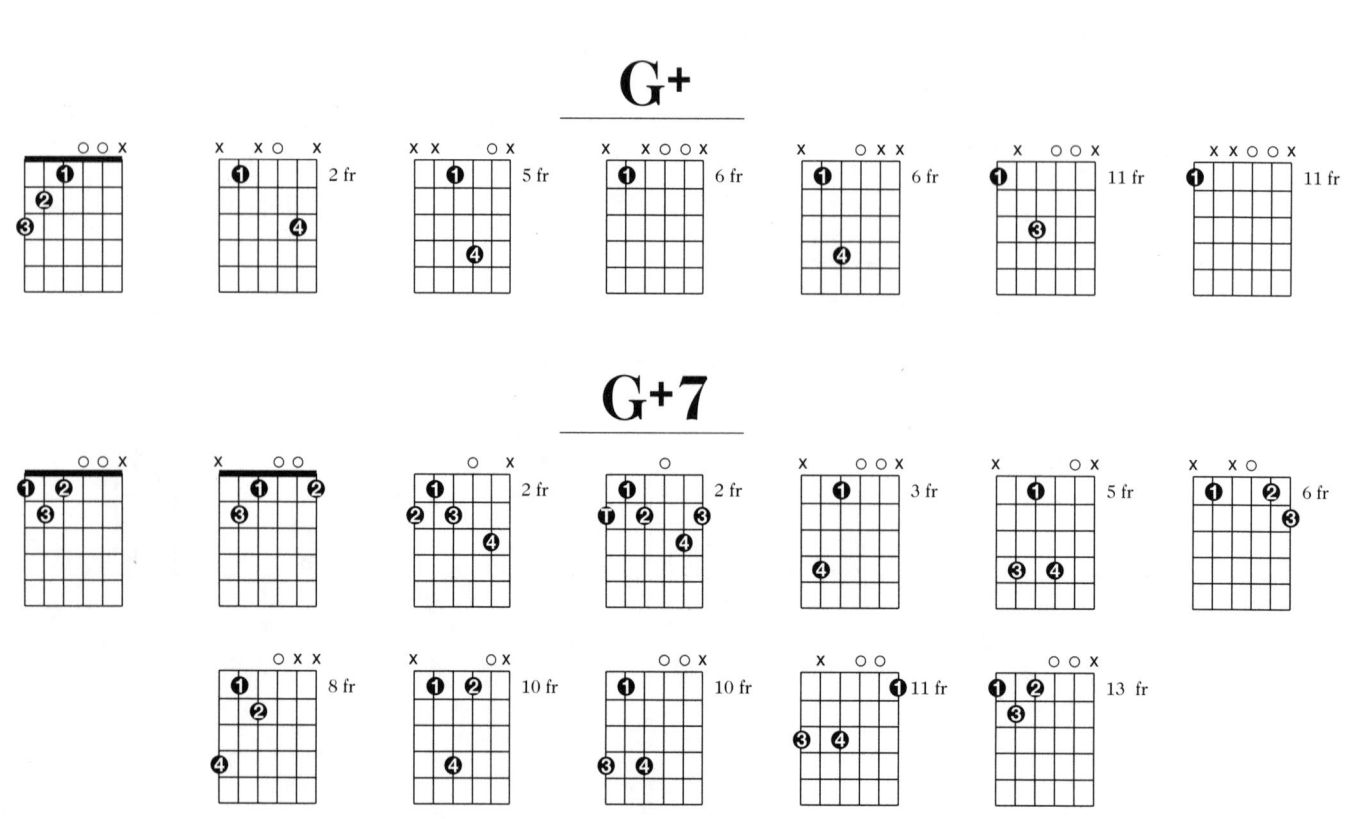

G

G

G°

G+

G+7

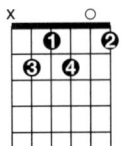

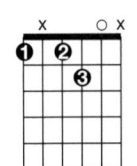

G+9

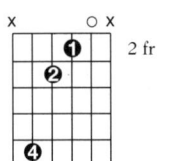

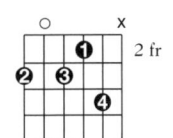

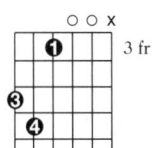

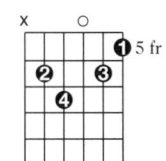

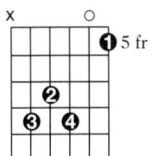

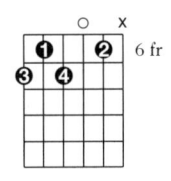

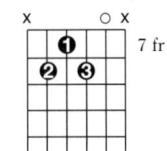

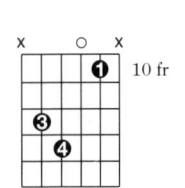

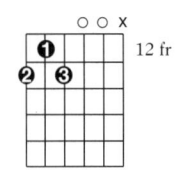

Gm

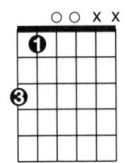

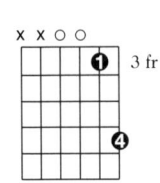

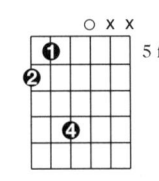

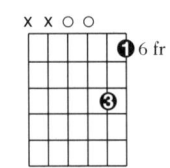

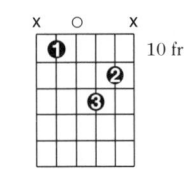

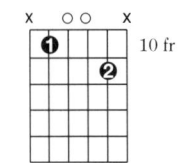

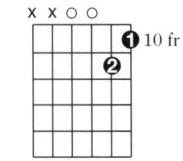

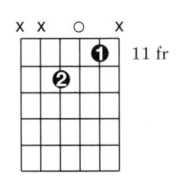

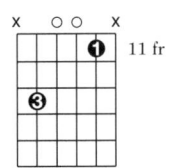

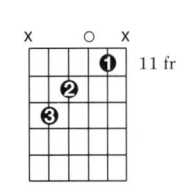

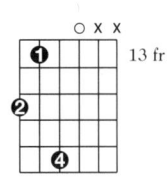

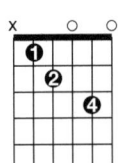

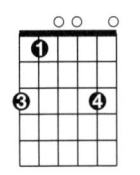

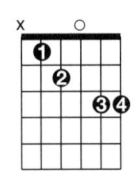

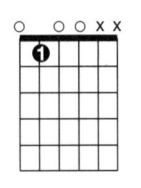

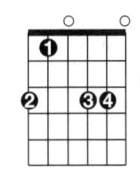

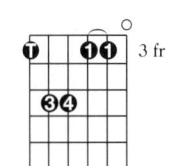

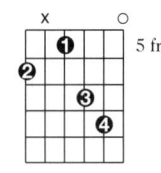

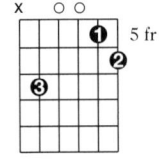

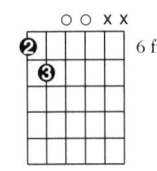

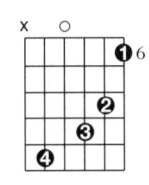

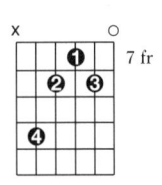

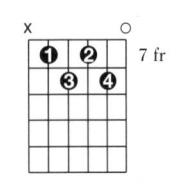

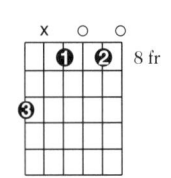

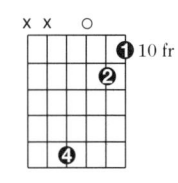

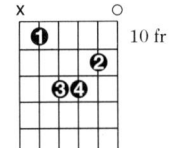

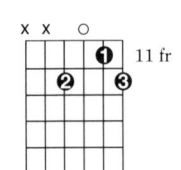

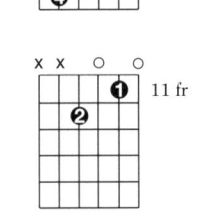

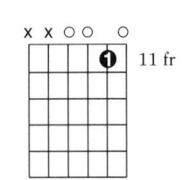

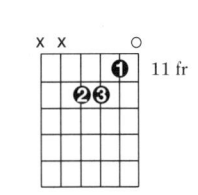

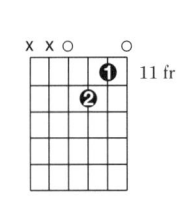

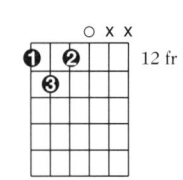

Gm6

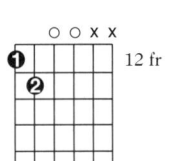

Gm6/9

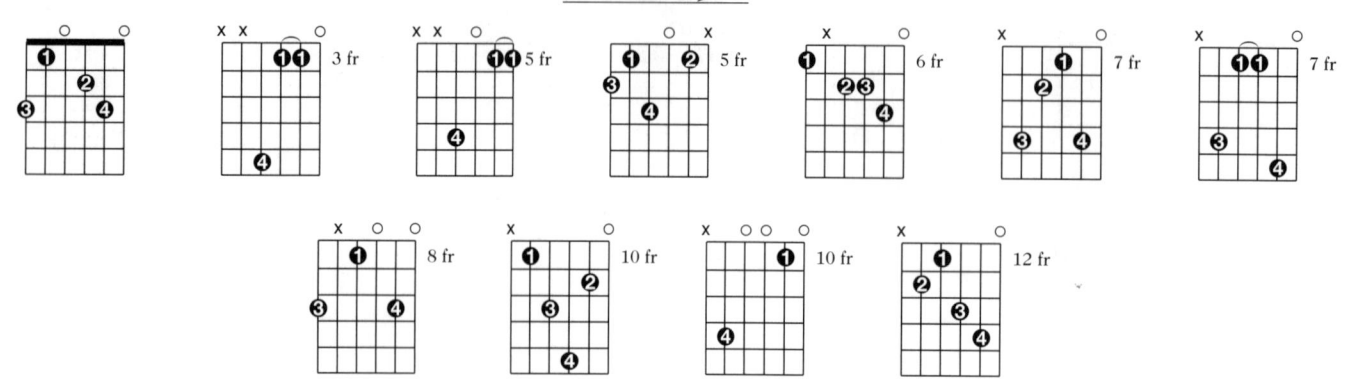

Gm13

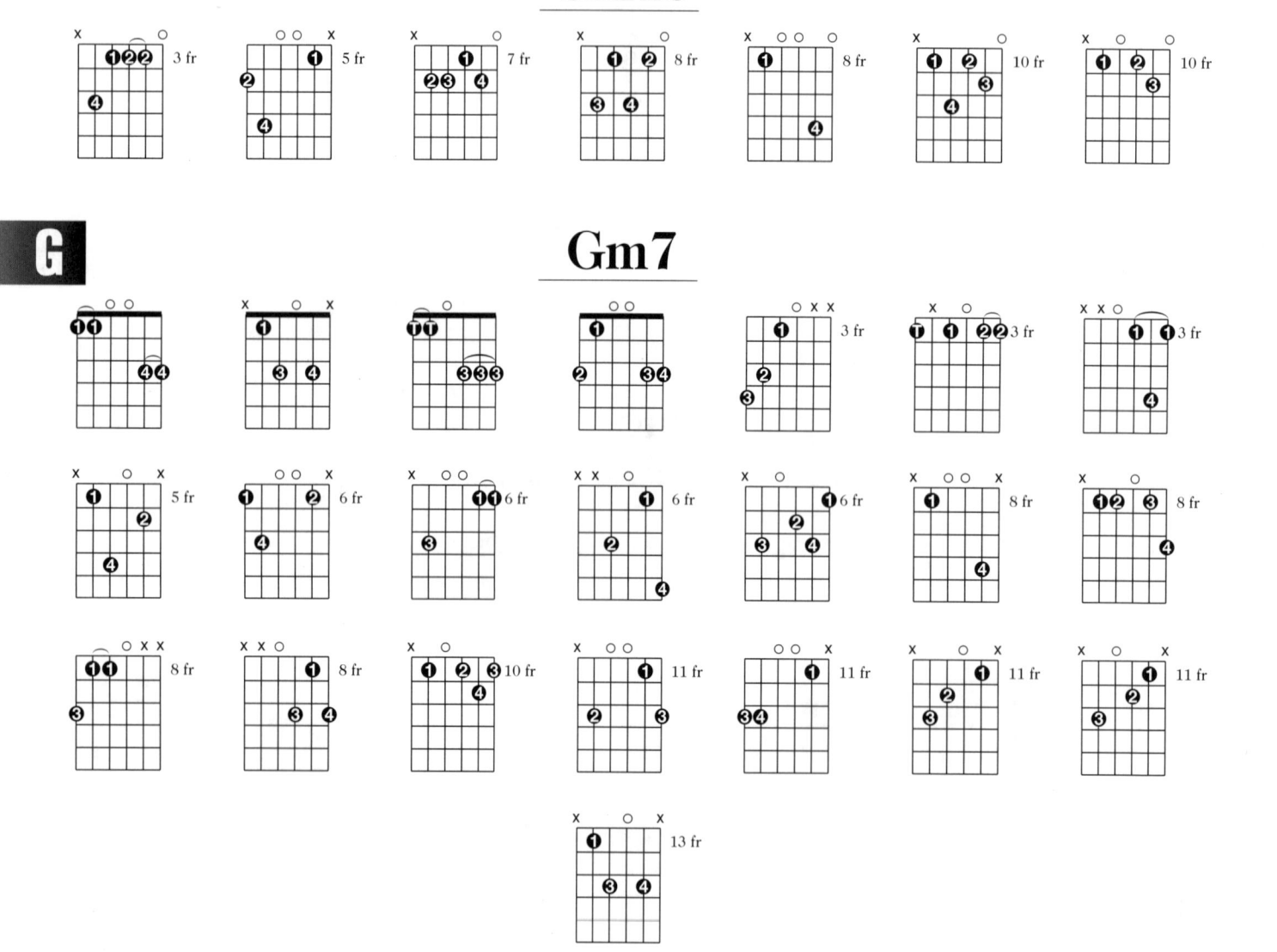

Gm7

Gm(add9)

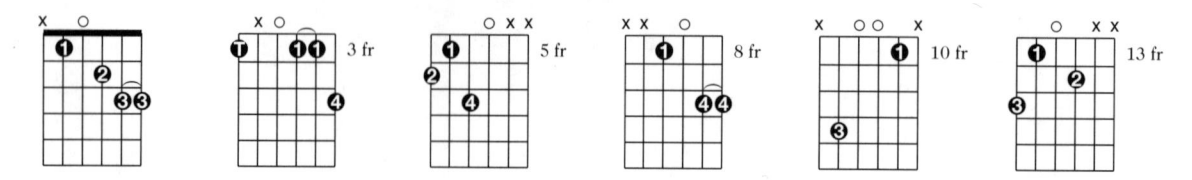

Gm9

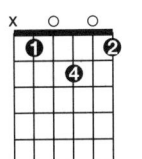

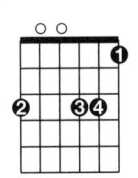

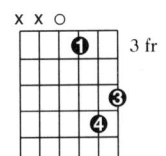

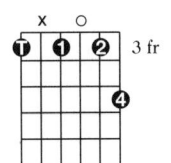

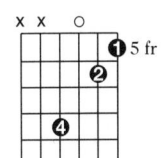

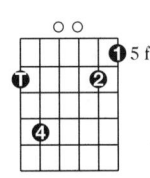

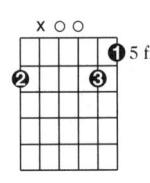

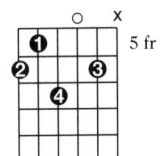

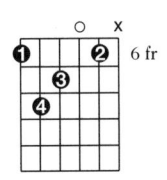

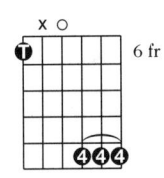

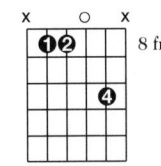

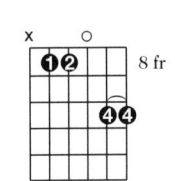

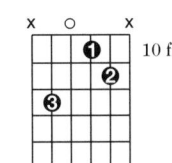

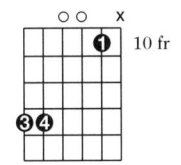

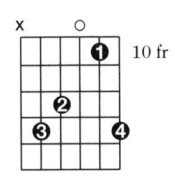

Gm11

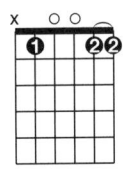

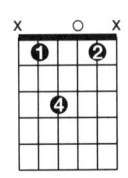

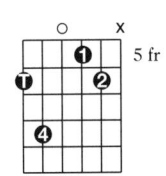

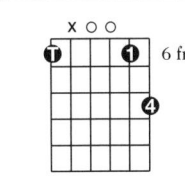

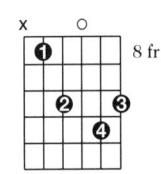

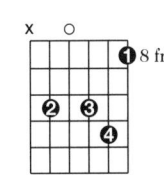

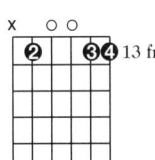

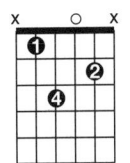

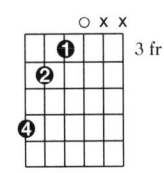

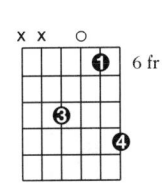

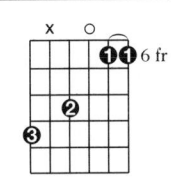

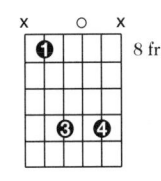

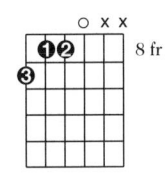

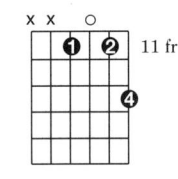

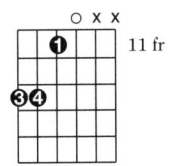

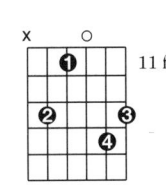

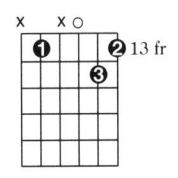

Gm7♭5

Gm9♭5

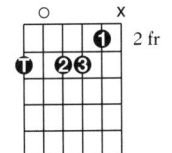

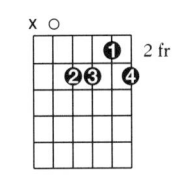

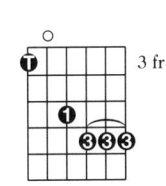

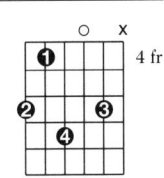

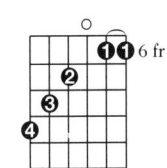

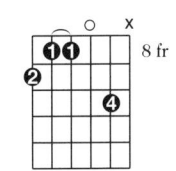

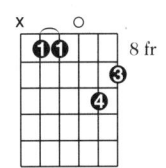

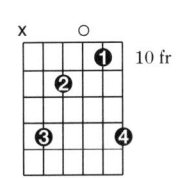

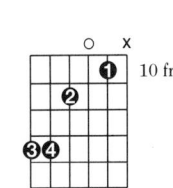

G6

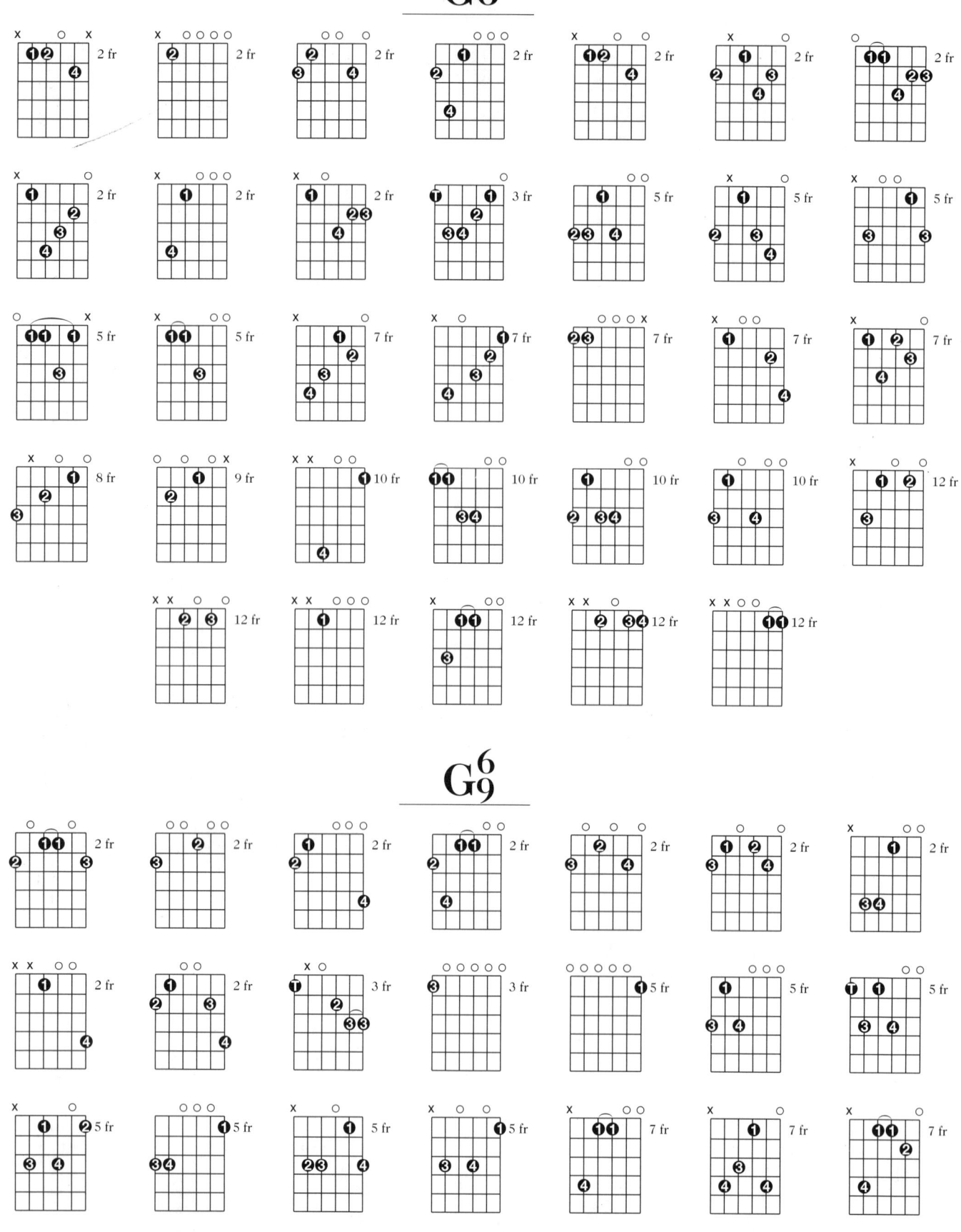

G6/9

92

G13

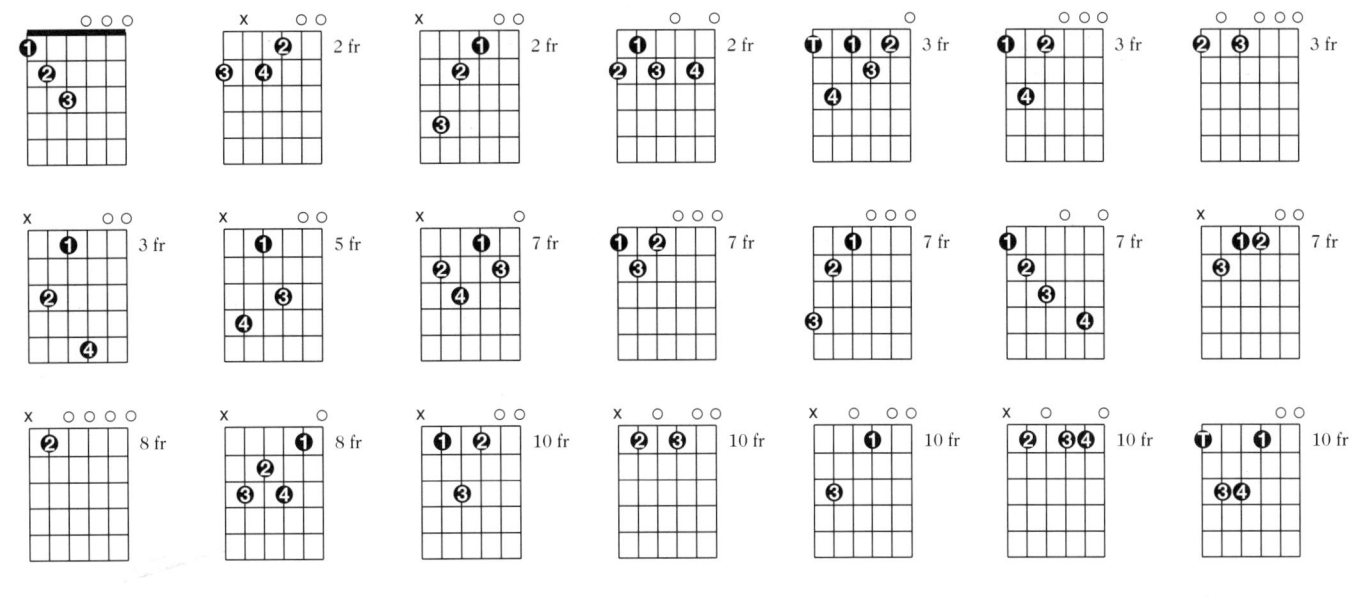

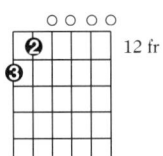

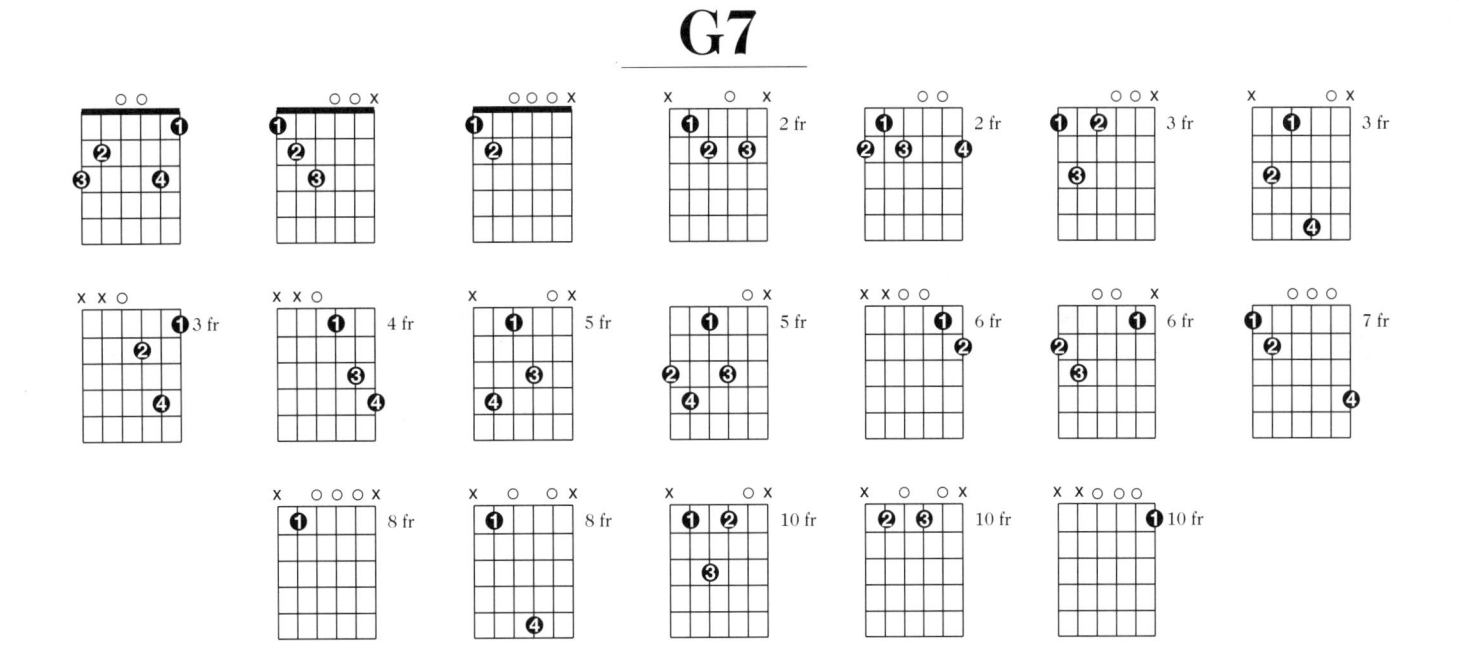

G7

G9

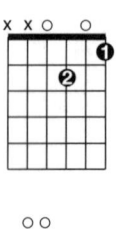

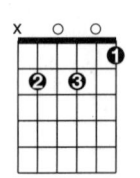

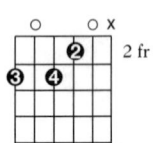

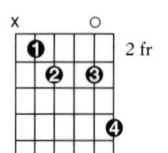

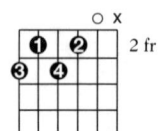

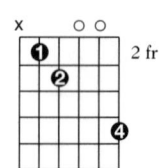

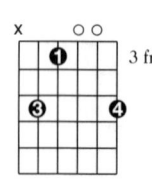

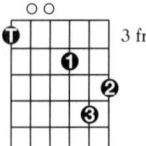

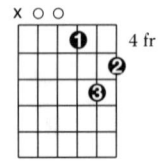

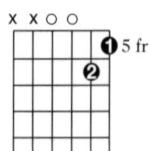

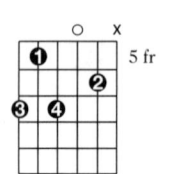

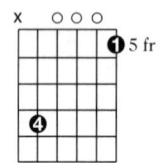

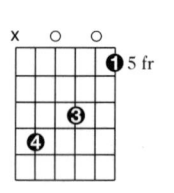

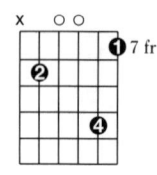

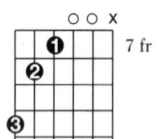

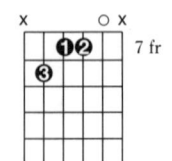

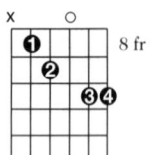

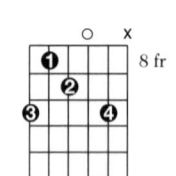

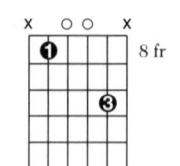

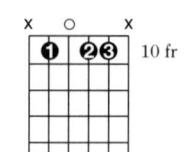

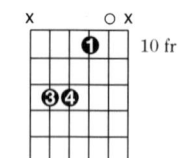

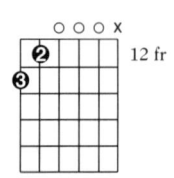

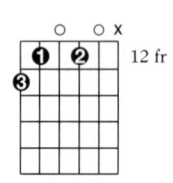

Gadd9

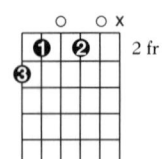

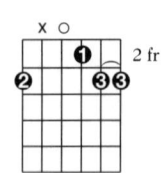

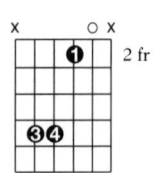

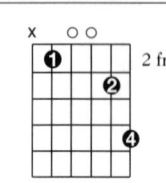

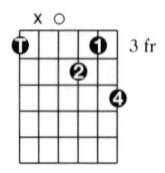

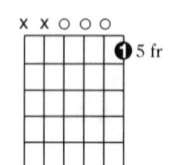

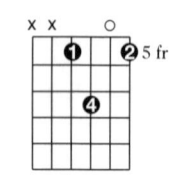

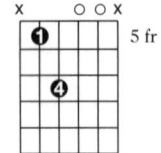

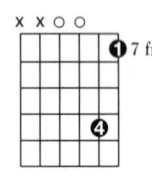

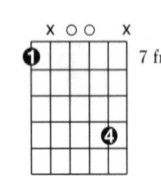

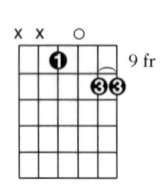

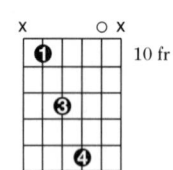

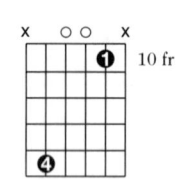

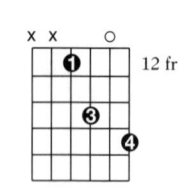

Gmaj7

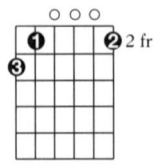

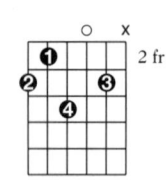

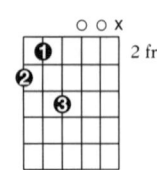

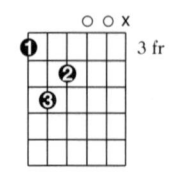

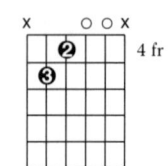

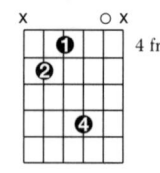

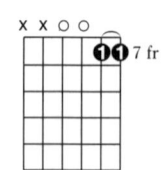

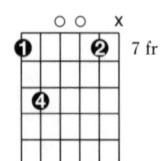

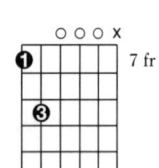

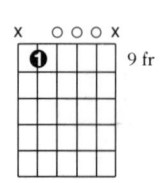

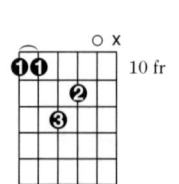

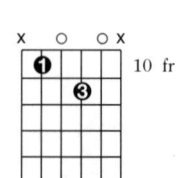

Gmaj9

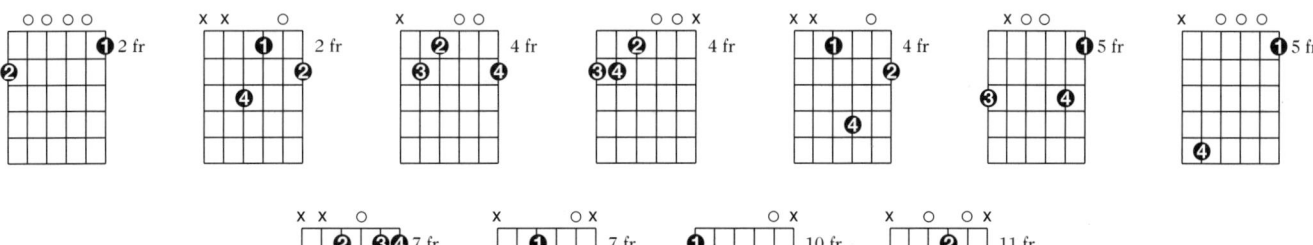

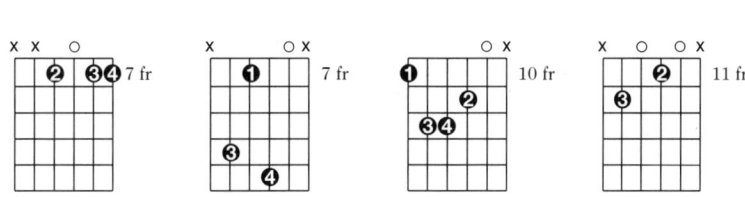

Gmaj13

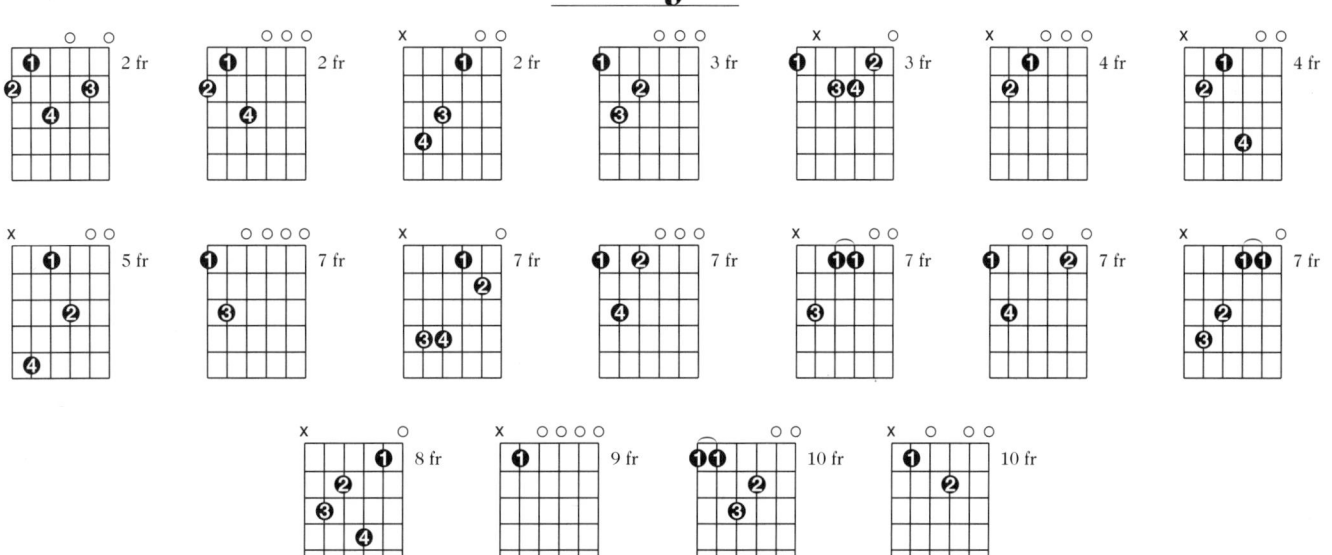

G7sus4

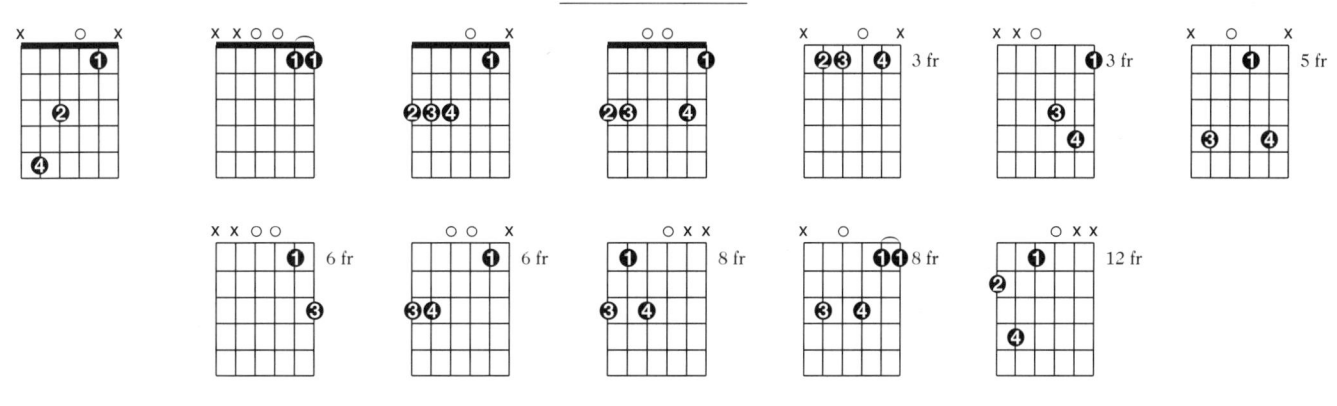

G11

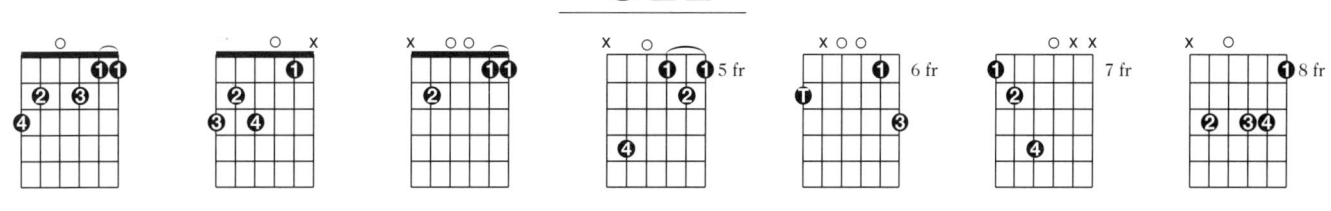

G7♭5

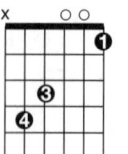

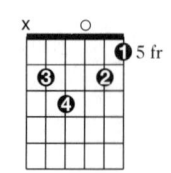

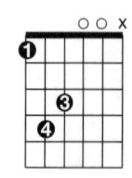

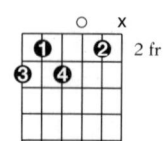

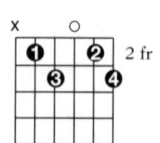

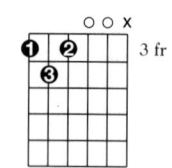

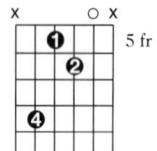

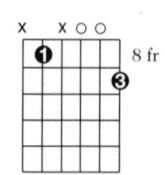

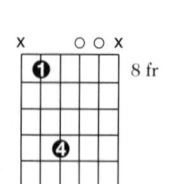

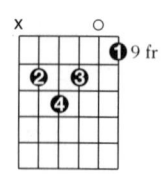

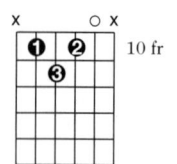

G9♭5

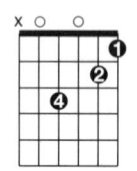

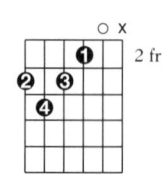

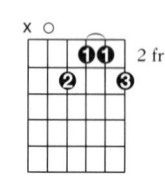

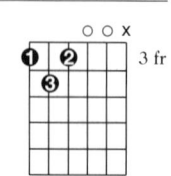

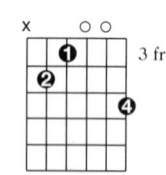

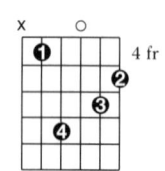

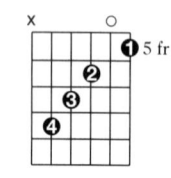

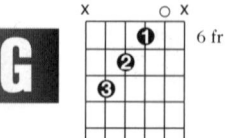

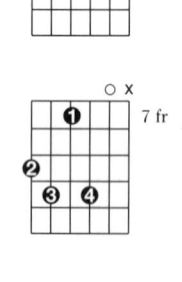

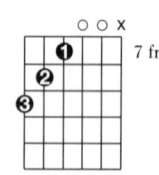

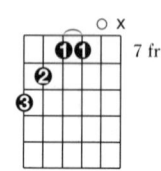

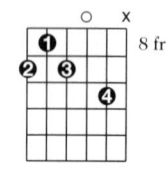

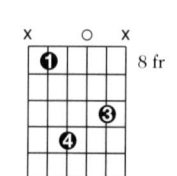

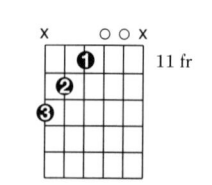

G9♯11

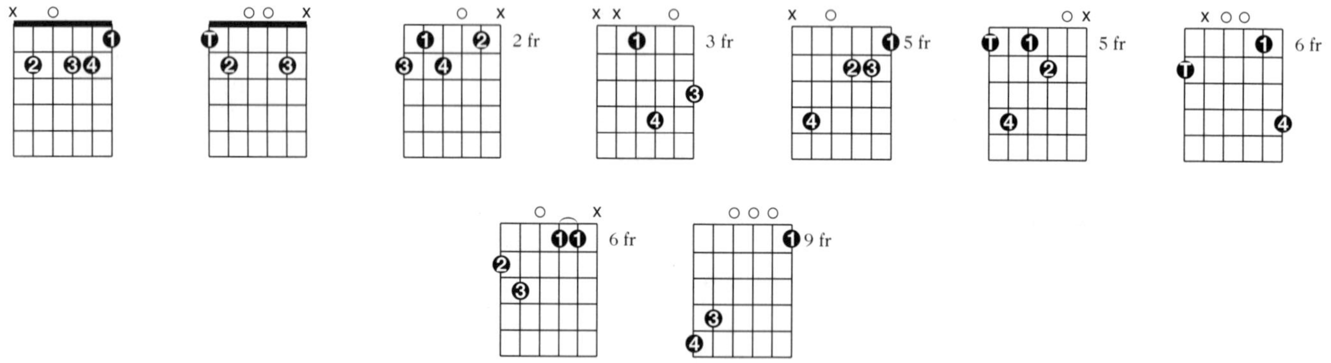

G13♭5

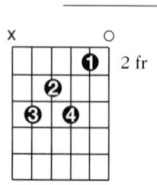

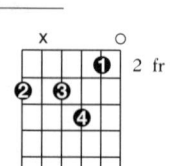

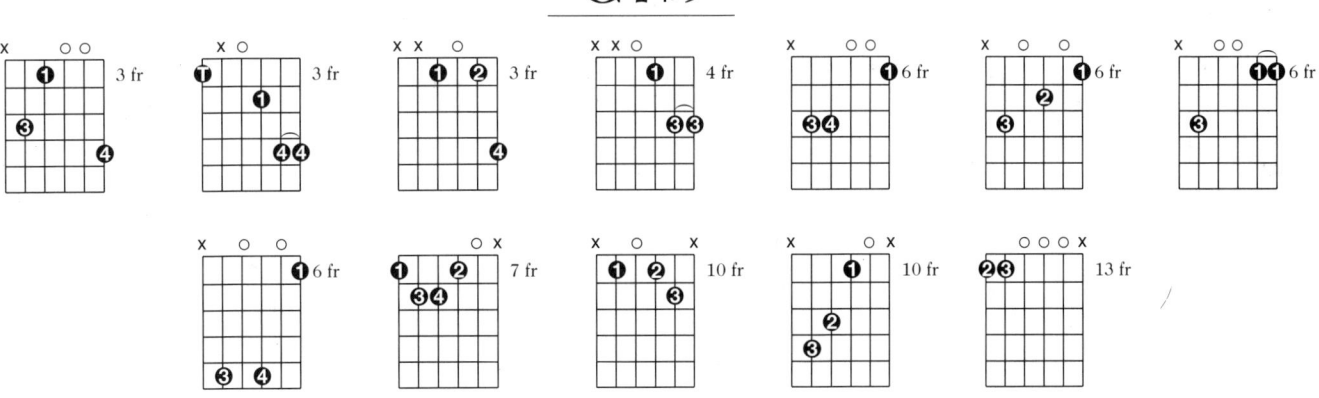

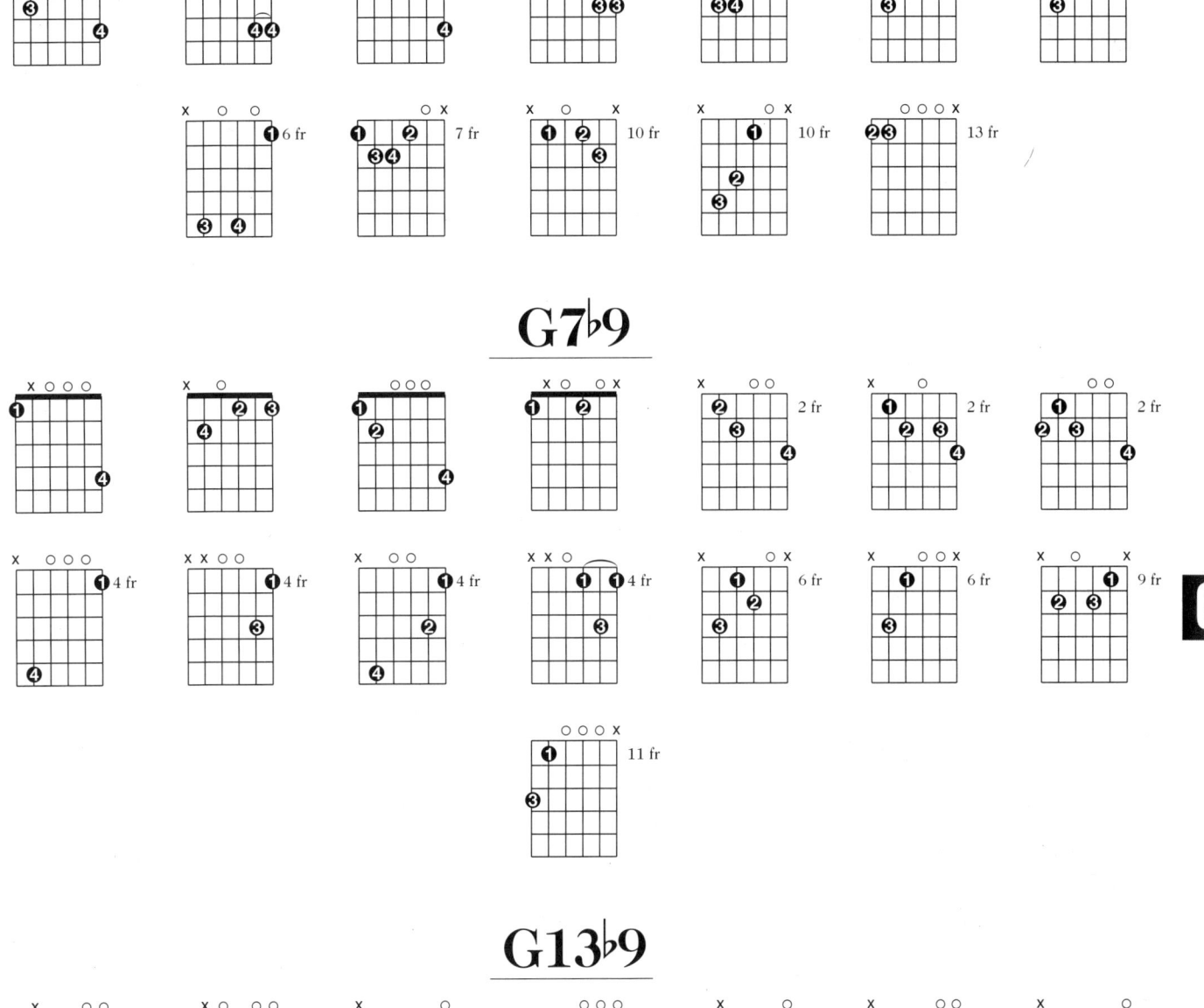

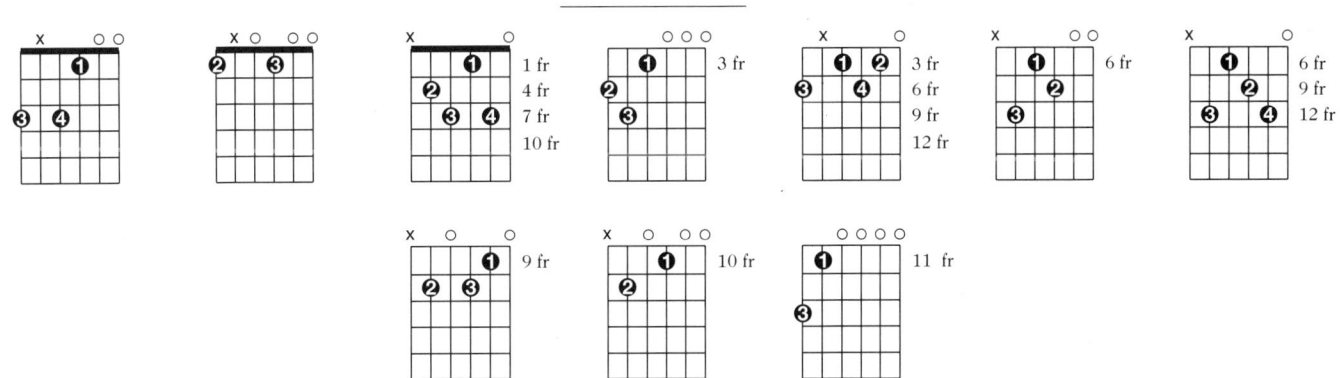

G7#9

G7♭9

G13♭9

G13♭5(♭9)

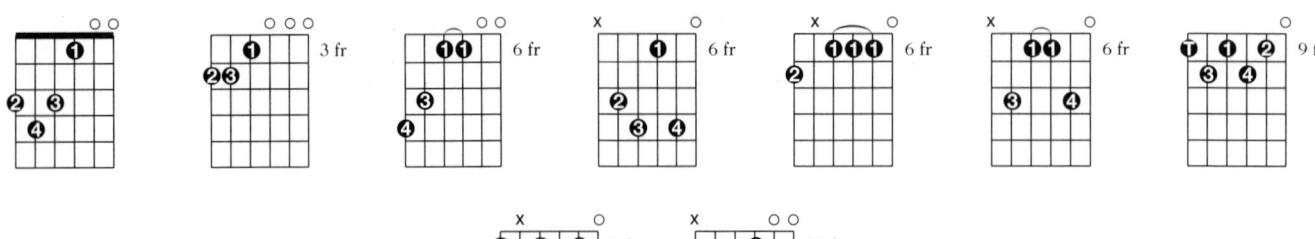

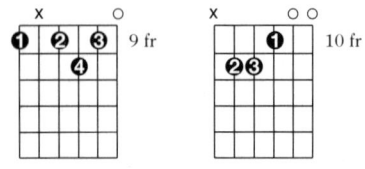

Gm(maj7)

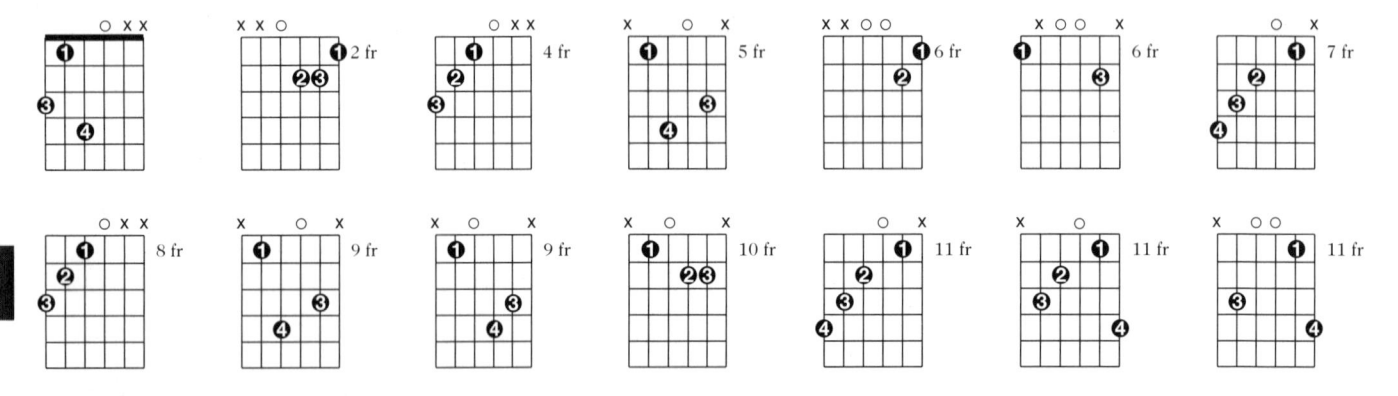

Gm(maj9)

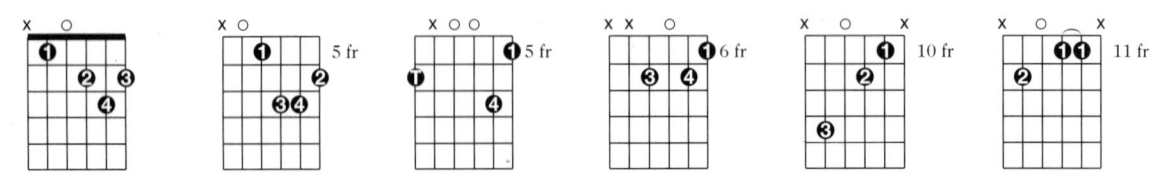

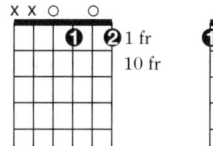

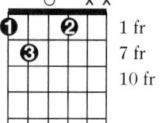

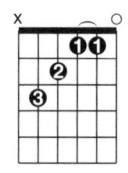

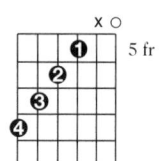

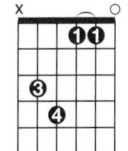

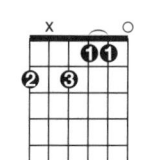

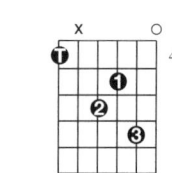

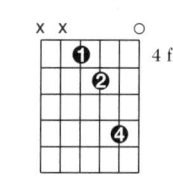

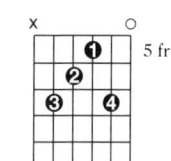

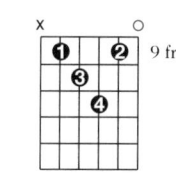

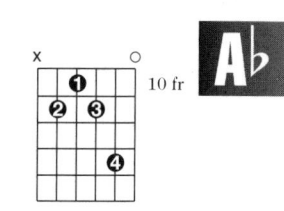

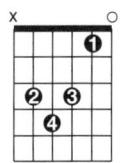

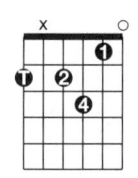

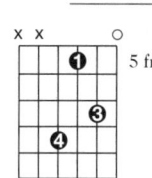

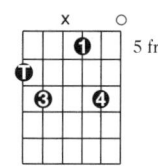

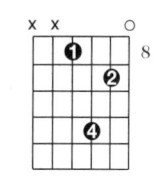

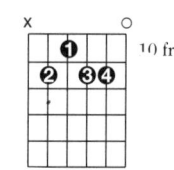

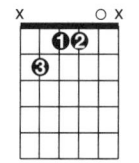

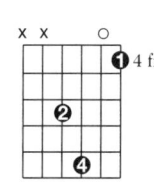

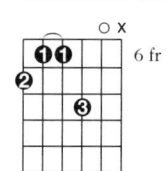

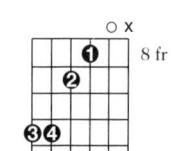

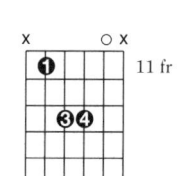

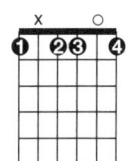

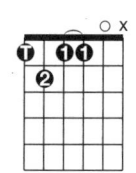

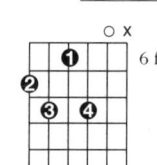

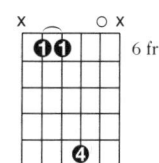

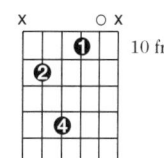

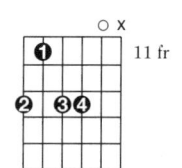

A♭

A♭°

A♭+

A♭+7

A♭+9

A♭m

A♭m6

A♭m6/9

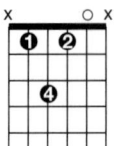

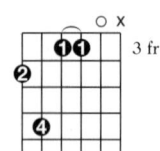

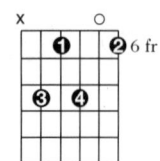

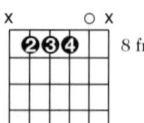

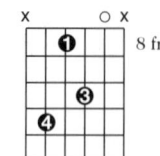

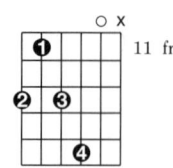

A♭m13

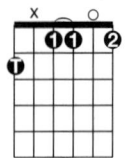

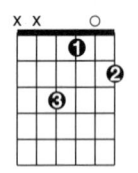

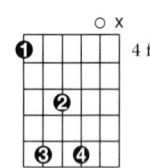

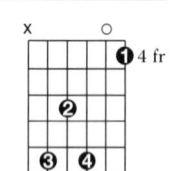

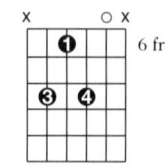

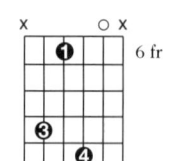

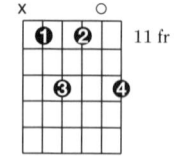

A♭m7

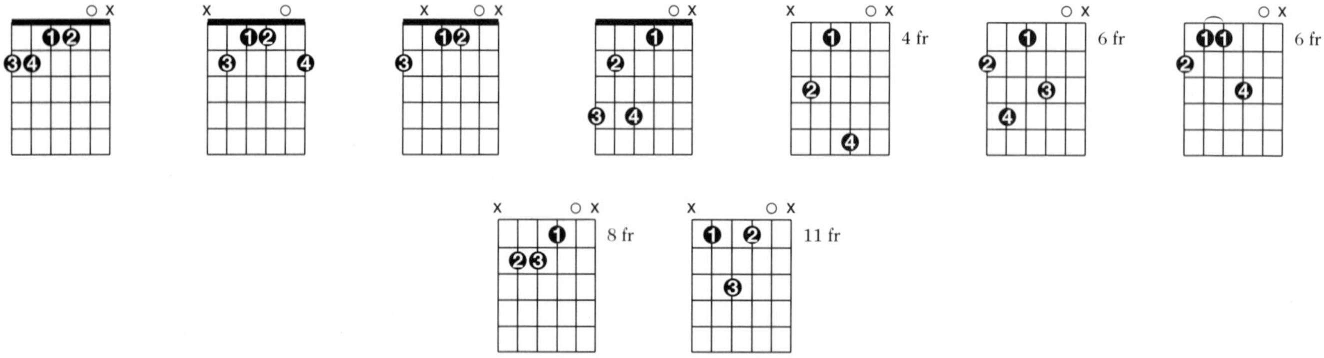

A♭m(add9)

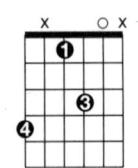

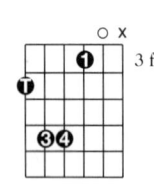

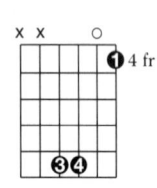

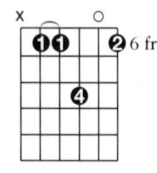

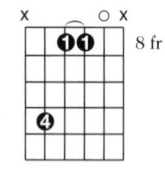

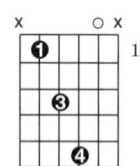

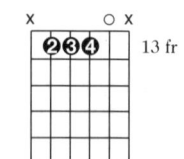

A♭m9

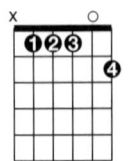

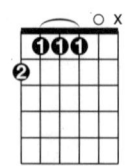

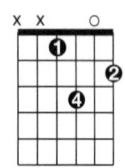

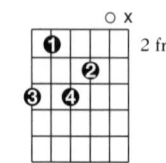

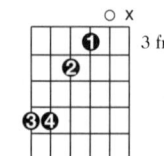

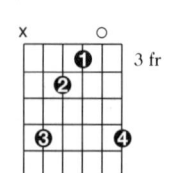

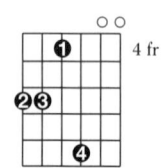

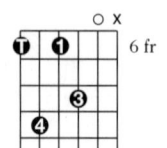

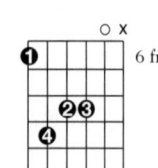

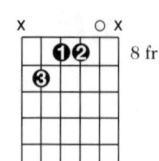

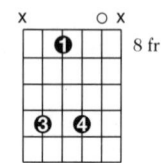

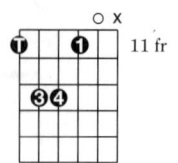

A♭m11

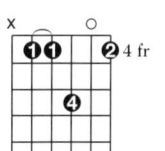

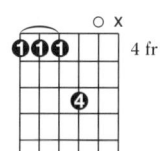

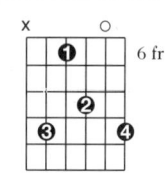

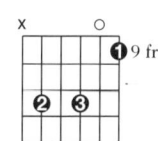

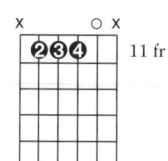

A♭m7♭5

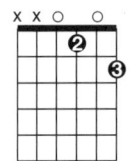

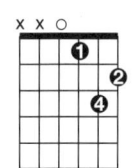

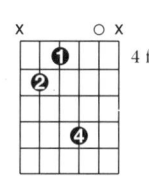

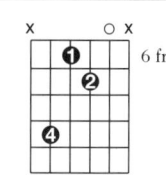

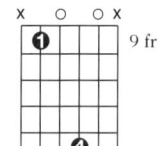

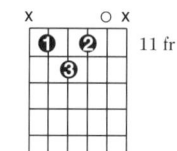

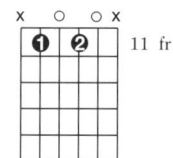

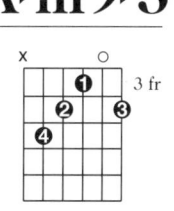

A♭m9♭5

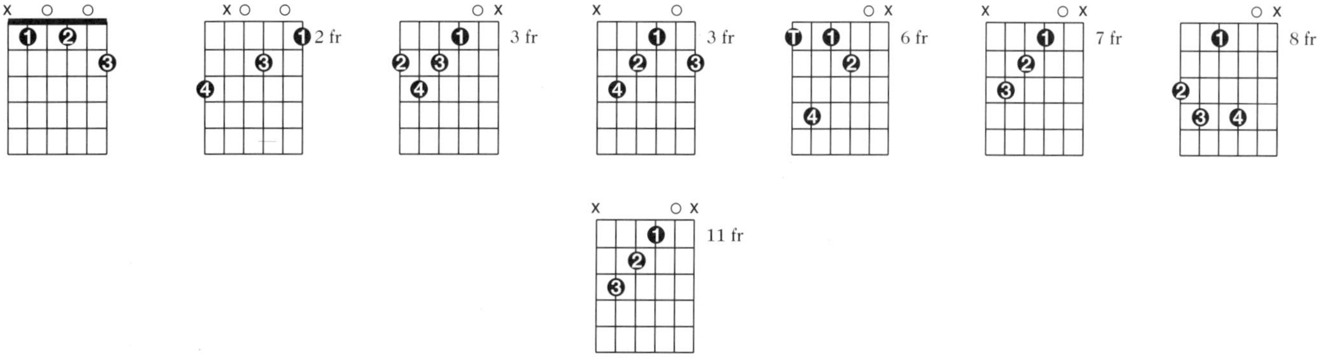

A♭maj7

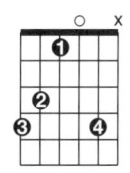

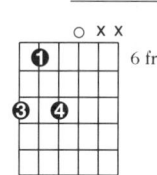

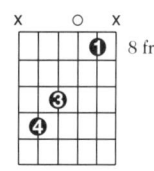

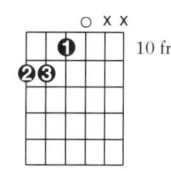

A♭maj9

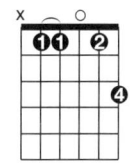

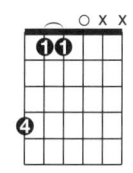

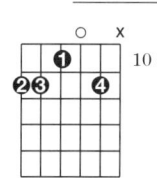

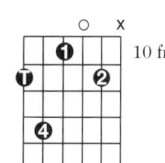

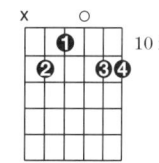

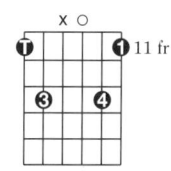

A♭maj13

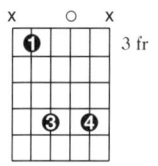

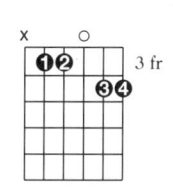

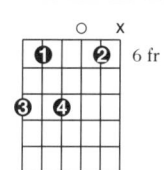

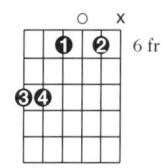

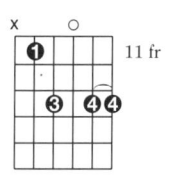

A♭

A♭7♭5

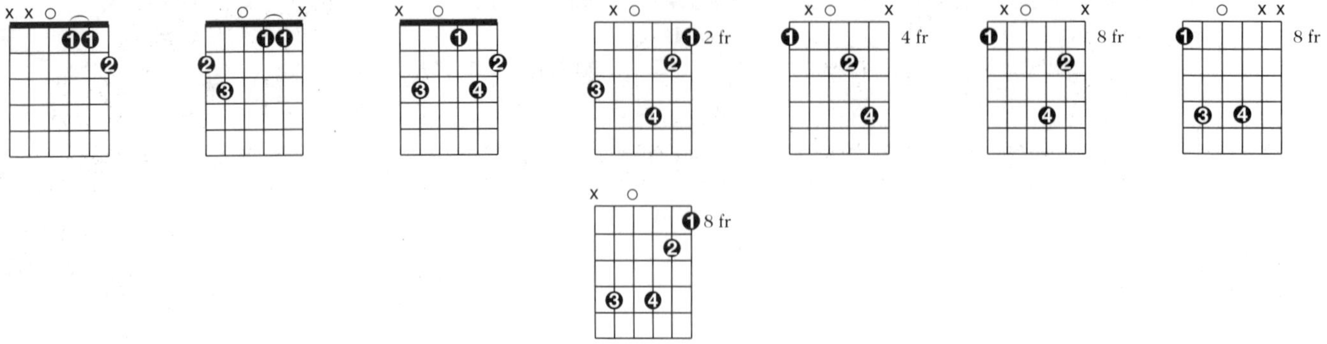

A♭9♭5

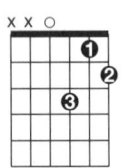

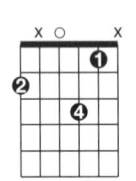

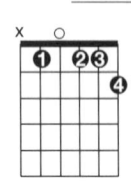

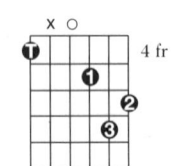

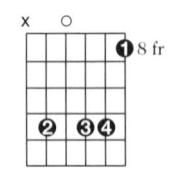

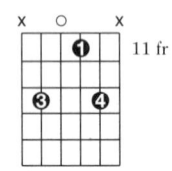

A♭9♯11

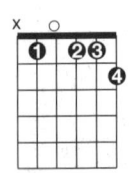

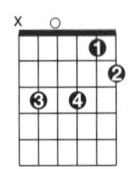

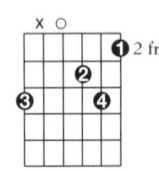

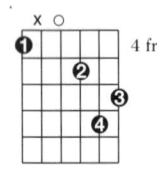

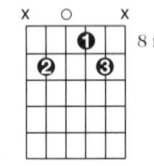

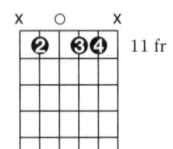

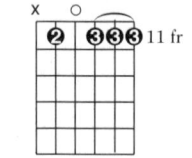

A♭7♯9

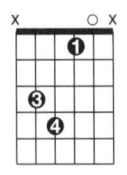

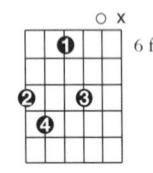

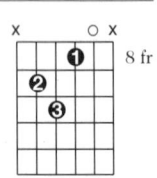

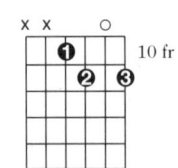

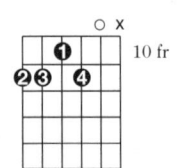

A♭m(maj7)

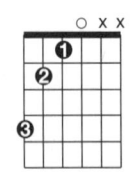

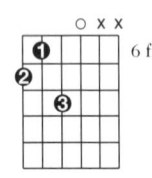

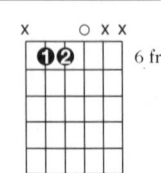

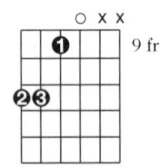

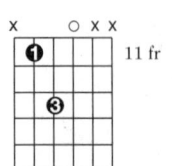

A♭m(maj9)

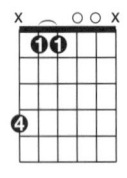

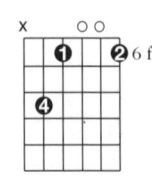

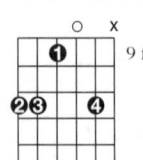

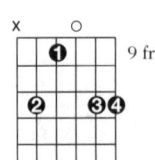

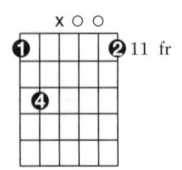

Improve Your Groove

ALL BOOKS INCLUDE NOTES & TAB

With Guitar Instruction Book/CD Packs From Hal Leonard!

Classic Rock Guitar Styles
by John Tapella

A complete guide to rhythm and lead guitar in the style of Led Zeppelin, The Who, Eric Clapton, Pink Floyd, The Rolling Stones, Doobie Brothers, The Grateful Dead, and more. Includes lessons on common riffs, progressions, scales, and techniques. The CD includes 25 tracks with music examples, complete pieces, and special jam progressions.
00695042 Book/CD Pack $16.95

Guitar Styles Of The '90s
by John Tapella

Explore guitar in the styles of bands like Pearl Jam, Nirvana, Soundgarden, and Stone Temple Pilots. The CD includes over 20 examples and four complete pieces. Book provides lessons on altered tunings, scales and solo techniques, common chords and rhythms, and more.
00695086 Book/CD Pack . . $14.95

Punk Guitar Method
by John Tapella

"This volume contains all the blistering moves, scales, chords, and rhythm charts you'll ever need..." —*Guitar School*. Take an inside look at the guitar styles of bands like the Sex Pistols, The Ramones, Green Day and The Offspring. Learn common chords, progressions, solo scales and techniques, rhythms and more. CD features 32 musical examples played out and two complete songs.
00695035 Book/CD Pack $17.95

Terrifying Technique For Guitar
by Carl Culpepper

The ultimate source for building chops while improving your technical facility and overcoming physical barriers. Covers: alternate, economy, hybrid, and sweep picking; symmetrical, chromatic, and scale exercises; arpeggios, tapping, legato, and bending sequences – over 200 exercises in all. CD includes full exercise demonstrations.
00695034 Book/CD Pack . . $14.95

Guitarists' Guide To Theory And Harmony
by Jeff Schroedl

This easy-to-follow method teaches how to solo over a chord progression. It covers riffs, blues-based music, extended chords, power chords, major scales and key signatures, triadic and seventh chord harmony, diatonic and non-diatonic progressions, and much more. The CD includes full band backing for reference and play-along.
00695081 Book/CD Pack $14.95

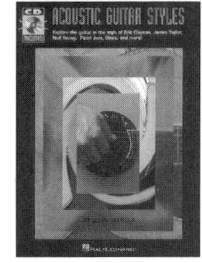

Acoustic Guitar Styles
by John Tapella

Explore guitar in the style of artists like James Taylor, Neil Young, Eric Clapton, Pearl Jam, Oasis, and many others. The book covers strumming and fingerpicking; standard, open, and altered tunings; working with a capo; picking techniques, chord embellishments, home recording, and more! The CD includes over 50 examples and five complete pieces.
00695105 Book/CD Pack . . $14.95

Acoustic Guitar of the '80s and '90s

Learn to play acoustic guitar in the styles and techniques of today's top performers. This book/CD pack features detailed instruction on 15 examples, including: Tears In Heaven • Patience • Losing My Religion • Wanted Dead Or Alive • and more.
00695033 Book/CD Pack $19.95

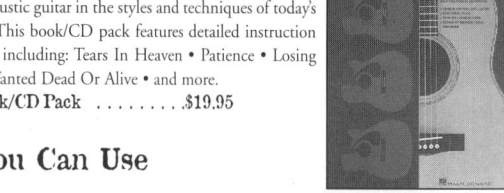

Blues You Can Use
by John Ganapes

A comprehensive source for learning blues guitar, designed to develop both your lead and rhythm playing. Covers all styles of blues, including Texas, Delta, R&B, early rock and roll, gospel, blues/rock and more. Includes 21 complete solos; blues chords, progressions and riffs; audio with leads and full band backing; and more!
00695007 Book/CD Pack $19.95

Power Trio Blues
by Dave Rubin

This book/CD pack details how to play electric guitar in a trio with bass and drums. Boogie, shuffle, and slow blues rhythms, licks, double stops, chords, and bass patterns are presented for full and exciting blues. A CD with the music examples performed by a smokin' power trio is included for play-along instruction and jamming. The music styles of Chicago and Texas bluesmen are presented along with rare photos of them with their favorite axes.
00695028 Book/CD Pack $19.95

Electric Slide Guitar Method
by David Hamburger

This book/CD pack is a comprehensive examination of slide guitar fundamentals in the styles of Duane Allman, Dave Hole, Ry Cooder, Bonnie Raitt, Muddy Waters, Johnny Winter, and Elmore James. Also includes: sample licks and solos; info on selecting a slide and proper setup; backup/rhythm slide playing; standard and open tunings; and more.
00695022 Book/CD Pack $19.95

The Guitar F/X Cookbook
by Chris Amelar

The ultimate source for guitar tricks, effects, and other unorthodox techniques. This book demonstrates and explains 45 incredible guitar sounds using common stomp boxes and a few unique techniques, including: pick scraping, police siren, ghost slide, church bell, jaw harp, delay swells, looping, monkey's scream, cat's meow, race car, pickup tapping, and much more.
00695080 Book/CD Pack $14.95

Guitar Licks
by Chris Amelar

Learn great licks in the style of players like Clapton, Hendrix, Hammett, Page and more. Includes two complete solos; 40 must-know licks for rock and blues; info on essential techniques; standard notation & tab; and more. CD features demos of every technique, lick and solo in the book
00695141 Book/CD Pack $14.95

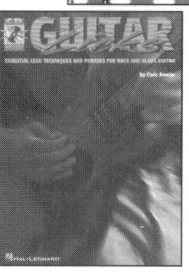

FOR MORE INFORMATION, SEE YOUR LOCAL MUSIC DEALER, OR WRITE TO:

HAL•LEONARD CORPORATION

7777 W. BLUEMOUND RD. P.O. BOX 13819 MILWAUKEE, WI 53213

Prices, contents & availability subject to change without notice.

THE HAL LEONARD GUITAR METHOD

MORE THAN A METHOD IT'S A SYSTEM.

This comprehensive method is preferred by teachers and students alike for many reasons:

- Learning sequence is carefully paced with clear instructions that make it easy to learn.
- Popular songs increase the incentive to learn to play.
- Versatile enough to be used as self-instruction or with a teacher.
- Audio accompaniments let students have fun and sound great while practicing.

HAL LEONARD METHOD BOOK 1
Book 1 provides beginning instruction which includes tuning, 1st position melody playing (strings 1-6) the C, G, G7, D7 and Em chords, rhythms through eighth notes, solos and ensembles and strumming. Added features are a chord chart and a selection of traditional songs, including "Amazing Grace," "Greensleeves" and "When the Saints Go Marching In." The optional outstanding recording features audio demos of several exercises with various accompaniments. Tracks include acoustic and electric examples with some played at two different speeds.
00699010 Book $5.95
00699026 Book/Cassette Pack $7.95
00699027 Book/CD Pack $9.95

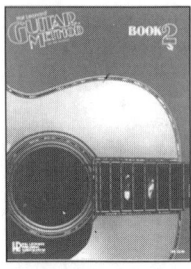

HAL LEONARD METHOD BOOK 2
Book 2 includes studies and songs in the keys of C, G, D, Em, and F, syncopations and dotted rhythms, more advanced strums, the most common 1st position chords, solos, bass runs and a variety of styles from bluegrass to blues-rock. A great selection of traditional songs including: "Simple Gifts," "Mamma Don't 'Low," "Roll in My Sweet Baby's Arms," "Jesu, Joy Of Man's Desiring," and many more. Pages are cross-referenced for supplements.
00699020 ....$5.95

HAL LEONARD METHOD BOOK 3
Book 3 includes the chromatic scale, 16th notes, playing in 2nd, 4th, 5th and 7th positions, moving chords up the neck (bar chords), finger picking, ensembles and solos, a wide variety of style studies and many excellent songs for playing and/or singing. Can be used with supplements.
00699030 ....$4.95

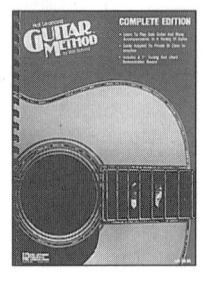

COMPOSITE
Books 1, 2, and 3 bound together in an easy-to-use spiral binding.
00699040 ....$14.95

GUITAR METHOD SUPPLEMENTS
Hal Leonard Pop Melody Supplements are the unique books that supplement any guitar method books 1, 2, or 3. The play-along audio features guitar on the left channel and full rhythm section on the right. Each book is filled with great pop songs that students are eager to play! Now available in book/CD packs!

EASY POP MELODIES
A unique pop supplement to any guitar method book 1. Cross-referenced with Hal Leonard Guitar Method Book 1 pages for easy student and teacher use. Featured songs: "Feelings," "Let It Be," "Every Breath You Take," "You Needed Me" and "Heartbreak Hotel."
0000697281 Book $5.95
00699148 Book/Cassette Pack $12.95
00697268 Book/CD Pack $14.95

MORE EASY POP MELODIES
A unique pop supplement to any guitar method book 2. Cross-referenced with Hal Leonard Guitar Method Book 2 pages for easy student and teacher use. Featured songs: "Long and Winding Road," "Say, Say, Say," "King of Pain," and more.
00699151 Book $5.95
00699149 Book/Cassette Pack $12.95
00697269 Book/CD Pack $14.95

POP MELODIES PLUS
Pop supplement to Book 3. Pop Melodies Plus features "Cool Change," "Daniel," "Don't Be Cruel," "Memory," "Maneater" and many more. 14 songs in all.
00699154 Book $5.95
00697270 Book/CD Pack $14.95

ROCK TRAX 1
Rock Trax is a supplement to any method book 1. It also teaches rhythm guitar, lead guitar and solo licks. The exciting play-along audio features a great-sounding rhythm section and demonstrates each exercise in the book. Rock Trax is unique because it provides the teacher with a program to teach rock guitar technique when the student begins lessons.
00699165 Book/Cassette Pack $12.95
00697271 Book/CD Pack $14.95

ROCK TRAX 2
This rock guitar supplement to any method book 2 teaches rhythm guitar, lead improvisation and solo licks. The tape provides eight background rhythm tracks and demonstrates both the solo licks and new rock guitar techniques.
00697272 Book/CD Pack $14.95

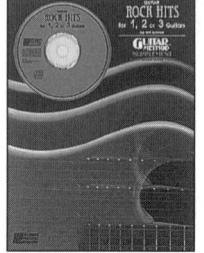

ROCK HITS FOR 1, 2, OR 3 GUITARS
Supplement to any method books 1 and 2. These arrangements are playable by 1, 2, or 3 guitars or class/ensemble. The audio features lead, harmony, and rhythm guitar parts with band backup on side A. Side B repeats the complete band accompaniments without guitar parts 1 or 2. "Practice notes" give the student additional playing tips. Contents: Sister Christian • Rock Around The Clock • Johnny B. Goode • Rocket Man • Sad Songs (Say So Much) • Hungry Like The Wolf • Maggie May.
00699168 Book/Cassette Pack $12.95
00697273 Book/CD Pack $14.95

INCREDIBLE CHORD FINDER
A complete guide diagramming over 1,000 guitar chords in their most common voicings. The book is arranged chromatically and each chord is illustrated in three ways for three levels of difficulty: the easiest form of the chords for the beginner and the more difficult versions for the intermediate and advanced players. Note names of each string are indicated on each chord diagram to let the player know what notes are being played in the chord.
00697200 6" x 9" $4.95
00697208 9" x 12" $5.95

BEGINNING GUITAR VIDEO
This video, especially cross-referenced with the Hal Leonard Guitar Method Book 1 and its supplements, Easy Pop Melodies and Rock Trax, teaches: • How to play chords • How to read music • How to play solos and duets • How to improvise rock • How to accompany singing in wide variety of musical styles. It's hosted by Will Schmid, one of the world's leading guitar teachers and authors, and features such great songs as "Every Breath You Take," "Mull Of Kintyre" and more. On-screen music, guitar diagrams, playing tips with close-up hand positions and demonstrations make for easy learning. Also includes Play-along Trax with full band accompaniment. 60 minutes.
00730627 ....$19.95

FOR MORE INFORMATION, SEE YOUR LOCAL MUSIC DEALER, OR WRITE TO:

HAL•LEONARD® CORPORATION
7777 W. BLUEMOUND RD. P.O. BOX 13819 MILWAUKEE, WI 53213

Visit Hal Leonard on the internet at http://www.halleonard.com
Prices, contents and availability subject to change without notice.